# NASIR KHUSRAW, THE RUBY OF BADAKHSHAN

To Dr. Robbins
for inspiring
me to do my
best. THANK YOU
Shanika
Sultan

**The Institute of Ismaili Studies**
Ismaili Heritage Series, 4
General Editor: Farhad Daftary

Previously published titles:
1. Paul E. Walker, *Abū Ya'qūb al-Sijistānī: Intellectual Missionary* (1996)
2. Heinz Halm, *The Fatimids and their Traditions of Learning* (1997)
3. Paul E. Walker, *Ḥamīd al-Dīn al-Kirmānī: Ismaili Thought in the Age of al-Ḥākim* (1999)

# Nasir Khusraw,
# The Ruby of Badakhshan

*A Portrait of the Persian
Poet, Traveller and Philosopher*

ALICE C. HUNSBERGER

I.B.Tauris
LONDON • NEW YORK
*in association with*
The Institute of Ismaili Studies
LONDON

New edition published in 2003 by I.B.Tauris & Co Ltd
6 Salem Road, London W2 4BU
175 Fifth Avenue, New York NY 10010
www.ibtauris.com

in association with The Institute of Ismaili Studies
42–44 Grosvenor Gardens, London SW1W OEB
www.iis.ac.uk

In the United States of America and in Canada distributed by
St Martins Press, 175 Fifth Avenue, New York NY 10010

First published in 2000 by I.B.Tauris & Co Ltd in association with
The Institute of Ismaili Studies

ISBN 1 85043 926 5

A full CIP record for this book is available from the British Library
A full CIP record for this book is available from the Library of Congress

Library of Congress catalog card: available

Typeset in ITC New Baskerville by Hepton Books, Oxford
Printed and bound in Great Britain by MPG Books Ltd, Bodmin

# The Institute of Ismaili Studies

The Institute of Ismaili Studies was established in 1977 with the object of promoting scholarship and learning on Islam, in the historical as well as contemporary contexts, and a better understanding of its relationship with other societies and faiths.

The Institute's programmes encourage a perspective which is not confined to the theological and religious heritage of Islam, but seeks to explore the relationship of religious ideas to broader dimensions of society and culture. The programmes thus encourage an interdisciplinary approach to the materials of Islamic history and thought. Particular attention is also given to issues of modernity that arise as Muslims seek to relate their heritage to the contemporary situation.

Within the Islamic tradition, the Institute's programmes seek to promote research on those areas which have, to date, received relatively little attention from scholars. These include the intellectual and literary expressions of Shi'ism in general, and Ismailism in particular.

In the context of Islamic societies, the Institute's programmes are informed by the full range and diversity of cultures in which Islam is practised today, from the Middle East, South and Central Asia and Africa to the industrialised societies of the West, thus taking into consideration the variety of contexts which shape the ideals, beliefs and practices of the faith.

These objectives are realised through concrete programmes and activities organised and implemented by various departments of the Institute. The Institute also collaborates periodically, on a programme-specific basis, with other institutions of learning in the United Kingdom and abroad.

The Institute's academic publications fall into several distinct and interrelated categories:

1. Occasional papers or essays addressing broad themes of the relationship between religion and society in the historical as well as modern contexts, with special reference to Islam.
2. Monographs exploring specific aspects of Islamic faith and culture, or the contributions of individual Muslim figures or writers.
3. Editions or translations of significant primary or secondary texts.
4. Translations of poetic or literary texts which illustrate the rich heritage of spiritual, devotional and symbolic expressions in Muslim history.
5. Works on Ismaili history and thought, and the relationship of the Ismailis to other traditions, communities and schools of thought in Islam.
6. Proceedings of conferences and seminars sponsored by the Institute.
7. Bibliographical works and catalogues which document manuscripts, printed texts and other source materials.

This book falls into category five listed above.

In facilitating these and other publications, the Institute's sole aim is to encourage original research and analysis of relevant issues. While every effort is made to ensure that the publications are of a high academic standard, there is naturally bound to be a diversity of views, ideas and interpretations. As such, the opinions expressed in these publications must be understood as belonging to their authors alone.

# Ismaili Heritage Series

A major Shi'i Muslim community, the Ismailis have had a long and eventful history. Scattered in many regions of the world, in Asia, Africa, and now also in Europe and North America, the Ismailis have elaborated diverse intellectual and literary traditions in different languages. On two occasions they had states of their own, the Fatimid caliphate and the Nizari state of Iran and Syria during the Alamut period. While pursuing particular religio-political aims, the leaders of these Ismaili states also variously encouraged intellectual, scientific, artistic and commercial activities.

Until recently, the Ismailis were studied and judged almost exclusively on the basis of the evidence collected or fabricated by their enemies, including the bulk of the medieval heresiographers and polemicists who were hostile towards the Shi'is in general and the Ismailis among them in particular. These authors in fact treated the Shi'i interpretations of Islam as expressions of heterodoxy or even heresy. As a result, a 'black legend' was gradually developed and put into circulation in the Muslim world to discredit the Ismailis and their interpretation of Islam. The Christian Crusaders and their occidental chroniclers, who remained almost completely ignorant of Islam and its internal divisions, disseminated their own myths of the Ismailis, which came to be accepted in Europe as true descriptions of Ismaili teachings and practices. Modern orientalists, too, have studied the Ismailis on the basis of these hostile sources and fanciful accounts of medieval times. Thus,

vii

legends and misconceptions have continued to surround the Ismailis through the twentieth century.

In more recent decades, however, the field of Ismaili studies has been revolutionised due to the recovery and study of genuine Ismaili sources on a large scale – manuscript materials which in different ways survived the destruction of the Fatimid and Nizari Ismaili libraries. These sources, representing diverse literary traditions produced in Arabic, Persian and Indic languages, had hitherto been secretly preserved in private collections in India, Central Asia, Iran, Afghanistan, Syria and the Yemen.

Modern progress in Ismaili studies has already necessitated a complete re-writing of the history of the Ismailis and their contributions to Islamic civilisation. It has now become clear that the Ismailis founded important libraries and institutions of learning such as al-Azhar and the Dar al-'Ilm in Cairo, while some of their learned *da'is* or missionaries developed unique intellectual traditions amalgamating their theological doctrines with a diversity of philosophical traditions in complex metaphysical systems. The Ismaili patronage of learning and extension of hospitality to non-Ismaili scholars was maintained even in such difficult times as the Alamut period, when the community was preoccupied with its survival in an extremely hostile milieu.

The Ismaili Heritage Series, published under the auspices of the Department of Academic Research and Publications of The Institute of Ismaili Studies, aims to make available to wide audiences the results of modern scholarship on the Ismailis and their rich intellectual and cultural heritage, as well as certain aspects of their more recent history and achievements.

To my daughter
*Adriane*
for the journey so far

True offspring of the Prophet, that man of faith,
Sworn foe of foes of the chosen family.

Not a man to enter into the fighting fields of dogs,
like a ruby in Badakhshan he hid himself away.

From 'The Tale of Nasir Khusraw and his Seclusion,' in
*Lisan al-ghayb,* attributed to Farid al-Din 'Attar

# Contents

# List of Illustrations

# Preface

Nasir Khusraw strides along the pages of many kinds of books – poetry, travel, philosophy, biography, social history, religious polemic, literary anthology, geography. He himself has written substantial volumes of the first three kinds, and tradition has included him in the others. He strides across centuries too, from the 5th/11th century when he flourished in Eastern Iran and Central Asia to the present day when Persian speakers quote his poems in everyday speech, as in the phrase, *Az ma-st ki bar ma-st* ('What comes from us returns to us').

If Nasir Khusraw is less well-known today, even in Iran, than other Persian poets such as Sa'di, Khayyam, Rumi or Hafiz, other travel chroniclers and historians such as Ibn Battuta or Ibn Khaldun, and other philosophers such as Ibn Sina, al-Farabi or Nasir al-Din Tusi, this may in part be due to his devoted allegiance to the Ismaili Shi'i faith. This allegiance put him at odds with both Sunni and Twelver Shi'i communities; and when Iran became officially Twelver Shi'i in the 10th/16th century his Ismaili philosophical texts and poetry were easily set aside. Also, rather than composing love poems or mystical odes, which have a more universal appeal, Nasir Khusraw focused largely on ethical and moralising poetry, admonishing the reader to attend to the task of spiritual improvement in place of chasing after the baubles of this material and materialistic world. In format, he generally writes these poems in the *qasida* form, each two to three pages in length, thus further lessening the likelihood of public recitation in full.

When I was invited by The Institute of Ismaili Studies to write a book bringing together all these elements of his life and writings (after having written a dissertation analysing Nasir Khusraw's doctrine of the soul as it is found in his six philosophical texts), the immediate question was one of structure. I decided that it could not be a three-part book (his poetry, his travels and his philosophy) for several reasons. The first was my suspicion that most readers would avoid the philosophy section. The second, and perhaps more important reason, was that a three-part book belies the unity within Nasir Khusraw's life and writings. His philosophy flows through his poetry, his travels were undertaken as a response to his conversion to Ismailism, and his keen poet's eye as well as his religious values are evident in his travelogue, the *Safarnama* – in the places he visits, the sights he delights at, and his careful observations of peoples, places and cultures. This inherent unity would also be lost if I had attempted another possible structure, a strict chronology of his life, because our information about different periods of his life is so skewed. We know the details of his seven-year journey, but we know almost nothing about him before his conversion; from his exile in the last years of his life we have practically all of his poetry and philosophy, but almost nothing of the years of preaching which led to the exile. I decided to set the question aside and see what Nasir had to say. I read carefully through the *Safarnama*, noting what he had noted, read the poems in his *Divan* to discover the main themes, and poured again over his philosophical works to see what topics I had passed over in my study of the soul.

The structure as well as the content of this book is a result of these examinations. The main line of narrative follows Nasir Khusraw's journey from his home in Khurasan, with the opening chapters setting the stage for his conversion and the decision to embark on such an expedition, leaving behind a family and a life as a leading financial officer in the court of the Saljuqs. On this evolving structure, filled out with his rich descriptions of the lands he travels through, I have hung the main themes of his philosophy, moving from the basic Ismaili tenet of the connected pair *zahir/batin* (exoteric/esoteric) to, for instance, the necessity of both knowledge and action. These themes are illustrated with examples from both his poetry and prose texts. Then, when we arrive in Jerusalem with the traveller, a secondary line of narrative begins, one which mirrors the structure of his cosmogony. Nasir Khusraw (along with some, but not all, Ismaili scholars of the Fatimid era) espouses an adapted form of Neoplatonic progression of creation from God to the material world. The basic lines of this progression are: God, Intellect, Soul, Nature, and the corporeal world. With this secondary structure, I use Jerusalem as a backdrop for the discussion of God, Cairo for the discussion of Intellect, and his return home for the discussion of Soul. In between is Mecca, the proper place for deep reflection on the meaning of pilgrimage. Once Nasir Khusraw has returned home, we share his pangs of exile, as well as the strength of faith which gives him hope.

With such a structure, I hope the probing, exploratory aspect of his personality comes through as well as his lessons on the inevitability of change. When things are going well, he takes care not to depend on them to last, and when things go wrong, he takes comfort that change can be counted on to bring better times. His philosophical ethics and the way he lived his life bear witness to how highly he valued the search for knowledge and an active public life for the betterment of individuals and society – values which he found amply expressed in the Ismaili Islam that he espoused. Nasir Khusraw's sincerity, courage and steadfastness of purpose make him an appealing character for people of all faiths.

A.C.H.
New York

# Acknowledgements

I am very grateful to the Institute of Ismaili Studies for its generous commitment to publishing this work as part of the Ismaili Heritage Series. Many friends and colleagues helped to sustain this book through its conception and growth. Foremost among the staff of the Institute, my very special thanks go to the head of the Department of Academic Research and Publications, Dr Farhad Daftary, for his unflagging enthusiasm, wise counsel, and broad knowledge; without his leadership this book would not have been accomplished. I want to express my appreciation also to the Department's publications editor, Kutub Kassam, for his keen attention to detail which cleaned up many errors and inelegancies of style; Dr Faquir M. Hunzai for taking the time to share his extensive knowledge of Nasir Khusraw which helped to improve the text in many places, and Dr Leonard Lewisohn for his valued comments and suggestions. My thanks go to Nicolette Loizou for word processing the first draft, and to Nadia Holmes for her superior editorial assistance through all the final stages, and also to the graduate students of the Institute for their responses to many of the ideas presented in this book.

Among those outside the Institute who contributed to the development of the work, I extend particular thanks to Professor Ehsan Yarshater for his careful comments on an early version of the first few chapters, and for granting generous permission, as editor of the Persian Heritage Series, to quote extensively from the translation of the *Safarnama* prepared by Professor Wheeler

Thackston. I am very grateful to Professor Mehdi Mohaghegh for his hospitality to me in Iran and for kindly sending me books from his own library. For reading or discussing certain portions of the text, I especially thank Professor Julie Scott Meisami, Professor Hamid Dabashi, Professor Michael Beard, Emilie Trautmann, Paul Carroll and Stacey Leichmann. I am indebted to Dr Pardis Minuchehr and Habib Borjian for sitting with me and reading Nasir Khusraw's poems in the early stages of this book, and to Manuchehr Kasheff for pointing out some of Nasir Khusraw's popular verses. Finally, to Shahrokh Vafadari I give my profound thanks for sharing his knowledge of Persian poetry and song.

# Note on the Text

The few editorial and transcription descriptions observed in this publication should be explained. For simplicity's sake, the subject's name is rendered as Nasir Khusraw, rather than the familiar and more technically correct Nasir-i Khusraw. More technically correct, because the *idafa* is not only an elision of Persian pronunciation but also an orthographic stand-in for *ibn*, meaning, correctly, 'son of Khusraw.' For the same reason, all diacritics have been eliminated, except the forward and backward apostrophe, respectively, for *hamza* and *'ayn* as in Qur'an and Ka'ba, and even they are dropped in some frequently used words such as Abbasid and Ismaili. The final 'silent' *h* is not written, whether from an Arabic or Persian root, e.g., Ka'ba (not Ka'bah) and *Safarnama* (not *Safarnamah*), except in some places where, in the original text, Nasir Khusraw himself (or a scribe) has written out the final letter as a *ta*, e.g., *kalimat*. Descriptions of each of Nasir Khusraw's edited books are found in Chapter 1, and the English translations of the book titles have been provided at first citation.

Unless otherwise noted (as in Chapter 4), all poetry selections are my own translations from Nasir Khusraw's *Divan*, edited in 1974 by Professors Mujtaba Minuvi and Mehdi Mohaghegh. Each selection is identified by the poem number given in the *Divan*, followed by the verse numbers. I have tried, as far as possible, to give a faithful approximation of the meaning of the verses, but have not attempted to create new poetry. Citations from the *Safarnama* are all direct quotations, with minor modifications in the system of spelling and transliteration from Professor Wheeler Thackston's translation, *Naser-e Khosraw's Book of Travels (Safarnama)*(Albany, N.Y., 1986). Selections from the Qur'an are taken from A. J. Arberry's translation, *The Koran Interpreted* (London, 1955).

Dates are given according to both Muslim and Christian calendars; thus Nasir Khusraw's date of birth, year 394 in the Muslim calendar, which corresponds to 1004 of the Common Era, is written 394/1004.

### ABBREVIATIONS

| | |
|---|---|
| *EI2* | *Encyclopaedia of Islam,* 2nd edition |
| *GR* | *Gushayish wa rahayish* of Nasir Khusraw, ed. and tr. Hunzai |
| *JH* | *Jami' al-hikmatayn* of Nasir Khusraw, ed. Corbin and Mu'in |
| *KI* | *Khwan al-ikhwan* of Nasir Khusraw, ed. Qavim |
| S | *Safarnama* of Nasir Khusraw, tr. Thackston, Jr. |
| *SF* | *Shish fasl* of Nasir Khusraw, ed. and tr. Ivanow |
| *WD* | *Wajh-i din* of Nasir Khusraw, ed. Aavani |
| *ZM* | *Zad al-musafirin* of Nasir Khusraw, ed. Badhl al-Rahman |

# Chronology

| | |
|---|---|
| 278–86/ 892–99 | The Samanids rule in Bukhara, patronising the arts and poets such as Rudaki. Some leading Samanids follow Ismaili Shi'ism. |
| 297/909 | The Fatimids establish Ismaili rule in North Africa and later extend it to Egypt, Syria, Palestine, and the Hijaz. |
| 341/952 | Birth of Kasa'i, one of the leading Iranian poets mentioned by Nasir Khusraw who wrote at the time of Sultan Mahmud of Ghazna. |
| 368/978 | Death of Daqiqi, one of the poets at the Samanid court, who commenced the Iranian national epic, later completed by Firdawsi. |
| 370/980 | Ibn Sina (Avicenna), the philosopher and physician, is born in Bukhara, of Ismaili parents. |
| 388/998 | Sultan Mahmud establishes his court in Ghazna, famed for its military conquests and its gathering of intellectuals, artists, and poets. |
| 394/1004 | Nasir Khusraw is born in Qubadiyan, near the city of Marv, in the Balkh district of Khurasan. |
| 401/1010 | Firdawsi completes the Iranian national epic, the *Shahnama*. |
| 427/1036 | The Fatimid Caliph-Imam al-Mustansir begins his sixty-year reign in Cairo. |
| 429/1037 | Tughril the Saljuq is proclaimed king in Marv, fracturing the Ghaznavid kingdom. |

| 431/1039 | 'Unsuri, chief court poet of the Ghaznavids, mentioned by Nasir Khusraw, dies. |
| 437/1045 | Nasir Khusraw begins his seven-year journey described in the *Safarnama*. |
| 442/1050 | Death of the famous Iranian scholar and world traveller al-Biruni. |
| 444/1052 | Nasir Khusraw returns home from his journey and begins his career as the Ismaili *hujjat* of Khurasan. |
| 463/1070 | Nasir Khusraw writes the *Jami' al-hikmatayn* for his Ismaili patron in Yumgan, Badakhshan. |
| 470/1077 | Approximate date of Nasir Khusraw's death in Yumgan. |
| 483/1090 | The Ismaili *da'i* Hasan Sabbah takes over the mountain fortress of Alamut in northern Iran. |
| 484/1091 | The theologian al-Ghazali appointed instructor at the Nizamiyya college in Baghdad. |
| 525/1137 | Death of Sana'i, the first great Sufi poet in Persian literature. |
| 527/1132 | 'Umar Khayyam, the poet and astronomer, dies. |
| 537/1142 | Birth of Farid al-Din 'Attar, poet of mystical stories, in Nishapur. |
| 610/1213 | Birth of the poet and prose-writer Sa'di of Shiraz. |
| 652/1254 | Beginning of the Mongol invasions of Iran. |
| 654/1256 | The Mongols capture the Ismaili stronghold of Alamut and less than two years later sack Baghdad, terminating the Abbasid caliphate. |

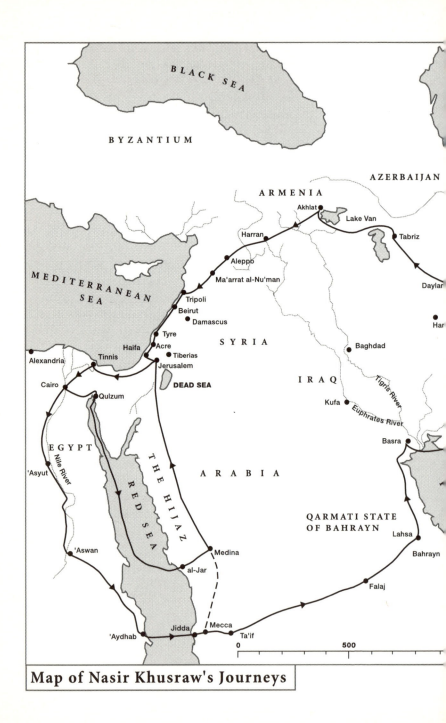

Map of Nasir Khusraw's Journeys

# CHAPTER ONE

# A Soul Higher Than Fortune

By words, the Prophet's religion spread throughout the earth;
and by words, he reached to heaven's highest dome.

*Divan*, 180:13

For over nine hundred years, Nasir Khusraw has attracted passionate attention, from admirers and critics alike. Delight in his mastery of poetical form and expression has led centuries of Persian speakers to rank him among the best of Persian poets. In addition, his personal record of the seven-year journey he took from Central Asia to the Mediterranean coast, Egypt, Arabia and back home again has been studied word by word for its detailed descriptions of cities, societies and customs. French and German scholars of the 19th century stood where he stood in Jerusalem and could count out the steps he had counted out centuries before. Appreciation for the serious intellectual content found throughout his writings, both in poetry and prose, early on earned him the title of 'Hakim,' that is someone revered for scientific knowledge and analytical ability. In some parts of Central Asia, people still claim descent from him. On the other hand, his success as a missionary for the Ismaili faith caused public and official opinion to turn viciously against him, forcing him to flee for his life. He spent the last fifteen years or so of his life in exile under the protection of a minor prince, in a remote place tucked away in the mountains of Badakhshan, slightly north of the Hindu Kush. He has been falsely credited with founding an eponymous religious sect, the Nasiriyya. Legends about him flowered so extravagantly that by 1574 a scholar was warned not to believe anything said about him. Today, his verses are still taught in Persian literature classes and, perhaps more significantly, are recited from memory and sprinkled throughout Persian conversations when a moral illustration is called for, as in the following example:

> Have you heard? A squash vine grew beneath a towering tree.
> In only twenty days it grew and spread and put forth fruit.
> Of the tree it asked: 'How old are you? How many years?'
> Replied the tree: 'Two hundred it would be, and surely more.'
> The squash laughed and said: 'Look, in twenty days, I've done
>     more than you; tell me, why are you so slow?'
> The tree responded: 'O little squash, today is not the day
>     for reckoning between the two of us.
> 'Tomorrow, when winds of autumn howl down on you and me,
>     then shall it be known for sure which one of us is the real
>     man!'
>
> (*Divan*, 256)

Nasir Khusraw has written in three distinct genres – travelogue, poetry and philosophy – each of which provides a window into his character. In addition, there exists a corpus of secondary literature of biographies, anthologies and geographies that cite him and his work. One of the earliest is a hostile account by his contemporary Abu'l-Ma'ali, who charges him with preaching heretical views. From then on, references to Nasir Khusraw, with varying degrees of fantasy and prejudice, show up regularly about once a century in the major intellectual compilations. Thus, while from his own words we can gain a picture of the man as he wished to be seen, from other writers we can glimpse something of the passions he aroused.

In an age when the international language of political and intellectual discourse from Spain to India was Arabic, Nasir distinguished himself by writing predominantly in his native Persian language. Most of his fellow Iranians – including the brightest stars of Islamic intellectual history, such as the philosophers Ibn Sina (Avicenna) and al-Farabi and some of his fellow Ismailis –

made sure to write at least some works in Arabic and thereby secured a broader reputation. For example, Ibn Sina's medical compendium, *al-Qanun*, translated from Arabic into Latin, served as Europe's main medical text until nearly the modern age and its title introduced the word 'canon' into European languages. Nasir Khusraw himself was certainly well-schooled in Arabic and there are some suggestions that he also composed works in that language.[1] But all that exists today is in Persian, and that raises some questions. If indeed he wrote only in Persian, it would throw a provocative light on someone who, in all other aspects, took a global view of life. If, on the other hand, he did compose in Arabic also but all that remains are his Persian works, it would illuminate something about the audience that received him and took his words to heart.

Nasir Khusraw's life can be divided into four periods: his early years up until his religious conversion at about the age of forty, about which we know very little; the seven-year journey, for which we have his *Safarnama (Travelogue)* and some references in his poetry; his return home to Khurasan as head missionary for the Ismailis in the region, for which there are some sketchy statements from him and from secondary sources; and finally his exile in the Pamir mountains of Badakhshan in the district of Yumgan, for which we have his poetry and some of his philosophical works with their dedications to the prince who gave him refuge.

## THE EARLY YEARS

Abu Mu'in Hamid al-Din Nasir ibn Khusraw ibn Harith al-Qubadiyani al-Marvazi, generally known as Nasir Khusraw, was born in 394/1004 into a family of government officials.[2] In his prose philosophical works, he usually records his entire name when claiming authorship; in the *Safarnama* he often refers to himself as 'Nasir'; and in the poetry he primarily uses his pen-name 'Hujjat,' which means 'Proof,' his title of elevated rank within the Ismaili missionary organisation, but also 'Nasir' and 'Khusraw.' Khusraw is the only Persian word in his name (all the others, apart from the place names, being Arabic or Arabicised), and it would certainly have been a point of great pride to this defender of

Persian culture and language. For example, Khusraw Parviz and Khusraw Anushirvan were powerful kings of pre-Islamic Iranian empires who established many of the administrative structures later adopted by the Islamic empire under the caliphs.

Nasir's place of birth, Qubadiyan, was a small town in the outskirts of Marv, a major city in the Balkh district of the great province of Khurasan, which extended in eastern Iran roughly up to the Oxus River. The provincial capital, Nishapur, and the city of Marv were important stopping points along the Silk Route and, in Nasir's time, cosmopolitan cities successfully mixing people from many ethnic groups and religions. Sizeable Jewish, Christian and Buddhist communities lived side by side with Muslims of both Sunni and Shi'i persuasions, producing a society rich not only in material wealth but also in intellectual, religious and artistic products.

In the 4th/10th century, several decades before Nasir's birth, the provinces of Khurasan and Transoxiana (in today's Central Asia) had been the locus of a Persian cultural renaissance, following several hundred years in which Arabic temporarily gained ascendancy after the military conquest achieved by the Arabs around the year 30/650. This 'Persian Spring,' as I would call it, resulted in a new language, New Persian, that richly suffused Arabic words into Middle Persian vocabulary and grammar, and provided the vehicle to express a Perso-Islamic cultural identity. One of the most significant early fruits of this new language was the composition of the Iranian national epic poem, the *Shahnama* (*The Book of Kings*), completed by Firdawsi in 401/1010, when Nasir Khusraw was five or six-years-old. Then, within decades, Nasir established himself as a master stylist in this new language in both poetry and prose, fully able to express himself in complicated metres in which rules of Arabic poetry govern Persian poetry, and in a clear prose style unencumbered by the linguistic ornamentation so favoured several centuries later.

Nasir followed family tradition and entered the government bureaucracy in some financial capacity, perhaps tax collection, for which he gained a measure of fame. 'I was a clerk by profession and one of those in charge of the sultan's revenue service' and 'acquired no small reputation among my peers,' he writes in his *Safarnama*.[3] In his early days, familiar first with the Ghaznavid

sultans and then working for their successors the Saljuqs, Nasir
Khusraw enjoyed a life of travel, study, poetry, wine, women and
friends. He had done well at school, having learned Arabic and
Persian with their rules of prosody, and studied philosophy, religious sciences, literature, history and mathematics. Later in life,
he wrote a book on mathematics, even though he could find 'not
one single scholar throughout all Khurasan and the eastern lands
like myself [who] could grapple with the solutions to these problems.' But he felt it his responsibility to take on the task, for
readers he would never see, 'those yet to come, in a time yet to
come.'4

Nasir Khusraw relished the opportunity to see new places and
to admire the accomplishments of the human hand and mind. In
his travels, he turned his keen eye toward both the physical and
administrative structures put in place by each society, such as city
walls, irrigation canals and road surfaces, as well as taxation conditions, employment practices and shop rental policies.
Intellectually precise and attendant to detail, nothing fell outside
his curiosity: he admired the luxurious feel of silks and damasks;
tested local superstitions; arranged a private preview of a royal
banquet; held poetry sessions with local poets; struck up conversations with peasants, shopkeepers and princes; visited Christian
shrines; noticed the presence of women in the cafés of Armenia;
compared fruit bazaars in Cairo, Mecca and Khurasan; delighted
at the sight of a child holding a red rose in one hand and a white
rose in the other; and struggled across the Arabian desert but
refused to eat the recommended lizards.

But, for Nasir Khusraw a more urgent current ran under such
delights of the world, namely his aching desire to have some purpose, some answer to the question of why all this exists. Why the
world, why human happiness, why human sadness, why beautiful
pearls within ugly, scabby oysters? He asked all the teachers and
clergy he knew, inquired of all denominations and schools of
thought, and read all the books he could, but no response was
adequate enough for him. This restless searching and inner dis-
content lasted until it all came together in the conviction that the
answers to these ultimate questions could be found in the doctrines of the Ismaili Shi'i faith.

At some point in his 40th year (or 42nd, depending on the source), Nasir experienced a spiritual upheaval. It culminated in the conviction that truth could be discovered in the Ismaili message. He also became convinced that he must change his life completely and use this truth to change the world. In his *Safarnama* he describes a powerful dream that shocked him out of his 'forty years' sleep,' and transformed his life into one of religious conviction and preaching. Elsewhere, in an autobiographical poem, he recounts his years of spiritual searching and credits his teacher, al-Mu'ayyad fi'l-Din al-Shirazi (d. 470/1078), with guiding him on the path of knowledge. Both accounts of conversion are valid psychologically and possible historically. For a dream or a quest need not be merely a literary convention or a topos of human mythology. People do have dreams and do have moments of exquisite clarity, which they interpret as having revealed a profound truth that thereafter guides their lives. We shall see in greater detail below how Nasir Khusraw had no doubt that the dream meant him to alter his ways radically and that his teacher showed him the new way.

### THE JOURNEY OF A LIFE

Following this conscious, vivid conversion, Nasir Khusraw quit his administrative post and set out from his home province of Khurasan, ostensibly to make the pilgrimage to Mecca. His route took him westward through northern Iran, across Armenia and Azerbaijan, down through Syria to Jerusalem, Hebron and other cities of the region. He spent three of the seven years of his journey in Cairo, the capital of the Fatimids and the heart of Ismaili power and intellectual life. The Fatimids directly challenged the Abbasid caliphate in Baghdad, both militarily and theologically. Their missionary network aimed not only to guide men and women to a life of intellectual and spiritual salvation, but also to attain the Shi'i vision of an Islamic state. While in Cairo, Nasir studied Ismaili doctrines, law and governance with other leading scholars. He also made four pilgrimages to Mecca. From his last pilgrimage, he continued north across Arabia, then through Iran, going eastward, back home to Balkh.

When Nasir left Cairo, he apparently left as the *hujjat* of Khurasan, the head of the Ismaili *da'wa* (missionary organisation) in his home province. The Fatimids had divided the Islamic world into twelve regions and assigned for each of them a supervisor, or *hujjat*, to direct and coordinate the propagation of the faith. For Khurasan, they could not have chosen a better person for their purposes than Nasir Khusraw. His love of his homeland now combined with his fervent commitment to guide others to the right path, just as he himself had been guided.

But the Ismaili faith, which is a branch of Shi'i Islam, was by no means universally appreciated. Both the Sunnis and some non-Ismaili Shi'is regarded the Ismailis as heretics. The significant difference between the Sunnis and the Shi'is (including Ismailis) is that in Shi'i theology the spiritual and temporal leadership of Muslims is believed to flow through the descendants of the Prophet Muhammad, specifically the progeny of his daughter Fatima and her husband 'Ali, a cousin of the Prophet. The early, pre-Fatimid Ismailis recognised a particular line of such spiritual leaders or imams. Subsequently, with the rise of the Fatimids, the Fatimid caliphs were recognised as imams by the Ismailis; and this line of Ismaili imams has continued to the present day. The other main branch of Shi'ism recognises twelve imams, the last of whom disappeared in mysterious circumstances in the year 260/874, and its followers are known as Twelver Shi'is (Ithna'ashariyya). Sunni theology, on the other hand, does not accord 'Ali such extraordinary veneration and generally accepts the progression of leadership as it unfolded after the Prophet Muhammad, that is, the first four caliphs, followed by the Umayyad and Abbasid dynasties of caliphs – an historical continuity which lasted over 600 years, from 11/632 to 656/1258, when the Mongols executed the last Abbasid caliph.

As equally long lasting as the theological difference between Shi'ism and Sunnism, was Shi'i opposition to the concentration of political power in the hands of the Sunnis. The Fatimid caliphate, which lasted from 297/909 to 567/1171, was the first and only major Shi'i ruling power until 907/1501 when Twelver Shi'ism was established as the state religion of Iran under the Safavids. Since the Fatimids directly challenged the authority of the

Abbasid caliphate, both doctrinally and politically, the Sunni Abbasids conducted a campaign of threats, killings and theological polemic against the Fatimids from their capital in Baghdad. Other than the Ismaili Fatimid caliphate in Cairo, most other political power bases were Sunni, and strongly so. Nasir Khusraw's employers before his conversion, first the Ghaznavids and then the Saljuq sultans, were all staunch Sunnis and showed their support for the Sunni caliph in Baghdad through decisive efforts to quell Shi'i activism, especially that of Ismaili missionaries working for the Fatimid caliph.

As the head of Ismaili missionary activity in Khurasan for the Fatimid *da'wa*, Nasir's missionary successes put his life into danger. Both the Sunni and the Twelver Shi'i religious scholars (*'ulama*), as well as the crowds of common people under their influence, threatened his life. We have no clear picture of how much or how frequent the persecution of Nasir Khusraw was, nor do we know what forms it took. But we do know that other Ismaili preachers were often put to death because of their work. So when public pressure against Nasir escalated even in his hometown of Balkh, he realised he had to flee. He found refuge further east, in a place called Yumgan, in the court of 'Ali b. al-Asad, an intellectual Ismaili prince in the mountainous region of Badakhshan.

### YEARS OF EXILE

In exile, remote, far from the intellectual centres of Cairo and his beloved Khurasan, Nasir Khusraw turned his energies inward, producing most of the written works we now have. Stylistically, his philosophical texts move methodically through the fundamentals of Ismaili faith, and his *Safarnama* displays a straightforward, even spare, language with only a few moments of personal expression for the reader. So it is in his poetry where Nasir portrays the greatest range and depth of his feelings. His poetry is filled with the despair and bitterness of his exile, calmed only at times by his unflinching conviction of the rightness of his actions and the surety of his ultimate salvation before God on the Day of Judgement. He heaps his anger on his countrymen for throwing him out of his own land and for being so ignorant as not to see the truth of his message. He bewails his exile, his suffering in intellectual solitude. He pounds his fist at the world for promising pleasure and delivering destruction. But he cannot escape the safety of his refuge. His protection tightens round him. Yumgan becomes synonymous with prison. In one poem, he sets the tone by calling to the wind:

> Pass by, sweet breeze of Khurasan
>> to one imprisoned deep in the valley of Yumgan,
> Who sits huddled in comfortless tight straits,
>> robbed of all wealth, all goods, all hope.
>>>> (*Divan*, 208:1–2)

One image in which our poet often found consolation was of a jewel in a mine. He sees himself as the one precious thing to be found in his entire surroundings. By extension, we are all jewels in the mine, buried beneath tons of muck and dirt, but surely there. No matter the external circumstances, no matter the physical conditions – and luxury and victory can be as deceptive as poverty and enslavement – each person is a work of God, a creation of intrinsic value. Each person contains a piece of eternity, a soul that is the true self. To find this essential self a person must work and dig. Without work, without sacrifice, without conscious effort, the jewel will not be found and will not shine. If the jewel does not shine it does not fulfil the purpose for which it was made. Intrinsic value must be brought into view.

The soul's purpose is to move toward God. For Nasir Khusraw, the conscious effort to find and polish the jewel, that is, to purify the soul of its base bodily surroundings, can only take place when the intellect (Arabic, *'aql*, or Persian, *khirad*) leads the way. Since it is the defining characteristic of human beings, not found in any other of God's creatures, the intellect is the tool for fulfilment in this world and salvation in the next. Through the intellect the human soul is able to learn the things it needs to learn in order to separate what is essential from what is not, the *batin* from the *zahir*, and thereby direct the person's actions to achieve the finest pleasures possible.[5]

Nasir's flight and exile provide the overt content of much of his later poetry. In his verses he allows full rein to his sense of separation and homesickness, pointing surely to one of the most compelling reasons for his enduring popularity, touching as he does upon universal feelings not only of loss and abandonment, but also of hope and confidence in the eventual triumph of good over evil. It is one of the ironies of oppression that the solution chosen to eliminate an enemy often guarantees that enemy's enduring fame. In Nasir Khusraw's case, no one knows the names of his oppressors, but his poems from exile, longing for his homeland, speak across the centuries to anyone whose world has been swept away by war, oppression or terror.

## THE CONTENT OF HIS WRITINGS

As a writer who wrote extensively in the Persian language, Nasir Khusraw is admired not only for his dedication to his mother tongue, but particularly for his imaginative rhetorical skill and his ability to create new words, in addition to new twists on old phrases. As a traveller who visited much of the Islamic world, his personal record of his seven-year journey continues to be scrutinised for all clues it might possibly offer to the history, politics, archaeology, administration, society, religion, customs and military defences of the region and time. As a preacher, he provides not only the tenets of faith in his works, but also the reasons for faith and prescriptions for living in faith. As a moralist warning of the dangers of troubling too much over the pains and pleasures of the world, his verses are recited to this day to illustrate the lessons of life and, also, to provide solace by diminishing vanity which places excessive importance on this life. As a thinker living in exile, his prolific literary output from his 'prison' of Yumgan stands as testimony to his passion and drive for life which were not extinguished even by his own very palpable despair. From whichever angle one chooses to look, what appears is a man trying to live life as ethically and purposefully as possible, one who has examined his past and then decided to make a fundamental change, one who has come to some sort of accommodation with the massive upheavals and disappointments of his life.

His answer was not, however, to fatalistically take refuge in the world's pleasures, or to retire from the world and ignore its social and physical attractions, as many ascetics and some Sufis did, but rather to reject the primacy given to these pleasures by many people and warn all who would be seduced by them. Nasir Khusraw is no ascetic. He chooses as his place of exile a prince's court, not a darvish's hut. Nor does he remove himself from an active life in the world. From his exile in Yumgan, he pours out his writings, 'a book a year,'[6] continuing to see the education of others as his personal responsibility.

## THE TRAVELOGUE

In his *Safarnama*, Nasir Khusraw leaves a record of the seven-year journey from his home in Khurasan to Egypt and back.[7] He adopts a personal style, often referring to himself as 'I, Nasir,' to explain something he did or saw in a certain place. From internal evidence, we can deduce that he wrote the *Safarnama* in a later period from notes that he had taken along the way. Writing in a comparatively simple Persian prose, Nasir Khusraw gains the reader's trust with his straightforward descriptions of cities and towns. He is not trying to impress anyone with his language skills but rather with the strange and wonderful things he saw during his travels. Thus, when words fail even him, as in this attempt to describe the sumptuous richness of Fatimid Cairo, we are also amazed at what he saw:

I saw such personal wealth there that were I to describe it, the people of Persia would never believe it. I could discover no end or limit to their wealth, and I never saw such ease and comfort anywhere (*S*, 55).

The account he did make, then, ought to be seen as a reserved response to exciting experiences. His serene, simple prose style, along with his gentle confessions of personal weaknesses, strike an authentic chord.

Unfortunately, the reports from Nasir Khusraw's sympathetic and discerning eye, open to all architectural and administrative achievements, did not enjoy a wide readership in the Muslim world. Certainly the *Safarnama* suffered from being written in Persian in a culture where Arabic was still the *lingua franca* of the intelligentsia from all lands, but perhaps even more for describing the glories of Ismaili political success. When the Fatimid state splintered and finally fell in 567/1171, the Sunnis again took over the reins of government in Egypt. Deprived of political rule and subject to persecution, the Ismailis once again resorted to the practice of *taqiyya*, or concealing their faith, and advertisements of the glories that had been Fatimid Cairo such as Nasir Khusraw's *Safarnama* were purposefully ignored.

### POETRY

Nasir Khusraw's poetry is located in several works, the main corpus having been collected into his *Divan*,[8] which now totals more than 15,000 lines. The poems in the *Divan* are primarily odes composed in *qasida* form, portraying lofty sentiments and thoughts in a formal and stately style. The *qasida* is characterised by a single rhyme carried throughout the whole poem. Each line (*bayt*) consists of two equal parts (*misra'*). Besides the odes, the *Divan* also contains shorter poems and quatrains. The poems in the *Divan* have, so far, received two major treatments in English: forty poems were translated by P. L. Wilson and G. R. Aavani in 1977,[9] and, more recently, Annemarie Schimmel has translated and discussed key themes in quite a number of selected verses.[10]

Nasir Khusraw also has two long free-standing poems, both of which were included in the 1925–28 edition of the *Divan*, even though there was some question of the authorship of one. The first, *Rawshana'i-nama (The Book of Enlightenment)* must be distinguished from his prose work of the same name – which surely marks Nasir Khusraw as the sole example of a Persian writer to have two different works, one in prose, the other in verse, bearing the same name. Fortunately, the prose work carries another name, *Shish fasl (Six Chapters)*, and for the sake of clarity will be referred to here as such. The second long poem, *Sa'adat-nama (The Book of Happiness)*, has caused considerable debate for over a century. As it had been traditionally attributed to Nasir Khusraw, it was included in the 1925–28 edition of the *Divan*, even though one of the editors considered it spurious. Malik al-Shu'ara states in his *Sabk shinasi* that it must have been composed by another person, a certain Nasir Khusraw-i Isfahani.[11] G. M. Wickens translated the *Sa'adat-nama* into English in 1955, without taking sides on its authorship. Given the doubts about its authorship, the present work makes no further reference to the *Sa'adat-nama*.[12]

### PHILOSOPHY

As the leader of the Ismaili *da'wa* in Khurasan, Nasir Khusraw produced a number of prose works on Ismaili doctrine, all of them in the Persian language as far as we know. To date, six of these works have been edited from manuscripts and several have been translated, at least partially, into Western languages. The six edited works are *Gushayish wa rahayish* (*Unfettering and Setting Free*), *Jami' al-hikmatayn* (*Uniting the Two Wisdoms*), *Khwan al-ikhwan* (*The Feast of the Brethren*), *Shish fasl* (*Six Chapters*, i.e., the prose *Rawshana'i-nama*), *Wajh-i din* (*The Face of Religion*) and *Zad al-musafirin* (*The Pilgrims' Provisions*). In addition to these, I. K. Poonawala has identified a number of manuscripts of other works by Nasir Khusraw, and Nasir himself refers to about ten other works, missing to this date.[13]

The *Gushayish wa rahayish*[14] is arranged as a series of thirty questions and answers dealing with theological issues which range from the metaphysical ('How can a non-body [such as God] create a body?') to the soteriological ('On the injustice of compelled acts and eternal punishment'). Most of the questions are concerned with the human soul, its relation to the world of nature, and its quest for salvation in the next world. They discuss whether the soul is a substance and whether it has been created, and how a person can know about God and His work. However interesting the questions, Nasir Khusraw's answers always remain general and synoptic, presenting succinct versions of his understanding of Fatimid doctrine on each of the topics. The work stands as a catechism identifying the key theological questions of the Fatimid *da'wa* and summarising its teaching on these issues.

In *Jami' al-hikmatayn*,[15] Nasir Khusraw contributes to the larger medieval goal of combining the two 'wisdoms' of philosophy and religion, specifically Greek philosophy and Islam. Our author not only attempts to bridge the methodological gap between the two, namely philosophy's method of arriving at knowledge through logical proofs and religion's method of arriving at knowledge through revelation from God, but also to show that the two are in essence the same, that is, they lead to knowledge of the same truth. The catalyst for Nasir's work was an Ismaili poem written by Abu'l-Haytham Jurjani a few decades earlier (in the 4th/10th century) which posed certain theological questions. This poem had come to the attention of the Ismaili prince of Badakhshan, 'Ali b. al-Asad, Nasir's protector. Curious, the prince asked him to respond to the questions, and the *Jami' al-hikmatayn* was his voluminous answer.[16] After establishing a theoretical foundation based on Aristotelian principles such as the different kinds of causes (including formal, efficient, final), Nasir Khusraw covers a wide range of topics, including proofs for the existence of the Creator, divine unity (*tawhid*), divine perfection, universal nature, the angels, *pari*s and *div*s, genus and species, various types of eternity, the properties of the moon, creation, the difference between perception (*mudrik*) and understanding (*idrak*), the relation between body, soul and intellect, the concept of 'I' or self, and the influence of heavenly bodies on human beings and souls. In addition, he includes a section on the poem's author and disparages theologians for destroying both religion and philosophy.

The third edited text, *Khwan al-ikhwan*,[17] is divided into 100 chapters. These chapters cover such topics as resurrection; how an incorporeal soul will be punished or rewarded; the necessity for carrying out the requirements of the religious law (*shari'a*); the meaning of the word *Allah*; the different ranks of Intellect and Soul; the difference between soul and spirit; how the 'many' of the world come from 'one' command of creation; the superiority of spiritual power over physical power; that the declaration of faith (*shahadat*) is the key to heaven; the difference between the Qur'an and the word of the Prophet; and why two prophets could not function at the same time. Chronologically, we know that this is one of Nasir Khusraw's later works since he refers in it to his *Gushayish wa rahayish*.[18] The *Khwan al-ikhwan* is remarkably similar to the *Kitab al-yanabi'* written in Arabic by his fellow Persian Ismaili philosopher, Abu Ya'qub al-Sijistani (d. after 361/ 971), a similarity which strongly suggests that Nasir may have merely translated his colleague's work into Persian, at least in part.[19] However, Nasir Khusraw's work contains unique sections not found in al-Sijistani's Arabic text and should therefore be studied as an independent text, for these sections may either represent lost parts of al-Sijistani's work, a portion of another work by him, or original writing by Nasir Khusraw himself.

The fourth edited text, *Shish fasl* (the prose *Rawshana'i-nama*),[20] presents a succinct version of the Fatimid Ismaili doctrine of creation, beginning with the concept of unity (*tawhid*), continuing through the succeeding Neoplatonic hypostases of Intellect, Soul and Nature, and ending with a discussion of human salvation and how it relates to the hypostases. However superficial this short treatment of these topics may appear, *Shish fasl* nevertheless serves a valuable purpose in laying out essential doctrines in compact form suitable for teaching purposes, a value visible in the work's popularity even today. It points to the widespread appeal of these doctrines among many Ismailis and thus a continuity of belief stretching back 900 years.

In the *Wajh-i din*,[21] Nasir Khusraw provides his most straightforward esoteric interpretation (*ta'wil*) of a variety of religious regulations and rituals, giving the inner (*batin*) meaning of certain externals (*zahir*) of religion. The book's fifty-one sections include, for example, his *ta'wil* of certain verses from the Qur'an, the call to prayer, ablutions for prayer, the five assigned times of prayer, the movements of praying, alms for the poor, the *hajj* (pilgrimage to the Ka'ba in Mecca) and certain prescribed punishments. Following Ismaili hermeneutics, he shows the parallels between the structure of the physical world and that of the spiritual world, and between the human body and the human soul. As an example of the latter, he explains that since drinking wine corrupts the body and usury corrupts the soul, both are therefore prohibited by religious law. For Nasir Khusraw the rectitude of religious law is revealed in its balanced concern for a believer's body as well as soul. The 'face of religion' can be seen as both that beautiful reality which needs to be veiled, as well as the superficial cover itself which hides the inner reality. By choosing this title, Nasir is also alluding to the verse in the Qur'an, 'All things perish, except His face' (28:88), meaning that when all superficialities are removed, only the reality of God remains.

In the last of his six works edited so far, the *Zad al-musafirin*,[22] Nasir Khusraw covers a wide variety of physical and metaphysical topics such as simple matter, bodies, motion, time, place, creation, cause and effect, and reward and punishment. But in keeping with the title of the book, he devotes most of his discussion to the human soul, that is, the pilgrim soul travelling through this physical world to salvation in the spiritual world. He discusses the fundamental substance of soul and its essential activities. He devotes one entire chapter to how the soul is united with the body and another to explain why. In another chapter he describes how individuals emerge in the physical world and later are annihilated. One chapter treats the experience of pleasure and heaven. He refutes the doctrine of metempsychosis (*tanasukh*), the theory that souls reincarnate in different human bodies over time. He argues for the necessity for the reward of heaven and the punishment of hell, that is, the ultimate state of the soul. Throughout the text, Nasir asserts that the most important provisions which the pilgrim needs for this journey are knowledge and wisdom.

# CHAPTER TWO

# Heretic, Magician or King?

I asked the prince of Badakhshan, Shah Sultan Muhammad.
He responded that everything about Nasir was a fable,
unworthy of any credence.

Dawlatshah, *Tadhkirat al-shu'ara*

Extending Nasir Khusraw's own use of the image of a jewel, we can say that trying to gain a true picture of him is rather like trying to see inside a jewel. The picture we have of him comes fragmented through several sources and we must move it from side to side, looking through different facets to see it entire. What he himself has written refracts off what others have written and the reader must take care in interpreting what is there, for some of the shadows are actually flaws.

Usually the biographer's task consists, in part at least, of correcting the received popular picture of the subject – showing the noble side of a scoundrel, the doubts of a world conqueror, or the crimes of a hero. The effort aims to round out the picture, to make the subject more human by taking away the mystique and mythology. But rarely is the biographer handed a stack of legends so convoluted and frequently repeated that one of the first books published has to carry the title, *Problems in Nasir-i Khusraw's Biography*.[1]

Over the centuries, accounts of Nasir Khusraw's life assert that he was variously a king, a heretic, a reincarnationist, the leader of a sect named after himself, that he built palaces and gardens by magic, that he lived on the top of a mountain eating only once every twenty-five days, that he lived to be more than 100-years-old, and that he subsisted solely on the smell of food.

To complicate matters further, there appeared in the 10th/ 16th century (500 years after he lived) a document purporting to be his autobiography. This pseudo-autobiography, *A Treatise on Repentance for Judgement Day*,[2] tells of the poet's early education, including his studies of magic and sorcery, his work under the Fatimid caliph in Egypt, his several narrow escapes from enemies, his flight to Badakhshan, and his last years in Yumgan. But this treatise also includes his deathbed scene. A later writer, speaking as his brother, has added a description of Nasir Khusraw's final hours, complete with the dying scholar's instructions for the distribution of his possessions. Not only does this in itself throw the entire work into doubt as an autobiography, but the document is replete with falsehoods concerning the specifics of his life, such as its claim that he studied sorcery. But it cannot be discarded entirely out of hand, for it reveals clues of the popular conception of this man; that is, what is remembered of the man can give us an inkling of the powerful effect he had on the public consciousness.

Other sources reveal additional problems. There are discrepancies in the dates of his birth and death, his place of birth, whether he converted to Ismailism before he went to Egypt or as a result of going there, whether he was a *sayyid* (a descendant of the Prophet Muhammad through his daughter Fatima), and the precise location of his missionary activities after his return home to Khurasan. In addition, along with such historical questions run questions of his poetic ability, some suggesting he was one of the best Persian poets,[3] and others claiming his art was compromised by its service to religious doctrine.[4]

## TRACKING DOWN THE SOURCES

Nasir Khusraw has attracted the interest of some of the finest minds over the centuries. Here, in chronological order, are brief descriptions of some of the citations in the rich literatures in Arabic and Persian of histories, geographies and biographies of poets.

The first of these sources mentioning Nasir Khusraw was written by a contemporary within fifteen years of the subject's death. In his book on religions, *Bayan al-adyan* (*A Description of Religions*),[5] Abu'l-Ma'ali reports that Nasir Khusraw was known as the leader of a region (*jazira*), had his home in Yumgan, and turned the people from the right path and took them down the path of heresy. The author states further that the Shi'is are divided into several groups, one of which is the Nasiriyya, the followers of Nasir Khusraw, and that several of his books, namely *Wajh-i din* and *Dalil al-mutahayyirin* (*The Guide of the Wanderers*), espouse heretical beliefs.[6] The biographer adds that many in the region of Tabaristan (near the Caspian Sea) had taken the wrong path and followed Nasir Khusraw's erroneous teachings.

Each of these points bears close inspection because in this blatantly hostile entry reside some seeds of truth. The Fatimid *da'wa* organisation divided the world into twelve regions or *jaziras* (literally, 'islands'), each headed by a chief *da'i* (missionary) with the rank of *hujjat* (proof). Nasir Khusraw, as we have seen, was named chief *da'i* of one of these twelve regions, his homeland of Khurasan, and therefore is known as the '*hujjat* of Khurasan.'[7] He himself mentions this frequently in his philosophical works and his poems. That this appointment meant a lot to him can be seen in his adoption of 'Hujjat' as his poetic pen-name. And, while it is true that he made his home in Yumgan (in his final years), it could hardly be said that Yumgan was the centre of his assigned region of Khurasan. Rather, Yumgan was a small backwater, its only claim to fame coming later, as the site of the preacher's exile.

As to heresy, it is commonplace for opponents of other people's religions to level against them the charge of irreligion. The opponents of the Ismailis were many and formidable, and the enemies of Nasir Khusraw called him irreligious and a heretic, a point about which he himself complains bitterly. Ironically, though, the one extant book of the two cited by Abu'l-Ma'ali to prove the preacher's heresy, the *Wajh-i din*, is one of the most explicit of his works to grapple with questions of faith and practice, the meaning behind the 'face' of religion. This work takes religious rituals and dogmas one by one and endeavours to show the underlying truths and purposes within each. Thus, rather than

a fair assessment of Nasir Khusraw's Shi'i faith, Abu'l-Ma'ali's preju-
diced judgement simply shows that he absolutely rejects Ismaili
doctrines.[8]

There is no arguing with the fact that Nasir attracted many
adherents to the Ismaili faith, but it is important to note that he
was famous within his own lifetime – this was not added centuries
later to embellish his biography. It is of great interest to read in
Abu'l- Ma'ali's contemporary account that Nasir Khusraw had so
many followers that there came to be a sect named after him.
Nasir himself cannot be the source of this notion, for a careful
review of all his philosophical writings reveals no unusual focus
on himself, no claims to personal leadership beyond the norm of
a missionary calling people to his faith, no arrogance beyond that
of someone who was well-educated and dared to write books. His
boasts of poetic prowess and lamentations from exile all fall within
the acceptable poetic and scholarly styles of his day. The Nasiriyya,
in fact, were a local Zaydi sect in the Caspian region whom Abu'l-
Ma'ali has wrongly attributed to Nasir Khusraw.

Others besides historians and geographers were moved by the
life and writings of Nasir Khusraw. The famous mystic poet, Farid
al-Din 'Attar (d. 617/1220), author of the *Mantiq al-tayr* (*The Conference of the Birds*) and *Tadhkirat al-awliya'* (*Lives of the Saints*),
reportedly penned a six-couplet poem in honour of Nasir
Khusraw's decision to remain in exile rather than to compromise
his commitment to the 'chosen family,' that is, the family of the
Prophet Muhammad. The poem appears, with its title, toward the
end of *Lisan al-ghayb* (*The Hidden Voice*), ascribed to 'Attar:

*The Tale of Nasir Khusraw and His Seclusion*

The cry of Nasir Khusraw when he dwelt in Yumgan
Arched even past heaven's nine-storied vault.

A little corner he took to hide himself away,
Hearing the Prophet himself had named the very spot.

True offspring of the Prophet, that man of faith,
Sworn foe of the foes of the chosen family.[9]

Not a man to enter into the fighting fields of dogs,

Like a ruby in Badakhshan he hid himself away.

'Mid the hidden hearts of mountains, he chose the corner of
    Yumgan,
So as not to have to look upon the horrid faces of his foes.

Now I, too, like that great prince, have found a little corner for
    myself,

Since in the search for deeper meaning he provided the
    provisions.

The next citation of Nasir Khusraw appeared in 674/1275,
just after the Mongols had conquered and ravaged Central Asian
and Iranian lands and destroyed the Abbasid caliphate (centred in Baghdad) itself in 656/1258. The chief judge in Shiraz,
al-Baydawi, wrote a history of Iran and its people, *Nizam al-tawarikh
(The Scales of Histories)*, in which he sifted through previous sources
and attempted to give a balanced account.[10] Al-Baydawi relates
that many stories are told about Nasir Khusraw – some say he is
a true believer, while others attack him for being an infidel who
believes in incarnation and for poorly defending his literary
ideas. Al-Baydawi states that Nasir's *Divan* is made up of 30,000
verses, 'full of wisdom and counsel,' a description which may
indicate that al-Baydawi had actually read the poems. Besides
poetry, al-Baydawi mentions two other works by Nasir Khusraw,
*Rawshana'i-nama* and *Kanz al-haqa'iq*, the second of which is no
longer extant. The chronicler adds other particulars of his life:
that Nasir came originally from Isfahan, that he was a contemporary of Sultan Mahmud of Ghazna and a friend of Ibn Sina,
and that his tomb is located in Yumgan, a town in Badakhshan.
He reports that the people of Quhistan are extremely devoted
to Nasir Khusraw, some saying he was a king, and others a *sharif*,
a descendant of the Prophet. He places the missionary's death
in 1049.

Several items in al-Baydawi's biography can be challenged at
once. Nasir Khusraw was not originally from Isfahan, according
to his own clear and ample statements in poetry and prose;[11] the
date of his death is incorrect;[12] and determining whether Nasir
Khusraw was a descendant of the Prophet has been the subject

of careful attention even in recent decades, with the conclusion that he was not and that the terms *sayyid* or *sharif* must be seen as honorific titles.[13] And while it is true that he was a contemporary of Sultan Mahmud, he could not have been a friend to Ibn Sina (d. 429/1037) who, while originally from the eastern Iranian provinces, was employed from the year 405/1015 (when Nasir Khusraw was eleven-years-old) in cities further to the west of Khurasan, such as Rayy and Hamadan. And as to whether they could have met along Nasir Khusraw's journey, the fact is that Ibn Sina died several years before Nasir commenced his journey in 437/1045.

Not only does al-Baydawi link Nasir Khusraw with the philosopher Ibn Sina, he includes a perceptive, though equally doubtful, tale of a meeting between our author and a famous Sufi mystic. This tale depicts Nasir Khusraw as a proponent of intellect (*'aql*) as the correct path to attaining true knowledge, and the Sufi as a champion of the superiority of love (*'ishq*) over intellect.

According to this story,[14] Nasir Khusraw travelled from Isfahan to Gilan to Rustamdar, where he engaged in intellectual debates with scholars who attacked him so violently that he had to flee for his life to Khurasan. After Nasir had been run out of town, he sought refuge in a Sufi monastery headed by Shaykh Abu'l-Hasan 'Ali al-Kharaqani (d. 425/1034). The shaykh knew of the scholar's predicament and instructed his own followers to allow Nasir to enter the enclave, but to misinform the traveller as to the identity of the person of the shaykh by introducing him as an illiterate landlord.[15] However, when Nasir Khusraw arrived and the greetings and introductions had been accomplished as planned, the guest did not fall for the deception. He, in fact, parried the gesture with his own attempt at hiding his erudition, saying, 'O great Shaykh, I would like to pass the discussions in silence and I would like to find a refuge among wise men.'

To which the shaykh replied, smiling, 'O you poor fool! How do you hope to be near me, you who have spent your years a prisoner to your imperfect intellect?'

Nasir replied, 'How is it known by the shaykh that our intellect is imperfect? For we say that the intellect is the first thing created by God.'

The shaykh answered, 'That is the intellect of the prophets. Do not be so sure of yourself on this issue. Your intellect is imperfect, like that of Avicenna! And you are both mistaken. The proof I give is the poem you composed yesterday in which you believe that the essence of the [Qur'anic] phrase "Be! And it is!" is the intellect. Rather, the essence referred to is love.' The shaykh then recited the first verse of Nasir's poem:

Above the seven heavens reside the two essences
More exalted than creation and all that is contained within it.[16]

(*Divan*, 112:1)

Nasir Khusraw was astounded at this miracle, for he had composed the *qasida* that very evening and had not revealed it to anyone. He then had full confidence in the shaykh and stayed some time in his service. While there, he occupied himself with ascetic practices and purifying his soul. After some time, he asked permission to leave for Khurasan where he was again hounded by religious scholars and clergy who found his message dangerous. Soon afterwards, Nasir Khusraw left Nishapur for Badakhshan.

This account about al-Kharaqani is most likely false because, as far as we know, it was only after his return from Egypt to eastern Iran in 444/1052 that Nasir's religious activity attracted the wrath of other religious scholars and leaders, whereas the Sufi died in 426/1034. However, Nasir Khusraw could have met al-Kharaqani decades before he embarked on his journey. Indeed, one of the first stops on his journey was at Bistam and the tomb of the Sufi master Bayazid, the very spiritual master claimed by al-Kharaqani.[17] Even if we dismiss this story for chronological reasons, we still need to look at the lesson it carried that made it attractive for centuries. The crux of the story is the contrast between two approaches to attaining knowledge – intellect or love. Nasir Khusraw is clearly seen as the espouser of intellect and rationality who is ultimately won over to the mystic's message of love. However charming this outcome, there is nothing in Nasir Khusraw's writings that would support the notion that he ever abandoned the vocabulary of intellect for that of mystical love. Deeply devout, deeply spiritual, and deeply devoted to the *ahl al-bayt*, the Prophet's family, he certainly was, but a Sufi, no.

Another sort of book appeared in the 7th/13th century, about the same time as al-Baydawi's history. This was al-Qazvini's annotated geography, *Athar al-bilad wa akhbar al-'ibad (Monuments of Lands and Remarks on the People)*,[18] which included an entry for the town of Yumgan. Further showing that Yumgan's only claim to fame was Nasir Khusraw, this two-page entry in a work of geography is nearly entirely devoted to one of the stories about his life. Al-Qazvini begins by stating that Yumgan is a well-fortified and impregnable city in the mountains of western Badakhshan, known for its mines of silver and something resembling ruby. He continues that, according to Prince Husam al-Din Abu'l-Mu'ayyad b. Nu'man, Nasir Khusraw had been a king of Balkh, but that after its people revolted against him he took refuge in Yumgan because of its strong fortifications. Once there, he used magic to have palaces and bathhouses built and gardens planted. According to al-Qazvini, the prince states that the buildings were described to him in the most fantastic terms and that, even in his day, the descendants of Nasir continued with these legends. This is the first mention of Nasir Khusraw's use of magic, whereby his powers of persuasion (acknowledged by his contemporaries) have been transformed into mythic proportions.

Some of the Mongol rulers, attempting to assess what exactly they were in charge of, commissioned their own studies of the conquered territories. In 1300, the esteemed physician and vizier Rashid al-Din Fadl Allah embarked on a major project to write a general history of the world. His *Jami' al-tawarikh* (*Compendium of Histories*), written under the order of the Mongol ruler Ghazan Khan, records this of Nasir Khusraw:

Nasir Khusraw travelled from Khurasan to Egypt due to the great reputation of Mustansir, and lived there for seven years. Each year he went on the Hajj pilgrimage and returned to Egypt. From the last Hajj he travelled to Basra and then returned to Khurasan. In Balkh, he carried out preaching for the Egyptian Alids. Enemies attacked him. He hid in the mountains of Yumgan and remained there for twenty years, surviving on water and plants.[19]

Except for some details of chronology (Nasir's journey actually lasted seven years, three of them in Cairo), this report represents one of the most accurate and restrained accounts about our author. Whether he was actually a vegetarian at the end, we do not know. In the later stages of his exile he may have turned to ascetic practices, but there is no advocation or evidence of any such tendency in any of his writings. On the contrary, one of his principal ethical positions is the responsibility of human beings to make use of the gifts of the body and nature given by God.

In the 9th/15th century, the highly esteemed poet and man of letters known as Jami wrote in the chapter on poets in his *Baharistan* (*Land of Springtime*)[20] that Nasir Khusraw 'used all the resources of the poetic art with complete naturalness and ability. He had complete control of the natural sciences, but was accused of holding erroneous religious views and to be inclined to irreligion and impiety. He wrote a book of his travels throughout most of the countries of the world and in addition wrote in verse about his engagements with the intellectuals of his day.'[21] Jami follows this introduction with the inclusion of several verses of Nasir Khusraw which he claims had been previously cited by the mystic 'Ayn al-Qudhat, but some scholars have raised questions about such citations.[22] This is the first account to unconditionally praise Nasir Khusraw's intellectual and artistic abilities. And the assertion of his 'complete control over the natural sciences' anchors Nasir's own claim to extensive scientific knowledge and also legitimises the title *hakim* (sage). Jami is also evidently familiar with Nasir Khusraw as the author of the *Safarnama*, though earlier chroniclers seem to have known more about the specifics of the travels themselves. In his comment about Nasir's conversations in verse with intellectuals, Jami could be referring to his confessional poem (see Chapter 4) in which the author lists the kinds of thinkers he consulted in his spiritual quest.

A contemporary of Jami, Amir Dawlatshah, produced in 893/1487 perhaps the most influential of such anthologies of poets, the *Tadhkirat al-shu'ara* (*Memoirs of the Poets*).[23] Copying extensively from al-Baydawi, Dawlatshah repeats the claim that Nasir Khusraw was originally from Isfahan and that he had proceeded from there to Gilan and Rustamdar, where he stayed awhile engaged in discussions with scholars and theologians. When Dawlatshah remarks that some reports claim Nasir to be a materialist (*tabi'i* and *dahri*) or to believe in the transmigration of souls (*tanasukh*) – positions Nasir Khusraw argued vigorously against – he ends it with the careful qualifier, 'but only God knows for sure' (*al-'ilm 'ind-Allah*), a sure sign that he had not read any of Nasir Khusraw's philosophical works. With the same scepticism, he rejects the notion that Nasir had discussions with Ibn Sina. But he follows al-Baydawi in repeating the story of the meeting with the Sufi al-Kharaqani, including even the first line of the *qasida* quoted miraculously by the Sufi. Dawlatshah also includes several other portions of Nasir's poems.[24] In addition to his obvious dependence on al-Baydawi's history, it appears that Dawlatshah carried out some original research. After reading a variety of sources, he summarises that 'some of them write that he is a sultan, others a king, others a prince, and others say he was a *sayyid*, and others that he spent time atop a mountain subsisting on the fragrance of food.' Dawlatshah dismissed such tales as popular rumour (*sukhan-i 'awam*), lacking any credibility. Seeking some clarification for the wide range of claims, he personally asked the then prince of Badakhshan, Shah Shahid Sultan Muhammad, about these accounts. Dawlatshah writes that the prince responded that all these stories were completely unfounded, 'that everything about Nasir was a fable unworthy of any credence.'

About a century later, a poet known as Dhikri came out with his *Khulasat al-ash'ar wa zubdat al-afkar* (*The Best of Poems and Finest of Thoughts*), a survey of poets since the time of Sebuktigin, the father of Mahmud of Ghazna.[25] On Nasir Khusraw, Dhikri translated into Persian a work in Arabic purported to be his autobiography under the title, *Risalat al-nadama fi zad al-qiyama* (*Treatise on Repentance to Serve as Provisions for the Day of Resurrection*). While the Arabic original is lost, Dhikri's 16th-century Persian translation was preserved by a later historian of poets, Hajji Lutf 'Ali Beg Adhar, who included the entire pseudo-auto-

biography in his 18th-century reference book of poets. As a result, details of this spurious work have become fixed in the popular
conception of Nasir Khusraw. It is too long to be reproduced here
in full, but a paraphrase of one section should give a flavour of
the details which make this piece so attractive.

According to Dhikri's account, Nasir left Egypt as a fugitive,
the victim of a political shake-up in the Fatimid court, and he
and his brother Abu Sa'id found refuge in Baghdad with the
Caliph al-Qa'im. During that time, Nasir went to visit the *da'i* of
Gilan, in the Caspian region. The *da'i* was so delighted with
having someone 'whose reputation as an intellectual, fully
steeped in the natural and occult sciences, was universal' that
he would not allow Nasir Khusraw to return to the caliph in
Baghdad who, after a while, had begun calling him back. It
seems that he remained in Gilan for quite some time, long
enough for Nasir Khusraw to be invested with the full powers of
a vizier and to complete a commentary on the Qur'an. Eventually Nasir handed over all political power and decision-making
to his brother in order to concentrate on his 'magic arts and
the evocation of spirits, which he held under his power.' It is
reported that, with the aid of one of these spirits, Nasir Khusraw,
perhaps trying to find a way to leave, was able to inflict the *da'i*
with an illness which no physician could recognise or cure.
Even though his familiarity with sorcery made him suspect, Nasir
was given permission to attempt a cure which required him to
leave Gilan and travel to Damascus where, he said, grew a plant
which could remedy the illness. Despite the opposition of religious lawyers and clerics, Nasir Khusraw was allowed to leave,
accompanied, however, by an escort of 300 men. On arriving
in Quhistan, some twenty-one farsangs away, Nasir Khusraw, with
the help of his brother, incited the influence of the planet Mars
so that all 300 men were overtaken with violence, killing each
other down to the last man.

Dhikri's account continues that Nasir Khusraw, his brother and
a disciple were thus able to escape eastward to Khurasan and to
the city of Nishapur, 'where he was unknown.' They lodged in the
safety of a mosque, but were soon found out by a man who had
known Nasir in Egypt. Nasir secured the man's silence with a

payment of 3,000 *mithqals* of gold. However, his disciple one day became caught up in a debate with religious experts during which his Ismaili beliefs must have become evident. He was pointed out to the crowd, which turned angry, then attacked and finally killed him.

Nasir Khusraw and his brother fled further east from Nishapur and took refuge in the province of Badakhshan. But even there, despite the careful watch and protection provided by the governor of Badakhshan, 'Isa b. As'ad al-'Alawi, he had to undergo a new persecution. The Qur'anic commentary he had written in Gilan had found its way to Badakhshan, and no one less than the zealous Sunni scholar Nasr Allah Sawiri denounced the ideas it contained and pronounced a death sentence on Nasir Khusraw. The two brothers fled deeper into Badakhshan, finally finding safety in a cave near Yumgan. According to Dhikri, they lived there for twenty-five years, devoting themselves to the most extreme ascetic practices. Dhikri records that some people believed that Nasir Khusraw ate but once every twenty-four hours, while others held that just the fragrance of food sufficed to sustain him.

In Dhikri's account, we now have in narrative form all the fantastical elements and all the suspicions against him woven together in a biography extolling his excellence as a poet.

Another misleading but important source, Khwandamir's *Habib al-siyar* (*The Friend of Biographies*)[26] declares:

Amir Khusraw is a major poet. He was a contemporary of the Fatimid Caliph al-Mustansir and was born in 359 [969]. Having arrived at the age of discernment, he made contact with the Ismailis, as a result of which he made haste to Egypt. He lived there seven years, making the pilgrimage each year. He limited himself strictly to Islamic dogma. After his last pilgrimage he left for Khurasan by the Basra road. He lived in Sawj, where he carried out missionary work on behalf of al-Mustansir and the Ismailis. Several enemies of the family of the Prophet fought against him. Frightened by these attacks, he took refuge in a mountain of Badakhshan where he remained for twenty years, satisfying himself on water and plants.

Khwandamir also refers to Nasir Khusraw's meagre intake of

food, which seems to have been copied from Rashid al-Din's *Jami'*
*al-tawarikh* of three centuries before. His mention of the *Safarnama*
seems to be the first time a chronicler had actually seen the book
itself, relaying details, for example, that it was after his last pilgrimage to Mecca that he turned north to Basra and then
homeward to the east. In addition, the enemies are specifically
labelled 'enemies of the family of the Prophet,' referring to attacks
by Sunnis. However, in spite of this positive entry, Khwandamir
introduces a serious problem. In calling our author Amir Khusraw,
he runs the risk of causing confusion with a later poet in India of
the same name.[27] While the titles of *hakim* and *khwaja* are legitimate for Nasir Khusraw (as well as *shah, sharif* and *sayyid* if we
accept them only as honorifics), Amir is not.

An 11th/17th-century work, Muhammad Muhsin Fani's
*Dabistan-i madhahib* (*Book of Religious Sects*) has been considered
by later scholars to be one of the more careful and accurate accounts, a feature especially important in a book on religious
differences.[28] For example, Schefer notes that its author has correctly timed Nasir's voyage and included some details of the exile
in Badakhshan. And, except for changing the name of the town
Sawj to Sabah, al-Khashshab agrees with Schefer that this is a de-
pendable source, citing Fani's interviews with the Ismailis of his
day. Fani writes, 'Ignorant people claim that Nasir was affiliated
with the Ismailis of Alamut, and certain writers have expressed in
their writings their regret to know that he attached himself to this
sect. But the fact is that the Ismailis of Alamut never had relations
with those of the West [i.e., Egypt]. We have heard this from Ismailis themselves about Nasir.' Fani is referring to the fact that
the division of the Ismailis into eastern (Nizari) and western
(Musta'li) branches came about after Nasir's death and the
caliphate of the Imam al-Mustansir (d. 487/1094).

In the late 12th/18th century, a court poet named Lutf 'Ali
Beg Adhar (d. 1195/1781) compiled an anthology of Persian poetry in which he also included biographies of the poets, remarkably
arranged geographically rather than chronologically. Called
*Atashkada-i Adhar* (*Adhar's Fire Temple*),[29] the anthology served as
one of Adhar's tools in his campaign to return Persian poetry to a
leaner, more classical style than the convoluted hyper-cerebral

'Indian' style then in vogue. Counting him as one of the early
Persian poets, Adhar gives Nasir Khusraw a substantial entry which
includes Dhikri's pseudo-autobiography discussed above and nine
selected poems or poem fragments. The selected poems themselves are noteworthy in that they provide a historical record of
what a poet of 200 years ago (Adhar himself) considered exem-
plary Persian verse. The influence of Adhar's entry cannot be
underestimated, especially given the fact that the fantastical images in Dhikri's piece were further broadcast when the
pseudo-autobiography was included in the first lithographed edition of Nasir's *Divan* (Tabriz, 1281/1864), and then translated
into French and portions of it included in Schefer's Paris publication of the *Safarnama* in 1881.

Toward the end of the 13th/19th century, an innovative and
much respected educator in the court of the Qajar kings of Iran,
Riza Quli Khan Hidayat (1215–1289/1800–1872), composed a
major biographical survey of poets, scholars and other literati up
to his own time. For Nasir Khusraw, this work, *Majma' al-fusaha*
(*The Conference of the Eloquent*),[30] gives a brief biographical introduction and includes quite a number of selections from his
poetry. Riza Quli Khan states that he has gathered nearly 12,000
verses from Nasir Khusraw's 'noble' *Divan*. If we compare this
figure to the 30,000 mentioned by al-Baydawi, we are led to
mourn the possibility that nearly 20,000 verses had been lost
through the six intervening centuries. Riza Quli Khan puts Nasir
Khusraw's date of birth correctly at 394/1003–4. In addition,
among Nasir's other works extant at the time, he lists *Zad al-
musafirin*, an Arabic *Divan*, *Dastur-i a'zam*, *Sa'adat-nama* and the
verse *Rawshana'i-nama*. In another of his works, volume nine of
*Rawdat al-safa-yi Nasiri* (*The Nasirean Garden of Purity*),[31] referring
to the king of the time, not Nasir Khusraw, Riza Quli Khan
states in the section on Khurasan that there exist in the mountains of Badakhshan, Hazara and Bamyan, Ismaili Shi'is who
follow the teachings of their *da'is*, especially the doctrines of
one called Shah Sayyid Nasir Khusraw 'Alavi. This branch of
the Ismailis is called the Nasiriyya. So, here again, we have the
followers of a sect identified by Nasir Khusraw's name, but this
time the reference is grounded within specific geographical

regions. Given the popularity he enjoys in those regions today, perhaps it is not too far-fetched to accept that Nasir Khusraw's fame (or notoriety) had persisted there over many centuries.

Sources over the past century or so are easier to come by, and the interested reader is invited to explore the works, particularly those of H. Taqizada, E. G. Browne, W. Ivanow, 'Ali Dashti, Y. al-Khashshab and Mehdi Mohaghegh. Several Russian and Tajik scholars have also contributed significantly, although the Soviet tendency to look for ways to view Nasir Khusraw predominantly as a defender of peasants is being reconsidered today. A good number of works have also been produced in Urdu. In 1976, an academic conference was held in Iran on the occasion of the 1000th anniversary of Nasir Khusraw's birth, and the published papers brought together the work of over thirty-five scholars.[32]

Two points remain. In the early years of the 20th century, learned people in Iran were able to recite certain verses used to discredit Nasir Khusraw's faith or, as Browne put it, to prove his atheism.[33] The verses do not prove any such thing, nor do they even indicate anything that could be termed 'irreligion.' Even if they are Nasir's poems, and there is much doubt about that, they reveal the questions any intelligent student of religion should be asking. The long life of these accusations, again, points to the enmity Nasir endured for his Ismaili beliefs. The second point, more positive, is brought out in a conversation between the eminent Iranian scholars Mirza Muhammad Qazvini and Dr Qasim Ghani, the gist of which was later published in 1942. In reply to Dr Ghani's challenge to name the best Persian poets, Qazvini responded, after a long disquisition on what constitutes good poetry:

The reply to this question has been generally agreed on for centuries, and the problem has been finally disposed of. Despite all differences of individual inclination and preference, despite the general divergence of opinion entertained by people on most matters, practically all are agreed on this one question; that the greatest poets of the Persian language since the coming of Islam to the present time (each one in his special variety) are the six following – Firdawsi, Khayyam, Anvari, Rumi, Sa'di, Hafiz. In my view, one can confidently add to these six the great philosopher Nasir Khusraw, since all the characteristic merits and artistic qualities that have established these six in the front rank of Persian poets are completely and in every respect present in the person of Nasir Khusraw ... .[34]

As this survey of the literary sources shows, a religious, literary and political persona took shape for Nasir Khusraw during his own lifetime, a persona which, fed by the twin fires of hostility and admiration, combined to make him appear either as a disreputable king deceiving his unwitting followers down the path of heresy with magic and sorcery, or as an ascetic philosopher urging his followers to stay fast to the path of salvation by heeding his own grasp of the truth apparent in his inspiring poetry, prose and character. Either way, the image of Nasir Khusraw ends up at the extreme, as simply an agent of evil or good. Such a caricature takes us far from the actual human being, who lived and developed over time, who faced the fears of a tortuous spiritual quest and whose passion for life was fuelled by the conviction that everything has a higher purpose, that a wise providence sustains the cosmos and all that is beyond the cosmos, and that his mission was to search for this providential wisdom and preach it to the world.

# CHAPTER THREE

# The Wonders of This World

Having heard a great deal about these banquets,
I was anxious to see one with my own eyes.

*Safarnama,* 56

The pearl sitting in its scabby shell and the ruby lying in its dirty mine symbolise for Nasir Khusraw the spiritual locked within the physical, the soul imprisoned within the body. He calls on his readers to discover the brilliance hidden within themselves. He exhorts everyone to put aside the pursuit of physical pleasures and seek out spiritual pleasures instead. He does this so often and so vehemently that it would be easy to consider Nasir Khusraw as only an unpleasant ascetic concerned solely with denouncing earthly things.

But how one-dimensional this characterisation is. For this is a man who does not just visit Jerusalem; he measures it, pacing out the dimensions of the city with his own feet, step by step. This is a man who does not just observe people at their daily work; he inquires what they are doing and why. This is a man who does not just listen to local lore; he tests it out. When told by local inhabitants that a certain valley near Jerusalem is called the Valley of Hell because from the edge one can listen and hear the cries of the people in hell, he goes to see for himself: 'I went there but heard nothing,' he records (*S*, 22).

At every turn, his attention to the details of the physical world reflects a mind amazed and appreciative of both the handiwork

of God and the achievements of human beings. In the record of
his journeys, in his poetry, and even in his philosophical works,
Nasir's acute eye and sense of wonder at all that exists reveal a
love of beauty and abundance of all sorts. Scores of his poems
contain a praise of nature so charming it cannot be credited to
his poetic virtuosity alone, but must indeed derive from some personal, heart-felt experience of life.

> What is the stew of speech? Meaning and allusion.
> Bring out new words again and again to brighten
>     up your own pot.
> We must not fear repetition in poetry,
>     because sweet speech is pleasant in the repetition.
> Even God's stew is tasty and fragrant and colourful,
>     made of apples and oranges, walnuts, quince and pomegranate.
>
> (*Divan*, 180:7–9)

Certainly, during his travels, Nasir Khusraw engages actively
with the world. In Beirut there is a kind of stone, he says, 'so hard
that iron makes no impression in it' (*S*, 15). He knows this, surely
not because some local told him, or else he would have said so as
he does in many other instances, but because he himself took up
a piece of iron and hit the stone, more than once, to test it.

Wonders of nature never cease to be worthy of Nasir's note-
book. He records endless details to edify and entertain the folks
back in Balkh: 'All along the way I noticed great quantities of rue
growing wild' (*S*, 20); and, near Haifa, 'we saw the bones of many
sea animals that had been fossilised because of constant pound-
ing by waves' (*S*, 19). Such a tale of the strange effects of the sea
would be particularly amazing to his audience living in a desert or
steppe climate far inland from the sea.

For Nasir Khusraw, all things from nature are meant to be used
as gifts from God, and human beings especially should employ
their intelligence and energy imaginatively to take what is given
and create useful and elegant products. Time and again, this traveller records his wonder at the variety of things that human
beings have been able to produce. In a moment of reflection
after praying in the mosque in Caesarea, he notices a marble

vase and then, with the eye of a poet and the mind of a physicist, marvels that even though it is 'as thin as Chinese porcelain' it can hold 100 maunds of water (*S*, 19). Close by the Friday mosque in Tiberias, the people have built a bathhouse over a hot spring, with water 'so hot that unless it is mixed with cold water you cannot stand it.' He obviously appreciates both the natural extreme and the human talent in harnessing something potentially harmful into something so useful to the community. From his comment, 'I went inside to try it out' we see he did not pass up the opportunity to try it out personally (*S*, 18). He does not want to miss an illuminating experience.

Just as human ingenuity has perfected the use of these two natural elements (a vase from stone and a healthy bath from scalding water), it has also produced new things that the world 'in all its greatness' has not been able to create. In the animal kingdom, the human mind has produced new animals (such as mules) from the union of horses and donkeys. Humans have even brilliantly combined the kingdoms of plant and animal to make an entirely new product, silk. Part of the glory of silk rests in the fact that such beauty comes from worms chewing on mulberry leaves. Humanity shines in being able to envision something beyond the immediate, to take a by-product of worms and weave it into fabulous, fanciful material (*KI*, 120).

Human beings also invent beautiful social events for their mutual delight. In Cairo, the caliph is famed for putting on a lavish feast twice a year, and Nasir employs all his powers of persuasion to gain a peek at this royal banquet hosted by the Fatimid Caliph-Imam al-Mustansir. As part of his argument, Nasir explains that he is not some uncouth provincial, wanting to ogle as a mere tourist. Rather, he would bring the eye of experience, having witnessed the renowned wealth and pageantry of the courts of Mahmud and Mas'ud of Ghazna.

Having heard a great deal about these banquets, I was very anxious to see one with my own eyes, so I told one of the [caliph's] clerks with whom I had struck up a friendship that I had seen the courts of the Persian sultans, such as Sultan Mahmud of Ghazna and his son Mas'ud, who were great potentates enjoying much prosperity and

luxury, and now I wanted to see the court of the Prince of the Faithful. [The clerk] therefore spoke a word to the chamberlain (*S*, 56).

When he finally manages a private tour the day before the
feast, he can scarcely contain his delight at the sights before his
eyes. He apologises to his readers that even the details he records
fall far short of conveying the almost unbearable luxury on dis-
play. This particular feast is prepared to celebrate the end of
the month-long fast of Ramadan in the year 441/1049:

Taken by my friend, as I entered the door to the hall, I saw construc-
tions, galleries, and porticos that would take too long to describe
adequately. There were twelve square structures, built one next to
the other, each more dazzling than the last. Each measured one hundred cubits square, and one was a thing sixty cubits square with a dais
placed the entire length of the building at a height of four ells, on
three sides all of gold, with hunting and sporting scenes depicted
thereon and also an inscription in marvellous calligraphy. All the
carpets and pillows were of Byzantine brocade and *buqalamun*, each
woven exactly to the measurements of its place. There was an indescribable latticework balustrade of gold along the sides. Behind the
dais and next to the wall were silver steps. The dais itself was such
that if this book were nothing from beginning to end but a description of it, words would still not suffice. They said that fifty thousand
maunds of sugar were appropriated for this day for the [caliph's]
feast. For decoration on the banquet table I saw a confection like an
orange tree, every branch and leaf of which had been executed in
sugar, and thousands of images and statuettes in sugar (*S*, 57).

Such sensuous detail cannot come from simple love of power,
wealth, or even the things themselves. There is deep admiration
for human ability – to design, to create, to organise – but most of
all, to envisage beyond the present. This admiration for the human desire to achieve more, to know more, stands at the basis of
Nasir Khusraw's philosophy of all existence. He sees the human
soul's fundamental activity (derived from its essence, its very substance, not imposed from the outside) to be the pursuit of its own
perfection or fulfilment. For him, this is demonstrated in each

individual's progression through life. For whenever one desired goal is achieved, a new desire takes its place. As soon as an infant learns to crawl it wants to walk. This progress through life is both physical and spiritual, a journey through all the elements of this world which goes hand in hand with the concomitant inner journey of spiritual growth. His conviction in the reality of human longing for such a pilgrimage towards self-realisation can be found throughout his writings and is apparent also in the stages of his own life.

### EARLY EDUCATION AND LIFE AT COURT

We know that Nasir Khusraw followed other members of his family into government service under the Ghaznavids and their successors, the Saljuqs. For example, after he returned from his seven-year journey, he found that one of his brothers was working in the entourage of Abu Nasr, the vizier of the prince of Khurasan.[1] Coming thus from a successful, highly placed and literate family, and judging from the high ranking writers and scholars he met along his journey, as well as his own intellectual output, we know that he received a full education in the literatures and sciences of his day, including theology, philosophy and mathematics.

In spite of some scholarly opinion to the contrary, there can be no doubt that Nasir was extremely well-schooled in Arabic learning, certainly in Qur'anic and *hadith* studies. His poetry and prose are suffused with allusions to, and actual portions of, Qur'anic verses, sayings of the Prophet and Arabic poetry. Sometimes in his poems Nasir uses individual words or phrases clearly taken from the Qur'an, such as *dar al-salam, ashab al-raqim* and *lu'lu' maknun.*[2] In other lines, he takes the meaning of the scripture and adeptly weaves it through his verses.

When Nasir Khusraw came to the town of Qarul, near Harran (probably modern Urfa, medieval Edessa), news of his arrival soon brought a hopeful admirer. A bedouin Arab, about sixty-years-old, came in and sat down next to the travelling scholar. Here, Nasir condescendingly expresses his amazement at someone unschooled in his own language, which was to Nasir Khusraw a foreign language in which he had obviously become proficient.

Teach me the Koran,' he said. I recited him the chapter beginning '*Qol a'udho be-rabbe'l-nas.*' He recited it back to me. When I had said the part that goes '*mena'l-jennate wa'l-nas,*' he said, 'Should I say "*a-ra'ayta'l-nas*" too?' 'There is no more to this chapter,' I replied. Then he asked, 'Which chapter has the part in it about the *naqqalat al-hatab?*' He did not even know that in the chapter called *Tabbat* the words *hammalat al-hatab* occur, not *naqqalat al-hatab!* That night, no matter how many times I recited the chapter beginning '*Qol a'udho be-rabbe'l-nas,*' he could not learn it. A sixty-year-old Arab! (*S*, 9–10)

### POETIC LESSONS

In medieval Muslim courts, poets often served as negotiators between rivals or as advisers to the king, steering him in prudent directions. Poets were also brought in to add cheer to sad situations or to magnify happy ones. Successful court poets were the celebrities of their day, rich and emulated, with multitudes memorising their words. But since the primary objective was the satisfaction of the ruler, their usual task was flattery. Those who failed to attend to either the psychological or political aspects of their employment found themselves poor, banished, or worse.

Nasir Khusraw ridiculed the life of the court poet, most likely owing to his experiences at the Ghaznavid and the Saljuq courts, where he witnessed first-hand the sycophantic capitulations of the official poets. Later, his forced exile embittered him even further to those who prosper through the flattery of the powerful. But this is not to say he did not know how to write panegyric verse – far from it. Even from his abode of exile, he pours praise on the Fatimid Caliph-Imam al-Mustansir, and in several of his philosophical works he praises the prince who gave him refuge in Yumgan. But Nasir's praise was wholly religious, inspired by his devotion to the Prophet's descendants. He himself made the distinction between praising someone worthy of praise and merely flattering the person who holds the purse strings.

As a sample of his themes, metaphors, and construction of a poem, I have translated here the first third of one of Nasir Khusraw's odes (no. 64 in the *Divan*).[3] The ode (*qasida*) was his favourite form of poetry. Part of the pleasure to be derived from reading this poem is to observe how it holds together structurally while moving forward through each distich, now lingering on an image, now reaching back to pick up a word from a previous line. While the translation can offer some sense of the poem's structure as well as some of the striking images that the poet invokes, it cannot do justice to the aural delights of alliteration, word play, and internal and final rhymes.

For example, the word translated here as 'azure' (*nilufar*) carries a lot of weight, for it not only means the sky-blue of the flower *nilufar*, designating either the morning glory, water lily or nenuphar, but the word itself derives from a combination of the Sanskrit words *nilu*, meaning dark blue, and *pala*, meaning flower. Until about 1600, the word *nil* was used in English for the indigo plant and dye. To the ear, Nasir Khusraw echoes the internal rhyme of *nilufar* in *nikuhish* (blame) and *nik* (good). To the mind's eye, the Wheel of Heaven is the revolving blue dome of the sky, very physical, with stars arrayed in fixed shapes, moving in unison like the spokes of a wheel, overseeing all the activity of the world beneath. Such a wheel of course is the wheel of fortune, that is, Fortuna or Fate. In the poem as in his life, Nasir repudiates the idea of fate and of blaming the stars for the troubles of one's life. We create our own evil stars, he says, and we pay the price. His line, 'When you are the author of your own ill-fated star, look not to Heaven for a lucky star,' is still a popular adage to Iranians today.

> Blame not the azure Wheel of Heaven;
>     away with such balmy notions!
> Note well that this wheel is above all actions
>     and it suits not the wise to blame the good.
> As long as the world is following its custom of torturing you,
>     you must learn the habit of showing patience.
> Take the heavy burden off your back today;
>     do not put off this advice until tomorrow!
> When you are the author of your own ill-fated star,
>     look not to Heaven for a lucky star.

The poet then moves into the theme of being true to oneself, to one's purpose, and to make one's actions match the inner self. For Nasir Khusraw, the inner self is the true self, its quality visible through external actions.

> How would you make your face an angel face?
>     By making your deeds the deeds of angels.
> Surely you have seen the tulips of the spring
>     shining like Capella in the fields?
> But even if a tulip did light up and shine like a star,
>     you would still see it as a tulip, just disguised.
> You are bright and capable,
>     why don't you take up the good features of the wise?

Here, tulips are the example of truthfulness. For even though tulips are brilliant and showy and we may therefore say they shine like stars (such as Capella), we know full well they are not stars. The outside is not what counts. Daffodils and orange trees, by the glorious colours in their flowers, fruits and leaves, fulfil their species, just as human leaders are bedecked in gold, silver and jewels, and privileged with banners, flags and pavilions. But a tree which chooses not to bear fruit, not to fulfil the highest role of its species, is burned in the fire, a direct reference to the punishment awaiting errant humans in Hell. To avert this end, humans must take up knowledge and learning, the finest fruits of human existence.

> See how the new-sprung daffodils, shining silver and gold,
>     resemble the colours of Alexander's crown!
> See how the orange trees, with multi-coloured fruits and
>     leaves, sing of Caesar's colourful pavilions!
> But the barren poplar remains with nothing,
>     for it made the choice to bear no fruit.
> If you turn your head away from learning,
>     you will never become an exalted leader.
> They burn the wood of trees with no fruit,
>     a suitable end to those without fruit.

Then, in the next line the poet pulls all these things together, along with the main image from the very first line, thereby achieving a structural cohesiveness, in a ringing manifesto of individual responsibility:

> But if your tree would choose the fruit of knowledge,
>     you would grasp the azure Wheel of Heaven in your hand!

In this, only the first third of one poem, we can see Nasir Khusraw's major themes of knowledge and of each person's duty to strive to attain it. We also see his vivid use of nature and colours, particularly the motif of trees, fruitful or barren. That the tree can choose to know, to be aware, and only thus bring forth fruit – this for the poet is the call to conscious searching for knowledge with which one can take control of the events in one's life. This search can take one far from home. We also see his sense of the passage of time, especially the passing of greatness, with his references to Alexander and Caesar. To the poet, they are as fleeting as flowers. Only knowledge endures.

### OF PERSIA AND PERSIANS

While the keeping of a travel diary is sometimes only a personal act, Nasir Khusraw clearly has an audience in mind as he makes his selections of what to record, and the audience is the Persian-speaking populace of Khurasan, the boundaries of which would then have extended deep into parts of today's Central Asia and Afghanistan. 'I saw such personal wealth [in Cairo] that were I to describe it, the people of Persia would never believe it' (*S*, 55); 'Every type of food, fruit, and other edible I ever saw in Persia was to be found [in Tripoli], but a hundred times more plentiful ... They make very good paper there, like the paper of Samarqand, only better' (*S*, 13). In Qa'in, the huge arch over the *maqsura* of the Friday mosque 'is much larger than any I have seen in Khurasan, but it is not in proportion to the mosque' (*S*, 102).

The traveller knows that the Khurasanians will be amazed by the diverse produce of warmer climates. In Tripoli, he writes, 'I saw a child holding both a red and a white rose, both in bloom,

and that was on the 5th of the last Persian month, Esfandarmadh
[i.e. late winter], old reckoning, of the year 415 of the Persian
calendar' (*S*, 13). But still he stands and takes notes, hoping that
a catalogue of empirical facts will testify to the truth of his observation, realising at the same time, however, that even such a list
will be difficult to believe.

On the third day of the month of Day of the Persian year 416 I saw
the following fruits and herbs, all in one day: red roses, lilies, nar-
cissi, oranges, citrons, apples, jasmine, basil, quince, pomegranates,
pears, melons, bananas, olives, myrobalan, fresh dates, grapes,
sugarcane, eggplants, squash, turnips, radishes, cabbage, fresh beans,
cucumbers, green onions, fresh garlic, carrots, and beets. No one
would think that all of these fruits and vegetables could be had at
one time, some usually growing in autumn, some in spring, some in
summer, and some in fall. I myself have no ulterior motive in reporting all this, and I have recorded what I saw with my own eyes, although
I am not responsible for some of the things I only heard, since Egypt
is quite expansive and has all kinds of climate, from the tropical to
the cold; and produce is brought to the city from everywhere and
sold in the markets (*S*, 53–4).

'I have no ulterior motive in reporting all this.' That is, the
traveller has no political, religious, or even commercial motive.
He simply mentions every person or geographical detail that
arouses his curiosity or which might interest the readers back home
in Khurasan. On the Ka'ba in Mecca, he notes, 'two large silver
rings sent from Ghazna are attached to the door too high for anyone to reach. Two other silver rings, smaller than the first two, are
attached to the doors such that anyone could reach them' (*S*, 76).
'The fine woollens imported into Persia and called "Egyptian"
are all from Upper Egypt, since wool is not woven in Egypt proper'
(*S*, 63). 'There were many pistachio trees inside the houses [in
Tun], although the people of Balkh and Tokharestan imagine
that pistachios grow only on mountains' (*S*, 101). And, for readers far from any ocean, he includes this piece of information about
a fish:

In the town of 'Aydhab [in Upper Egypt] a man whose word I trust told me that once a ship set out from that town for the Hijaz carrying camels for the emir of Mecca. One of the camels died so it was thrown overboard. Immediately a fish swallowed it whole, except for one leg that stuck out of the fish's mouth. Then another fish came and swallowed whole the fish that had swallowed the camel. That fish is called *qarsh*. I saw in that town a fish skin that in Khurasan is called *safan*. We in Khurasan had thought it was a kind of lizard, but here I saw that it was a fish because it had fins like a fish (*S*, 66).

Besides details of things, the traveller also mentions any Persian he comes into contact with along the way, such as in the town of Basra in today's Iraq: 'At that time, the emir of Basra was the son of Abu Kalijar the Daylamite king of Fars. His vizier was a Persian, Abu Mansur Shahmardan by name' (*S*, 90). Also in the south, along the Persian Gulf coast of Fars, in the town of Mahruban,

I saw the name of Ya'qub son of Layth written on the pulpit of the Friday mosque and asked how this had come to be. They told me that Ya'qub son of Layth had conquered up to this town but that no other emir of Khurasan had had the might to do it (*S*, 97).

However, Nasir Khusraw's interest in things Persian goes beyond finding such curiosities for his fellow countrymen. He is convinced of the superiority of the Persian language, its literature and its culture over others, and he rarely misses an opportunity to point it out. Nasir cherishes his native tongue and protects it from exposure to both the 'swine,' unworthy princes who only ask for poetry to flatter themselves, and ignorant barbarians, those incapable of grasping the subtleties of the Persian language. He chastises other poets for cheapening themselves and their language by composing poetry merely for money. 'You versify lies out of greed,' he accuses, but

I am one who refuses to throw beneath the feet of swine
   this precious pearl, the Persian language.

(*Divan*, 64: 32)

To appreciate the complexity of Nasir Khusraw as a human being, we have to look at and acknowledge the fact that sometimes his pride in the Persian language and heritage comes at the expense of others. While this aspect of his personality may be difficult to accept today, it is vital to see Nasir both as an inquisitive explorer and as a man of learning insistently proud of his past and the accomplishments of his culture. Part of his critical attitude relates to the decline he sees in this culture and part refers directly to the negative turns in the political events of his day. Nasir suffers deeply the loss of Persian-speaking Khurasan to the Saljuq Turks whom he disparages as untutored barbarians fit only for servanthood. In one poem, he anchors these sentiments in the repeated rhyme word *shud*, meaning 'became' or 'turned into,' so that each line works to drive home the point of change and reversal that he witnessed all about him:

> The land of Khurasan, once the home of culture,
> Has now become a mine rich in barbarian demons.
>
> Wisdom once had a home in Balkh, but its house
> Now lies in ruins, its fortune overturned.
>
> If the kingdom of Khurasan was once like Solomon's,
> How has it now become the kingdom of the cursèd devil?
>
> The land of Khurasan once feasted on religion,
> Now religion has become the companion of avaricious Qarun.[4]
>
> The house of Qarun has now made all Khurasan
> A model for the world entire of how sinister fate unfolds.
>
> Their slaves at one time were the Turks.
> But sometimes things turn this way and sometimes that,
>
> So now they themselves are slaves to the Turks.
> Has not the star of Khurasan turned sinister and dark?
>
> Even the servant of the Qipchaq is now a lord[5]
> And the free-born wife willingly a handmaid.
>
> Consequently, if the deficient man becomes a lord,
> Learning declines and vice increases.

I shall not give my heart to the slaves of this world,
Even though you have pledged your heart to Fate.

You might place your trust in the sinister wolf,
But the wise consider the wolf as not to be trusted.

(*Divan* 37: 16–26)

The poet also heaps scorn on the illiterate nomads whom he encountered during his journey in the Arabian peninsula. Although he was deeply attached to the holy cities of Mecca and Medina, and fully conversant with Arabic language and literature, he found that 'There is little civilisation in Arabia, its people being desert nomads, herdsmen, and tent-dwellers' (*S*, 71). His travels in the remote parts of Arabia brought him into direct contact with an age-old way of life accustomed to surviving on the little that is available.

Among one tribe [of Arabs], some seventy-year-old men told me that in their whole lives they had drunk nothing but camels' milk, since in the desert there is nothing but bitter scrub eaten by the camels. They actually imagined that the whole world was like this! … Along the way, whenever my companions saw a lizard they killed and ate it. The Arabs, wherever they are, milk their camels for drink. I could neither eat the lizard nor drink camels' milk; therefore, wherever I saw a kind of bush that yielded small berries the size of a pea, I picked a few and subsisted on that (*S*, 83–4).

### A KEEN APPRECIATION

Not only in the Cairo court of Caliph-Imam al-Mustansir did Nasir Khusraw stand amazed. Twelve months before the feast of Ramadan in Cairo, he had stood in Jerusalem gazing at al-Aqsa Mosque and recorded its structural details. While we may complain that his ledger-like listing of features nearly masks the sense of wonder which he feels and actually expresses, the sheer quantity of detail can be taken as the expression of his awe.

In that place is a skilfully constructed edifice with magnificent carpets and an independent staff who are always attendant. On the

outside again, along the southern wall and beyond the corner, there
is an uncovered courtyard about 200 ells long. The length of the
mosque along the west wall is 420 ells, with the *maqsura* to the right
along the south wall; it [the mosque] is 150 ells wide. It has 280
marble columns supporting a stone arcade, the tops and bottoms of
which are decorated and the joints filled with lead so that the construction is extremely tight. Between every two columns is a distance
of six ells, and the ground is flagged in coloured marble tile, the
joints again caulked in lead. The *maqsura*, in the middle of the south
wall, is large enough for sixteen columns and an enormous dome
inlaid in tile, as has been described. It is filled with Maghrebi carpets,
lamps, and lanterns, each hung by a separate chain. There is a large
*mehrab* inlaid with tile; on either side of the niche are two marble
pillars the colour of red carnelian, and the whole low wall of the
*maqsura* is of coloured marble. To the right is Mo'awiya's *mehrab*, and
that of Omar to the left. The ceiling is covered with wood carved in
elaborate designs. Along the wall of the *maqsura* toward the courtyard are 15 gateways and ornate doors, each of which is 10 ells tall
and 6 wide, 10 of them on the wall that is 420 ells long and 5 on the
wall that is 150 ells long. One of these gates in particular is done in
such beautifully ornate brass that one would think it was made of
gold burnished with silver. It has the name of the Caliph Ma'mun on
it and is said to have been sent by him from Baghdad (*S*, 26–7).

Nasir clearly seems to have also enjoyed the colourfully tiled
gate of Jerusalem, perhaps not only for aesthetic reasons but indeed because the tiles spelled out the titles of the Fatimid caliph.

It has a splendid gateway ... adorned with designs and patterned with
coloured tiles set in plaster. The whole produces an effect dazzling
to the eye. There is an inscription on the tiles of the gateway with the
titles of the [caliph] of Egypt. When the sun strikes this, the rays play
so that the mind of the beholder is absolutely stunned (*S*, 24).

Over and over again in his travels, Nasir Khusraw admires what
human beings do with the things of this world – how they use
their creativity and intelligence to make the world better. He delights in learning about the different ways that people around

the world have found to feed, clothe, house and manage their societies, as in these examples from Armenia, Ramla and Sidon:

[In Armenia] I saw men who roamed about the mountainsides and cut a wood something like cypress. I asked what they did with it, and they explained that when one end of this wood is placed in fire, pitch comes out the other end. It is then collected in pits, put into containers, and sent all over for sale (S, 7).

There is much marble here [in Ramla], and most of the buildings and houses are made of sculpted marble. They cut the marble with toothless saws and Meccan sand. The saw is drawn along the length of the shaft, not across the grain, as with wood. From the stone they make slabs. I saw all colours of marble – speckled, green, red, black, white, and multicoloured (S, 20).

The bazaar [of Sidon] is so nicely arrayed that when I saw it I thought the city had been decorated either for the arrival of the [caliph] or because of the proclamation of some good news. When I inquired, they said that the city was customarily kept that way. The gardens and orchards were such that one would think an emperor had laid out a pleasure garden with belvederes, and most of the trees were laden with fruit (S, 15).

But lest a reader think Nasir only recorded items of beauty and novelty or was starry-eyed and uncritical in his observations, we have the example of his opinions on the city of Ta'if not far from Mecca: 'The entire district of Ta'if consists of a wretched little town with a strong fortress. It has a small bazaar and a pitiful little mosque ... they showed me a small, ruined fortress, which the Arabs said had been Layla's house, although they tell many such strange tales' (S, 82–3).

Though, as we shall see later, much of Nasir Khusraw's poetry warns against succumbing to the attractions of this physical world, the mantle of asceticism slips easily off his shoulders. For us to see Nasir solely as a moralising despiser of the world requires us to shut out not only the content of much of his writing but also the underlying personal and spiritual motivations which directed the activities in his life. His decision to travel across the world took

place after his decision to devote himself to religion. When he
returned home from his voyage he chose not to withdraw into
solitary piety, or even to establish himself in the communal life of
a monastery, but rather to assume the post of head of the Ismaili
*da'wa* in Khurasan. He tells us that he planned eventually to make
another journey, to see the countries and cities of the east. This
proud intellectual is noticeably uneffusive about his conversations
with intellectuals he meets on the way, but abundantly generous
with descriptions of the shapes and materials of city walls and the
ingenious solutions the inhabitants have devised to overcome
natural and human obstacles. While he often rails at the incon-
stancies of life, Nasir Khusraw never thinks of relinquishing the
world or disengaging himself from its activities; in fact in his last
years he bemoans each sign that he is far from the centre of things.

# CHAPTER FOUR

# The Turning Point

And I reflected that until I changed all my ways
I would never find happiness.

*Safarnama,* 2

The Qur'an promises an after-life, with reward or punishment, depending on the actions taken by the person in this life. For Nasir Khusraw the gravity of this promise came brilliantly to life one night in a dream which caused him to change his ways dramatically. He has recorded this moment of insight in two of his works: in prose in his *Safarnama* and in a long poem in his *Divan*. Both the prose and the poetic versions highlight different events and illustrate his reactions in a slightly different light, and each reveals different facets of his personality and spirituality.

### THE PROSE VERSION

In the *Safarnama* Nasir recounts the whole story of his conversion in the first two pages, often with a succinctness so cryptic that the reader is left wishing he had been more generous with words and details.

The author of the *Safarnama* is compiling the work after the fact. He has his notes in front of him, complete with dates, distances and names of cities. He weaves them together with a minimum of commentary, too infrequently adding an editorial comment on his reaction to what he had experienced, or remarking on why he chose to include a certain anecdote. Given that they provide Nasir Khusraw's explanation for the circumstances and rationale of not only his physical journey but also his spiritual conversion, the first two pages thus contain some of the most significant sentences in his entire corpus. They are packed with meaning.

Nasir begins by simply stating his name and occupation (establishing his familial and geographic lineage), along with some, barely modest, self-assessment:

Thus writes Abu Mu'in Hamid al-Din Nasir son of Khusraw of Qubadiyan in the district of Marv:
    I was a clerk by profession and one of those in charge of the sultan's revenue service. In my administrative position I had applied myself for a period of time and acquired no small reputation among my peers (S, 1).

Then the chronology begins. He nails down the beginning by giving exact names, dates and places. He gives the full name of the ruler of Khurasan – Chaghri Beg, brother of Tughril Beg together the founders of the Saljuq dominion who had swept the Ghaznavids out of the way. Nasir Khusraw relates that he was travelling in an official capacity in the service of the Saljuqs, perhaps collecting taxes, but the purpose is not spelled out, accompanied by a number of good friends and colleagues. They arrive at the town of Marv al-Rud on the day of a special planetary conjunction.

In the month of Rabi' II in the year 437 [October 1045], when the prince of Khurasan was Abu Sulayman Chaghri Beg Daud son of Mika'il son of Saljuq, I set out from Marv on official business to the district of Panj Deh in Marv Rud, where I stopped off on the very day there happened to be a conjunction of Jupiter and the lunar node. As it is said that on that day God will grant any request made of him, I therefore withdrew into a corner and prayed two rak'ats, asking God to grant me true wealth (S, 1).

But while Nasir half thinks this may be only popular superstition ('as it is said') that God will grant requests based on astrological occurrences, it seems that he is the only one of the group ready to acknowledge the possibility of God granting his wishes on this day. He has to separate himself from them in order to pray. Given the chance to request something from God he asks for true power. The Persian word for his request, *tavangari*, combines the senses of 'power' and 'wealth,' and with the addition of the word 'true' (*haqiqi*), we see another clue already of Nasir's personal spirituality and quest for inner understanding.

When I rejoined my friends and companions, one of them was reciting a poem in Persian. A particular line of poetry came into my head, and I wrote it down on a piece of paper for him to recite. I had not yet handed him the paper when he began to recite that very line! (*S*, 1)

It should be noted how unremarkable it is for Nasir that these businessmen and bureaucrats should be reciting poetry. Poetry at that time, as today, forms a fundamental part of Persian culture; even unlettered people recite poetry. Certainly for an educated, lettered man, the ability to recite poetry well is much appreciated, especially the ability to find the exact line to illustrate and define the mood of the moment. Among friends, reciting poetry often becomes competitive.

So, on completing his prayers, he finds his friends entertaining themselves with recitations. Nasir Khusraw's way of joining the group again is to jot down a verse for his friend to recite when he finishes the first one. He takes it as a personal answer from God when his friend spontaneously begins with that very same poem without even seeing the paper: 'I took this to be a good omen and said to myself that God had granted my behest.'

The government official ambitious for riches and power now balances his accounts in the currency of poetic inspiration. Poetic vision is surely a gift from God. And Nasir's understanding of this event as a moment of divine presence takes place even before his spiritual conversion; this means that spiritual reflection was a part of his personality. His official trip is going very well – with good friends, good poetry, and God granting wishes through auspicious planets. At his next stop he adds some wine to the mix.

From there I went to Juzjanan, where I stayed nearly a month and was constantly drunk on wine. (The Prophet says, 'Tell the truth, even if on your own selves') (S, 1).

From this public confession of extended drunkenness (including his explanation to justify why he is confessing), Nasir Khusraw moves his narrative directly into the description of the transformational dream he had during his month in Juzjanan. The contrast between the bold confession, dutifully following the Prophet's command to tell the truth, and the grinding-to-a-halt impact of his dream could hardly be sharper. For it is not just that he received a sign from God, since it seems in any case that he was accustomed to seeing God's signs in everyday events. But this time he saw and understood in a way he had not previously. The significance of his dream, however, dawns on him only in the morning, in wakefulness. In addition, the details of the dream not only stay with him in sharp clarity but carry with them another message. Rather than brushing the details aside by saying 'It was just a dream,' he experiences them as having a profound significance for the salvation of his soul. He takes the message seriously, a clear warning to reform his life. We may ask if this is merely a dream stimulated by a sense of guilt, caused by remorse for his excessive drinking and the physical wretchedness most likely accompanying it. After all, such regret after excess is not uncommon – but his reaction is extraordinary. It is the unusual person who actually hoists the camel's rope over his or her shoulders and sets out for a holy city a world away.

The journey Nasir recounts in his *Safarnama* will take him seven years. Here, beginning in the sentence immediately following his admission of excessive drinking, and employing the same economic phrasing that characterises the rest of his diary, he presents the rationale for embarking on his journey:

One night in a dream I saw someone saying to me, 'How long will you continue to drink of this wine, which destroys man's intellect? If you were to stay sober, it would be better for you.'

In reply I said, 'The wise have not been able to come up with anything other than this to lessen the sorrow of this world.'

'To be without one's senses is no repose,' he answered me. 'He cannot be called wise who leads men to senselessness. Rather, one should seek out that which increases reason and wisdom.'

'Where can I find such a thing?' I asked.

'Seek and ye shall find,' he said, and then he pointed toward the *qibla* and said nothing more. When I awoke, I remembered everything, which had truly made a great impression on me. 'You have waked from last night's sleep,' I said to myself. 'When are you going to wake from that of forty years?' And I reflected that until I changed all my ways I would never find happiness (*S*, 1–2).

Notice that there is no metaphor in the dream itself. The wine and the drunkenness stand for those things in this world. Only when he is awake does the poet reach for a metaphor, that of sleep and wakefulness, and judges that his life up until that moment has been one of slumber.

Lending further credibility to the recital of the dream, the man in the dream is not identified, even though he speaks with authority, and the profundity of his message survives beyond the confines of the dream into the light of day. If Nasir Khusraw had wanted to embellish his dream for others, or even for himself, in his later reflections on the dream he could have interpreted the man to be the Prophet Muhammad, the archangel Gabriel, or one of the Shi'i imams, all of whom were known to appear to believers in their dreams. He claims none of these. Also, the *qibla* is the archetypal temple itself, that is, the Ka'ba in Mecca, the direction of prayer and the goal of Muslim believers. Nothing requires it to be a metaphor for Cairo, the seat of the Fatimid Ismaili state.[1] For Nasir Khusraw, Mecca holds all the power and attraction it does for any Muslim believer. He eventually made four pilgrimages there and cherished his time as a *mujawir*, a pilgrim tending to the shrine of the Ka'ba.

It is not fruitful, and certainly misleading, to read a hidden meaning into every word Nasir Khusraw writes. For example, his remark about the need to drink wine because of its ability to soften the sorrows of life is not a metaphor for spiritual wine. Rather, his admission reveals a person already struggling to make sense of life and its pain. Before the dream, he had often opted to numb the pain with wine, he says, in order 'to lessen the sorrow of this world.'

The three sentences uttered by the man in the dream contain the seeds of all that follows in Nasir's life: attend to the clarity of your senses; always seek to increase your reason and wisdom, and guide others to that wisdom. On awakening, he accepts the precepts of his dream and determines to find a way to change his life accordingly. Finally, near the end of December, he acknowledges his change of heart to God.

On Thursday the 6th of Jumada II of the year 437 [19 December 1045], which was by Persian reckoning the middle of the month of Day, the last month before the year 414 of the Yazdigirdi era, I cleansed myself from head to foot, went to the mosque, and prayed to God for help both in accomplishing what I had to do and in abstaining from what he had forbidden (S, 2).

Upon his return home to Marv after completing his official trip, he made the decision public.

Taking leave from my job, I announced that I was setting out for the pilgrimage to Mecca. I settled what debts I owed and renounced everything worldly, except for a few necessities (S, 2).

Thus, it appears that Nasir's official duties continued after his dream for another four to six weeks, during which time he struggled to find a way to reckon with the dream. At some point along the way he made the decision to leave, and then made the announcement upon his arrival home in Marv. Two-and-a-half months later, he departed, accompanied by one of his brothers and an Indian servant.

Nasir Khusraw began his journey on 23 Sha'ban 437/5 March 1046, setting out for the great city of Nishapur. It took him six weeks to arrive at this crossroad of cultures and religions, entering the city on 11 Shawwal/21 April. A lunar eclipse occurred that day, he tells us, no doubt pleased at another auspicious sign from the heavens.

### THE VERSE VERSION

The other place to look for clues to this radical change in Nasir Khusraw's life is his poem which begins with the line, 'O well-read and world-travelled one' (*Divan*, 242). Because the poem offers critical clues to his intellectual and spiritual development, a major portion of it is reproduced here, in Ivanow's translation with minor modifications.[2] When reading the poem, we may notice when the poet keeps the narrative close to historical anecdote and when he moves over to allegory. Nasir provides two chronological anchors, both his own date of birth and the age when he started on his serious spiritual quest. Following an opening in which the poet asks how long he will concern himself with earthly blessings for the body instead of the blessing of knowledge for his soul, the poem continues:

> Unlock thy heart, and take the Qur'an as thy sole guide,
> So that thou mayest know the right path, and that the door
>     of salvation might become opened to thee.
> I would not be surprised if thou dost not find that path easily,
> Because I was like thyself, lost and bewildered for a long time.
> When 394 years had passed since the emigration (*hijra*) of the
>     Prophet,
> My mother gave birth to me, bringing me into this dusty abode,
> As an unconscious growing being, similar to the plants
> Which are born from black soil and drops of water ...

Here, Nasir outlines the classic understanding of human conception and maturation. The human being progresses through the hierarchy of life, moving from seed, clot, plant and animal, and then on through levels of increasing consciousness. The poet reports that he began his consciously organised search for wisdom when he was 42-years-old, a search which involved reading books and listening to those who were learned in an array of fields, including both physics and metaphysics.

> When the heavens had measured out forty-two years of life to me,
> My conscious self began to search for wisdom.
> I listened to the learned, or read books in which they explained

The constitution of the celestial spheres, the movement of time
    and elements.

Then he provides us with a glimpse of his personal psychology.
His next line, 'Feeling that to me my own body is the dearest,'
forms the logical assumptions on which he bases his questions for
the world. What is interesting is that he does not apologise for
placing himself at the centre, at the very beginning of his rational
structure. Thus, from his grand sense of his self – actually his physical self – he infers that there must be a superior person amongst
human beings, a someone 'most precious of all that had been
created.' Ivanow translates this passage as follows:

Feeling that to me my own body is the dearest,
I inferred that in the world there must be someone who is the
    most precious of all that had been created,
Just as the falcon is the noblest of the birds,
    or the camel among the quadrupeds,
Or the date palm amongst the trees, or ruby amongst the jewels,
Just as the Qur'an amongst the books,
    or Ka'ba amongst the houses,
Or the heart amongst the organs of the body,
    the sun amongst the luminaries.

His spiritual quest then is to find the most perfect human being in the entire world. Since every genus and species in the
created world – from the starry heavens down to minerals deep
within the earth – has its own highest examplar, among humans
there must also be someone 'most noble.' But all his questioning of the learned men in the major schools of Islamic thought
proves fruitless.

As I pondered over this, my soul was filled with sad thoughts.
I began to ask questions from thinking people of their opinions:
From the Shafi'i, Maliki, Hanafi, I asked what they had said.
I began to search for the guidance of the Chosen One of God
    (i.e., the Prophet).
But when I asked (my teachers) about the reasons for (various)

injunctions of the religion, or the verses of the Qur'an on which
they are based,
None proved to be helpful, one resembling the blind, and the
other the deaf.

Particularly troubling for Nasir Khusraw is the 'verse of the oath'
in the Qur'an (48:10), because it seems to give special status to
those who lived at the time of the Prophet Muhammad, those
who were able to personally give their allegiance to God and His
Prophet. This refers to a specific historical event in the early years
of the Prophet's ministry. Six years after the migration from Mecca
to Medina (the *hijra*), the Prophet and a number of his followers
gathered under a tree in a place called Hudaybiyya. When the
Prophet asked for the allegiance of his followers, they all placed
their hands on the Prophet's hand according to the Arab custom,
thus demonstrating their fealty. That God accepted their oath is
evident in the words, 'God's hand is over their hands.'

For Nasir Khusraw, this stretching out of God's hand must occur in timeless time as well. God must be eternally stretching out
His hand for those who pledge their fealty to Him. It is incompre-
hensible to him that at any point in history God would pull back
His hand. For him it is inconceivable that this oath is not still
being demanded of believers by God, an idea associated with the
issue of God's justice. For, to those under the tree at Hudaybiyya,
God promised Paradise. So if there is no such tree now, no person to whom to give allegiance with outstretched hand, then
presumably there is no Paradise for those who come after that
moment in time. Since it would be unjust of God to limit His
demand of allegiance and promise of Paradise to one small group
at a particular point in time, the opportunity for the oath must be
present at all times. In every age, there must be someone who will
provide personal contact with the Prophet in order to keep the
connection.

Once I happened to read in the Qur'an the 'verse of the oath,'
The verse in which God said that His hand was stretched above.
Those people who swore allegiance 'under the tree'
Were the people like Ja'far, Miqdad, Salman and Abu Dharr.

I asked a question from myself, what had happened to that
   tree, that hand;
Where can I now find that hand, that oath, that place?
The answer to this was only 'There is now neither the tree, nor
   that hand;
That "hand" has been scattered, the assembly has dispersed.'
All of them were (sincerely) devoted to the Prophet and were
   rewarded with Paradise,
Particularly for having taken that oath, being chosen from
   amongst the ordinary mortals.
Said I (to myself): 'In the Qur'an it appears
   that Ahmad
Is the announcer and preacher (of the truth),
   the light shining (in darkness). [33:45–6]
If any unbeliever wishes to extinguish that light,
   blowing with his mouth,
God will relight it again, despite the efforts of all the unbelievers.
   [9:32]
How has it come about that today there is neither that hand
   nor those men?
The word of God, surely, cannot turn out to be untrue.
Whose hand should we touch when swearing allegiance to God?
Or should not (divine) justice treat equally those who came
   first and those who came later?
Was it our fault that we were not born at that time?
Why should we be deprived of personal contact with the
   Prophet, thus being (unjustly) punished?

Nasir's incomprehension leads to spiritual disillusion and discouragement, particularly concerning the limitations of the physical world, including time. He is troubled by the gap between what human beings are able to imagine and what they are actually able to achieve, constricted as they are by the 'limiting laws' of the three physical realms – mineral, plant and animal. Because he sees the immense potential of human beings, he bemoans the physical fetters that bind them to the world and thus hinder the attainment of their spiritual aspirations.

My face became yellow as a flower from sorrow at being unable
    to find an answer to this;
My back bent prematurely from sadness
    when I reflected how much human existence
Depends on the limiting laws of the inanimate world,
    vegetative force and animal life.

The next line marks a transition point, enlightening him with an understanding from which he can begin to draw hope.

Today, this animate soul and corporeal body of mine
    are of the Elect,
For I am both a simulacrum of Time itself
    as well as the darkening temporal realm.[3]

What Nasir Khusraw means by this line is that human beings are not just creatures endowed with a physical and material nature. They consist of both body and soul, and therefore are not completely bound by the limitations of the physical world. The human soul is the individual's link to eternity. As a combination of physical body and eternal soul, Nasir sees that he combines within himself all the characteristics of the macrocosmos. He identifies himself with the Universal Soul, the Soul of all humanity, the Universal Human. His whole being encompasses the Aeon in so far as his soul is animated in the eternity of meta-time, while his corporeal nature or body is aware at the same time of the darkness inherent in the human condition of mortality and temporality.

From this realisation, Nasir shifts into a few metaphor-filled lines to praise those who have knowledge. But why should praise for the learned be the first step after the realisation that humans are both body and soul, partly bound by the world and partly not? Because it is the eternal part of humans that does the learning. It is the soul that drives the human being to seek knowledge, and is the faculty which gains and keeps knowledge. For Nasir Khusraw, knowledge is the essence of human existence, just like the gold in the ore and the aroma in the musk.

The learned are (in this world) like musk,
   their learning like its aroma,
Or they are like a mine in which knowledge is enshrined as gold.
When musk loses its aroma, or ore is emptied of its gold,
Musk becomes worthless, the ore contains only specks of gilt.
When the aroma and gold are symbols of knowledge, let me then
Get up and search for 'musk' where it can be found,
   that exalted scroll.

Knowledge, therefore, is the object of Nasir Khusraw's search,
to seek knowledge wherever it can be found. He embarks on his
journey, asking questions of every kind of person he can find and
suffering physical hardship all along the way.

Then I rose from my place and started on a journey,
Abandoning without regret my house, my garden, those whom
   I was accustomed to see.
From the Persian and Arab, Indian and Turk,
From the inhabitants of Sind, Byzantium, a Jew, from everyone,
From the philosopher, the Manichee, Sabaean, from an atheist,
Did I inquire as to what interested me, with much persistence.
Very often I had to spend nights sleeping on hard stones,
With no roof or cover over my head except clouds.
Now roaming low, swimming as a fish in the sea,
Now high in the mountains loftier than [Gemini].
Now I passed through countries where frozen water was as hard
   as marble,
Now through countries in which the earth was as hot as embers.
By sea, by land, sometimes even if there were no roads,
By hills, by sandy desert, across streams and precipices,
Now with the camel's halter rope over my shoulder as a true
   camelman,
Now carrying my belongings on my shoulders as a beast of
   burden.
In this way did I wander from town to town, making inquiries,
Wandered in search of the truth over this sea to that land.

Our author poses particular questions about the balance between faith and reason, or more accurately, between blind conformance to religious dictates (*taqlid*) and the understanding of such dictates through reason. He defends both the role of reason in the life of faith and the reasonableness of the required religious duties (*shari'at*). At the same time, he absolutely rejects *taqlid*, as in these lines translated by Ivanow:

> They said that injunctions of the *shari'at* do not conform with
> reason,
> Because Islam was established by the mere force of
> the sword.
> This I answered with a question: 'Why then are prayers not
> prescribed to the children and weak-minded,
> If reason was not required for the discharge of religious duties?'
> I could never accept the blind following of prescribed forms
> (*taqlid*), without any demand for explanations.
> The Truth cannot be proved by blind acceptance.
> When God wishes to open the gate of His mercy,
> Every difficulty is raised and obstacles become (easily)
> overcome.

Then he finds the answer and his poetry slips immediately into metaphor:

> And then came the day when I arrived at the gate of the City to
> which
> The luminaries of the heaven were slaves, and all kingdoms of
> the world subordinated.
> I came to the City that resembled a garden full of fruit and flowers
> Within its ornamented walls, with its ground planted with trees,
> Its fields resembling the pattern of precious brocade,
> Its Spring of Water which was as sweet as honey, resembling
> Kawthar,
> The City in which houses are virtues,
> The Garden in which pine trees are Reason,
> The City in which the learned are dressed in brocade,
> Not (spun by women or woven by men).

It was the City in which, when I arrived, my reason told me:
Here it is where thou shouldst seek for what thou needest.
Do not pass through it in haste.

On one level, the City signifies Cairo, the flourishing capital of the Fatimid empire. As the political and religious centre of the Ismaili world, Cairo and its caliphs were great patrons of artists, scholars, jurists and philosophers. To house and support their intellectual outreach the Fatimids established a major institution of learning, al-Azhar, in 358/969, which still ranks as one of the leading universities for the study of Islamic theology and sciences.[4] On this level the city of Cairo itself incarnated the virtues of knowledge, rewarding the learned with beautiful robes of honour and money enough to buy their own brocade, rather than the rough, woollen cloaks of ascetics. Splendour and wisdom walked hand in hand in Cairo, as Nasir Khusraw attests in his descriptions of the three years he spent within its walls. For him, Cairo is a grand city, a beautiful garden in which the very 'pine trees are Reason.'

But on another level, the City alludes to the Tradition (*hadith*) of the Prophet Muhammad, 'I am the City of Knowledge and 'Ali is its Gate.' For Nasir Khusraw, the City represents the knowledge inherited by the living Ismaili Imam, the descendant of the Prophet and guardian of 'Ali's esoteric knowledge.

The only way to enter this 'City of Knowledge' is through the Imam of the Time, who is therefore in Ismaili doctrine often termed the Gate (*bab*). It was in Ismaili Islam that Nasir found the answers to his spiritual search, and which at the same time allowed for the full expression of his philosophic and poetic insights.

In the next line of the poem, the 'Warden of the Gate' refers to Nasir Khusraw's teacher, al-Mu'ayyad fi'l-Din al-Shirazi (d. 470/1078), the chief *da'i* in Cairo and as such the highest dignitary of the Ismaili religious establishment under the Imam al-Mustansir bi'llah (427–487/1036–1094).[5] Al-Mu'ayyad is the person who helps this seeker of wisdom find the knowledge he has been searching for.

And I went before the Warden of the Gate, and told him what
    I was after.

He said: 'Cease worrying, the jewel has been found in thy mine.
Beneath the ideas of this world there lies an ocean of Truth,
In which are found precious pearls, as well as Pure Water.
This is the highest Heaven of the exalted stars.
Nay, it is Paradise itself, full of the most captivating beauties.'

Here we see two of Nasir Khusraw's most fitting metaphors,
the jewel in the mine and the pearl hidden in the ocean. But they
are not just poetic conventions; he is using them to convey deep
religious significance. Within these two major themes of Nasir's
religious beliefs are distilled his metaphysics and his ethics for
living. Of the Ismaili doctrines the poet is drawing on here, foremost stands the principle of *zahir* and *batin*, that is, the distinction
between the exoteric and the esoteric, between the external, manifest world of physical existence and the inner, hidden world of
spiritual reality. Al-Mu'ayyad, the 'Warden of the Gate,' assures
the traveller that there is indeed an eternal support, a veritable
ocean of truth that underlies, supports and feeds the entire physical world in which we live. That ocean is the whole realm of the
*batin*, the abode of spiritual truth (*haqiqat*).

In Nasir Khusraw's poetic imagery, this ocean contains two
things of value: precious pearls and pure water. The metaphori-
cal significance of pearls is readily obvious. A pearl is a tiny, rare
item of beauty and wealth hidden within coarse surroundings (the
scabby oyster shell). In this poem the pearl of knowledge is external to the seeker, and to find it he must descend into the ocean's
dark and dangerous depths. For the believer who finds it, the pearl
brings infinite spiritual satisfaction in this world and assures him
of salvation in the next. Likewise, the water in the physical ocean
is vital for life, and is also used for mundane activities like transportation, cleaning and gathering many types of food. Oceans
also contain countless unknown creatures which live in a world
all their own. In Ismaili religious symbolism, water stands for the
hidden world of esoteric reality, in fact for the entire esoteric realm
that sustains the exoteric. This 'pure water,' like physical water,
nourishes life, transports the seeker to a farther shore, washes
away error and sin, contains glorious spiritual foods, and holds
within itself a vast territory of unfamiliar characters.

The second image in these lines of poetry, expressed in the phrase 'the jewel has been found in thy mine,' is the pronouncement that the most wonderful treasure, the essential component for understanding the truth lies within Nasir Khusraw himself. In this sense, the jewel is the soul itself, hidden within the body. A jewel (and thereby the soul, too) needs to be found (often a difficult task) and then polished (requiring hard work and special talent) in order for it to become perfect and to realise its unique capabilities. The jewel even takes on a second level of meaning. Besides representing the soul in the mine of the body, it represents any individual person within the troubles of the physical world, and it certainly denotes a sage surrounded by ignorant, hypocritical people. This jewel image must have become particularly comforting to Nasir in the last years of his life in the valley of Yumgan, where he was not only cut off from his home in Khurasan and the intellectual vitality of Cairo, but also very much surrounded by the forbidding mountains of the Pamirs and Hindu Kush. Like the image of the pearl in the ocean, the jewel of knowledge and wisdom lies within every person, only to be extracted by plumbing the depths of the psyche.

Upon hearing such counsel from his new teacher, Nasir Khusraw begins at the beginning, laying out the questions of religion that had troubled him so long.

> Hearing him say this, I thought he was Ridwan himself,
> So much was I struck with his wise words and admirable utterances.
> Then said I unto him: 'My soul is weak and frail.
> Do not look at this my strong body and pink cheeks.'
> But I never take a medicine without first trying and testing it,
> When I feel pain, I never would think or listen to what is unlawful.
> Said he: 'Do not worry, I am here to heal thee.
> Tell me all, describe thy pain.'
> And I began to ask him of the things that were first and those
>     that were last,
> Of the cause of the order of the world which is basis of things
>     as they are,
> Of what is genus and the way in which species is formed.
> I asked about the All-Powerful, predestination and fate,

Both of which are (never) inseparable from each other.
But how should one be given precedence over the others?
I asked him of the mechanism of the palpitation of day and night
    – how from these
The beggar becomes rich, and darkness becomes lit?
I asked about the Prophets (and their contradictory messages),
Of the reason for the prohibition of drinking blood or
    intoxicating wine.
Then I inquired as to the foundation of *shari'at,*
And why these five prayers have been prescribed.
I asked about the fast that the Prophet ordered to be observed
    during the ninth month of the year,
(Why should *zakat* [religious tax] be different for silver and gold
    coins,
Why a fifth on booty and a tithe on irrigated land?)
Why should this be one-fifth, and that one-tenth?
Why the brother takes one share while the sister only half?
I also asked about the cause of the uneven distribution of
    happiness:
Why does it (often) happen that a devotee is aggrieved while
    the oppressor is happy?
Or why one pious man is unhappy while another happy?
Or why one unbeliever enjoys his life while another is aggrieved?
Why one is of solid health and good-looking while the other
    is born blind, or of weak health from birth?
But God always acts in perfect justice – then
Reason cannot be satisfied by what it, in its imperfection, sees.
I see that it is the day, but thou sayest that it is night.
I ask thee to prove that contention, but thou in reply drawest
    thy dagger.
Thou sayest that at a certain place there is a Sacred Stone,
And everyone who performs a pilgrimage to it becomes free
    from sin.
Azar preached the religion of idolatry, and thou preachest the
    worship of that stone:
Then truly now thou art the same to me as Azar![6]

The teacher offers him the 'medicine' that will provide the antidote to scepticism, and finally cure such spiritual pain. Nasir Khusraw accepts it and then experiences tremendous joy, praising al-Mu'ayyad for enabling him to lay his hand 'into the Prophet's hand for the oath, under the same exalted tree, full of shadow and fruit.'

> When I mentioned all these questions, the wise one lifted his
>     hand, touching (with it) his breast.
> May a hundred blessings be now on that hand and that breast!
> He said: I shall give thee that medicine, tried and tested,
> But I have to affix a strong seal on thy mouth.
> He, that wise guide, summoned, as two legal witnesses, the world
>     and man (macrocosm and microcosm),
> And also all that can be eaten and used as drink.
> I expressed acceptance and he then sealed the medicine,
> Giving me a dose of it to take as a nourishing extract.
> My suffering disappeared, my speech became free,
> My yellowed face became scarlet through joy.
> He raised me from dust to the sky, as a ruby;
> I was like dust and became like precious amber.
> He it was who laid my hand into the Prophet's hand for the oath,
> Under the same exalted tree, full of shadow and fruit.

To describe his transformation, Nasir Khusraw then compares himself to a base stone that has been turned into a ruby by holding it up to the powerful rays of the sun, according to the popular explanation for the formation of rubies. 'I am that ruby now,' he declares. And just as the ruby cannot return to its former base state, Nasir Khusraw now cannot be less than the ruby that he is. Likewise, out of possessive jealousy, he says, the initiate cannot divulge his teacher's name, but the poet manages to weave the related word *mu'ayyid* (helper) into the lines.

> Hast thou ever heard that a sea comes from fire,
> Or that the fox becomes a lion?
> The sun has the power of turning stone into ruby
> Which no force of elements can turn again to its original state –

I am like that ruby now, and the sun is he
By whose light this dark world becomes lit.
Out of jealousy I cannot tell thee his name in this poem,
I can tell thee only so much that Plato would have been fit to
    become merely one of his (attendants).
He is the teacher and healer (of souls), helper (of religion)
    (*mu'ayyid*), from God.
It is hardly possible to imagine anyone equalling him in
    wisdom and knowledge.
May that City be prosperous whose Warden of the Gate he is!
May the Ship be safe whose anchor (captain) he is!

In his closing verses, Nasir Khusraw continues his panegyric on
his teacher al-Mu'ayyad and requests that he extend Nasir's greetings to the 'Owner of the treasury of knowledge and wisdom, and
of the House of God,' that is, to the Ismaili Caliph-Imam, al-
Mustansir bi'llah. The poet even includes a request of which singer
should sing the poem before the court, a certain Abu Ya'qub,
who lives on in history only in this citation by Nasir Khusraw.

O thou, whose well-reasoned poetry is the standard of wisdom!
O thou, whose prose is a model for philosophy!
O thou, under whose patronage learning is organised as
    arrayed troops!
O thou, at whose greatness's door knowledge has pitched its camp!
I request thee to convey greetings from this obedient slave,
The greetings, moving and lasting (as the glittering of a) jewel
    which shines as a moon,
The greetings (fresh as) a drop of dew in the petals of a
    narcissus or *shamshad*,
The greetings delicious as the breeze blowing over the beds of
    lilies and jasmine!
The greetings as pleasant and inspiring as the union with beauties,
The greetings as clear and eloquent as the words of great poets,
The greetings, as full of wishes of prosperity and happiness as
    the clouds of spring with rain water,
The clouds that descend from the mountains pouring the rain
    as delicious as drops of musk!

The greetings as true and blessed as the spirit of Jesus, son of Mary,
Sublime and harmonious as the blue sky.
(Convey all these) to the owner of the treasury of knowledge
    and wisdom, and of the House of Ma'mur,[7]
The owner of the Great Name by whom eternity exists,
To him born under the blessed planet for divine victory,
The pride of (humankind), the crown of the universe,
The image and flesh from flesh of his great ancestor and forefather,
Who is himself like the Prophet in counsel and Haydar in battle!
When he rides out, the world is filled with the light of his glory,
And the dust of earth becomes amber under the hooves of his
    horse!
Let the praises of these greetings glorifying that supreme lord
Be recited in the assembly on my behalf by Abu Ya'qub.

Nasir Khusraw ends the poem with praise for al-Mu'ayyad, gratitude for his teachings, and hope that the Imam will always have a
subject as worthy as al-Mu'ayyad. It would be like having a garden
enhanced with stately cypress trees.

Then praise to the one who has freed me,
My teacher, the healer of my soul, the embodiment of wisdom
    and glory.
O thou, whose face is knowledge, whose body is virtue and
    heart – wisdom,
O thou, instructor of humanity and its object of pride!
Before thee once stood, clad in that woollen cloak,
This man, emaciated, with pale face.
It was the truth that except for thy hand I ever touched with my
    lips
Only the Black Stone and the grave of the Prophet.
Six years (after this) I remained as an attendant of (the
    Prophet's) blessed image (i.e., the Imam),
Six years I sat in attendance as a servant at the door of the Ka'ba.
Wherever may I happen to be for the rest of my life, always
I shall use my pen, inkstand and paper only to express my
    gratitude to thee.
So long as cypress trees sway under the blows of the breeze,

Let the presence (of the Imam) be adorned by thee as the
garden is adorned by cypress trees!

## THE TWO ACCOUNTS COMPARED

The first difference to note in comparing these two 'confession'
pieces is that the poem contains no mention of the dream related
in the *Safarnama*. The poem instead shows Nasir Khusraw's arrival at spiritual awakening to be the direct result of a conscious
questioning of religious doctrines. When he was 42-years-old he
began asking scholars of all persuasions (he mentions three, the
Shafi'i, Maliki and Hanafi schools of law) for their interpretations
of specific Qur'anic verses or established dogma. These official
answers did not satisfy him. 'None proved to be helpful, one
resembling the blind, and the other the deaf.' From the poem
it is obvious that his primary concern was to determine the
existence of one person, a spiritual leader, 'someone who is
the most precious of all that had been created,' one who would
provide that 'personal contact with the Prophet' enjoyed by the
companions of the Prophet, those who knew him personally
when he was alive. This person would be able to explain to him
the true meaning behind the words of God. For just as God
'stretches out His hand' for believers to swear allegiance to Him,
and just as the companions had held out their hands in a public pledge of fealty to Muhammad's leadership under the tree
at Hudaybiyya, Nasir Khusraw asserts that successive generations
of believers also need to have someone to stretch their hands
out to, in order to confirm their allegiance to God. 'What happened to that tree, that hand?' he asks. If there is no comparable
person available to believers at later times in history, Nasir
Khusraw argues that God's justice can legitimately be called
into question. It would be unjust of God to have shown preference to those who lived at the time of the Prophet, rewarding
them with Paradise 'for having taken that oath,' and then leaving people of later generations without a hand to guide them.
'Was it our fault we were not born at that time?' he asks.

A question should be raised here, before proceeding with further analysis of the contents of this poem. How should the poet's

statements be read? When he writes that he seeks to find the leader, and compares the learned and their knowledge to musk and its fragrance, or to a mine and its gold, we are clearly dealing with simile. But when he writes that he sets out on a journey, 'abandoning without regret my house, my garden, those whom I was accustomed to see,' we have to exercise caution before calling it metaphor and dismissing its overt meaning. The poem may be endowed with rhythm and rhyme and laced with metaphor, but much of its content is corroborated in the sparsely-worded prose of his travel diary. The *Safarnama* mirrors the quote above about beginning his trip and also gives examples of his meeting and discussing religion with people from as many different backgrounds as he can. This latter trait is found in other works, such as the *Wajh-i din*, in which he says he has heard many arguments from knowledgeable Hindus about their practices and holy texts.[8] He writes in the poem of his passing through extreme climes and living in precarious physical conditions. He records in the *Safarnama* some specifics about these adventures – the dangers of travelling through the desert in Arabia, the wretchedness of arriving in one town so bedraggled that he and his brother were even refused entry to the bathhouse, and the despair of truly fearing for his life.

Further on in the poem, Nasir Khusraw clearly states his rejection of *taqlid*, the unthinking following of prescribed actions or explanations of the faith, in favour of individual reasoning and understanding of religion. He argues with anonymous adversaries that Islam requires the use of reason for the proper discharge of religious duties. For why else would the *shari'a* remove the requirement for prayer from children and the weak-minded, that is, those deficient in reason? Nasir's emphasis on reason here is entirely consistent with his other writings, both poetry and prose, where reason takes on a pivotal role in human existence and salvation.

Up to this point, the poem is descriptive. The date, names, places and concerns he enumerates can be found in his other writings. There is some use of simile ('the learned are like musk') but not in a manner which obscures meaning. But when he writes, 'And then came the day when I arrived at the gate of the City to which the luminaries of the heaven were slaves, and all kingdoms of the world subordinated,' we are in the realm of allusion. As mentioned earlier, the City can be both Cairo, the Fatimid capital, where Nasir Khusraw stayed for three of his seven years' journey, as well as a metaphor for the Ismaili Imam, the Prophet's descendant, and his realm of truth, the Ismaili gnosis which is the goal of Nasir's quest for knowledge. The 'Warden of the Gate,' however, is clearly not the Imam but Nasir Khusraw's teacher, al-Mu'ayyad fi'l-Din al-Shirazi, the chief *da'i* in Cairo.

Having found the 'Warden of the Gate,' Nasir warns him that he will not meekly accept whatever he is told, for 'I never take a medicine without first trying and testing it,' and then details many of the inconsistencies he and others have found in religious doctrines and practices. Why does the brother inherit one share while the sister only half? If God is just, why are some good people miserable and some bad people happy? Why isn't the veneration of the Black Stone in the Ka'ba considered idolatry? In response, al-Mu'ayyad places his hand on his own heart as a sign of humility and promises to give a tried and tested medicine to help answer these knotty problems. He then places a 'strong seal' on Nasir Khusraw's mouth. But what is this? Is it some kind of initiatory ritual or a metaphor for esoteric teachings? Could it also be a vow of secrecy, not to divulge inappropriately any of the esoteric Ismaili teachings? Possibly all of these. The lessons Nasir Khusraw learned, and learned well enough to teach them, can be found in his philosophical books.

Nasir Khusraw's ethics derive from these convictions. There is one truth for which one should do everything in one's power to find. This ultimate truth is beyond this world, so the rewards of this world must not be taken as one's final goal. Since human beings inhabit a physical world while the truth is beyond it, they must seek the truth through a combination of spiritual and physical means. Within each person resides the key to seeking and understanding the truth. This jewel within must be brought out and allowed to shine forth. From this foundation of beliefs, Nasir Khusraw derives the rationale for the activities of his life, his commitment to the Ismaili cause, and indeed the entire corpus of his writings which have come down to us.

# CHAPTER FIVE

# Knowledge and Action

Light the candle of wisdom within your heart
and hurry, heart aglow, toward the world of light.

*Divan*, 78:15

Consistent with any true conversion of the heart, and certainly
conforming to his personality, Nasir Khusraw looked for ways to
make this inner change manifest in his external life. What he would
later preach to others, he first practised himself. He saw very clearly
that to walk in the ways of his new faith, he would need to learn as
much about it as possible and then match his actions to this
knowledge.

He needed to learn the teachings of the Imam in Cairo and,
intellectual that he was, to study and immerse himself in the fine
points of Ismaili theology and philosophy. This learning suffused
his actions, whether the required actions of the *shari'a* (such as
prayers and fasting) or the more personal expressions of his faith
(such as study, travel, teaching and writing). In fact, through living this interconnected cycle of knowledge and action, he would
embody, actually enact, the underlying *zahir/batin* doctrine of the
Ismaili faith.

## UNDERSTANDING ZAHIR AND BATIN

When Nasir Khusraw writes in the *Wajh-i din*, 'The price of each
jewel is determined not by its external qualities, but by its inner

qualities' (*WD*, 81),[1] he illustrates one of the most important lessons of his newly converted life. For while it may appear that the value of a jewel comes from the brilliance and colour it displays, he points out that its value in fact derives from something other than such external attributes. A jewel's value must derive from the fact that human beings recognise an inner quality in jewels which forms the basis for their ranking certain jewels over others. Extrinsically, one could say, there is nothing which makes a ruby more valuable than a turquoise; red and clear are not necessarily more valuable than blue and opaque. It is only through human appreciation of the intrinsic qualities of these jewels that they have been assigned different comparative values. It is the same with gold, the philosopher explains:

Gold has not become as costly as it is simply by being yellow and melted. For if that were the case, brass – which is also yellow and melted – would be equally costly. Rather, its price relates to the virtue (*ma'na*) that lies within it, separate from brass. This is the subtle (*latif*) virtue and the subtle soul recognises that virtue (*WD*, 81).

True as this may be for jewels, that which is within determines the true value, Nasir Khusraw finds it true of everything else, even brass and gold. That is, everything manifest has a hidden quality which is not only the essence of the thing, but which indeed carries the explanation, the meaning, the true significance of the thing.

In Ismaili thought, whatever is in the world consists of two parts, exoteric and esoteric, *zahir* and *batin*. Whatever is *zahir* is known by the external senses of sight, hearing, touch, taste and smell, through specialised organs, such as eyes, ears, hands, tongue and nose, but 'that which is *batin* is hidden from these external senses' (*WD*, 78–9). Nasir Khusraw explains that 'the position of the Shi'is' is that the *zahir* consists, in part, of those acts which can be observed or otherwise felt by the senses, such as prayer (*namaz*), fasting (*ruza*), charity (*zakat*), pilgrimage (*hajj*) and holy war (*jihad*), as well as of all that is made of bodies that exists in heaven and earth and in between. The external senses perceive only bodies and not the *batin*, which is 'what you call those things which the senses have no part in perceiving,' such as the knowledge of unity, proofs of prophecy, Heaven and Hell, reward and punishment, resurrection and judgement, and the corruptibility of the earth. Thus, even religion requires the full use of both aspects of being. The believer is required to employ his external senses to carry out the external duties of faith, and also to employ his internal senses to understand and know the meanings of the faith.

In life, for example, Nasir Khusraw explains, we can physically pronounce the phrase 'In the name of God, the Merciful, the Compassionate,' by moving our tongues against our palates and raising our voices, and all listeners will hear it in the same way because it is perceived by the external senses, the *zahir*. But the *batin* of this doxology, its inner meaning, is not something obviously equally to both ordinary listeners and the wise, even though both hear the same words, because people are not equal in their ability to understand. He points out that if the hidden meaning (the *batin*) of this phrase were as obvious as the *zahir* of its words, everyone who heard it would understand (*WD*, 80–1). Thus, the fact that people can agree on the external but disagree on the internal demonstrates the existence of both levels.

Furthermore, even 'the seasons are not known by the senses, [nor] that a year has twelve months, and it is not obvious that the month of Ramadan is the ninth month of the Arabs' year' (*WD*, 81). That is, we may think we know it is winter because of the cold and snow, and we may think a year has twelve months because we can count the heavens' revolutions, and we may count and observe that the ninth month of the Muslim calendar is Ramadan; but, declares Nasir Khusraw, none of these is 'obvious.' The recognition of each requires powers of intellection and abstraction unique to human beings. Winter is an abstract designation. A year is an abstract organisation of days. Ramadan has far deeper significance than merely being the ninth month. Animals may experience cold, but they do not perceive an underlying meaning called 'winter.' Animals may perceive the light of day and the dark of night, but not the progression of days which make years. They cannot count the months or know their inner significance.

Animals only know the *zahir* of things, while [human beings] know the hidden meanings of things. This is why human beings are the overlords of animals (*WD*, 29).

With this line of reasoning, Nasir Khusraw is trying to point out that human beings have assigned names to things according to a hidden ideal, or 'form' in the Platonic sense, not simply by comparing their external features. For example, whenever we see a new chair, one we have never seen before, we know it is a chair, not because we have seen one which exactly matches it in all its external details, but rather because it corresponds to our inner idea of a chair. This abstract conception of the constitution of a chair is an indicator of its inner reality, the *batin*.

Other pairs of opposites follow the same polar pattern of *zahir* and *batin*. 'This' world, the apparent, physical world is gross, while 'that' world, the invisible, spiritual world, is subtle. The *batin* of 'this' physical, sensible, world is 'that' world which is spiritual, non-sensible. To prove his point, our author presents a list of other opposites: the human body (gross and visible) and the human soul (subtle and hidden); created (manifest) and creator (hidden); the bad when manifest to the good, and the good when hidden from the bad; fear and hope; theory and practice. One element of each pair is apparent to the senses, while the other is hidden. But each does not, and cannot, exist without the other. Like the two sides of a coin, one may seem to be solely in evidence at any time but the other still necessarily exists.

Nasir Khusraw applies the logic of this dynamic between pairs to religion as well. The scriptures and the law are both manifest. That is, the Qur'an as the Book of God is visible and tangible to everyone, as is the *shari'a*, the law of Islam. But their inner meanings and esoteric interpretations (*ta'wil*) are hidden to those who do not know, while obvious to those who do know (*WD*, 82). Knowledge is therefore that which clarifies, that which illuminates both structure and content. What the scriptures actually mean can be determined only by knowledge. The human body is required to obey the commands and fulfil the exoteric religious strictures and duties stipulated in the Qur'an and the *shari'a*. The human soul, however, needs to know the inner meanings and significance of these acts and the scriptures on which they are based. This physical world and all it has within it is merely a stepping stone – but a necessary stepping stone – to that spiritual world beyond. Knowledge and the act of knowing are that which separates the ignorant from the knower.

> Look with the inner eye at earth's hiddenness,
>     for the outer eye cannot see it.
> What is the hiddenness of the world? The noble ones
>     see the esoteric, but not the exoteric.
> Not with iron should the world be chained,
>     but with chains of wisdom it should be bound.
> Two things bind the world together, knowledge and devotion,
>     just as liberation lies in both these as well.
> Your body is a mine, your soul the jewel of knowledge and devotion;
>     so to these two commit yourself, body and soul.
>
> (*Divan*, 5: 1–5)

Of all the polarities here, one of the most important and far-reaching is that of 'this world' (the physical world) and 'that world' (the spiritual world). For, aside from the duality itself with its built-in contrast of opposites, there also exists a correspondence between the two worlds, in which the two parallel structures constantly interact with each other. For example, 'that' world (which is the creator, *sani'*, of 'this' world) is subtle (*latif*), a point Nasir Khusraw proves by its effects in this world (*WD*, 40). This subtleness, however, must not be construed with weakness. Traces of that world pass into the bodies of this world which the bodies cannot obscure or block out. For example, iron is forged in fire and thereafter always carries the essence of fire. According to Nasir Khusraw, the heat and brightness sometimes found in iron (as accidents) are the essence (*jawhar, ya'ni dhati*) of fire. This is proven when an iron object is placed near a hot flame, and the heat, which is fire's power (its *latif* quality), comes through on the other side of the iron. The heat would not be able to do this if iron did not share a trace of the essence of fire. Insofar as fire is the source of heat, and iron merely possesses the capacity to receive heat, fire is considered the 'creator' of the traces of iron.

Thus, the creature always retains an open channel to its creator, with all the implications that this entails.

A second connection between that world and this, the creator and the created, is that the other world is fully alive, indeed the source of life. 'Surely the last abode is life, did they but know' (Qur'an, 29:64). For Nasir Khusraw, this world is essentially lifeless in that it receives all its sustenance from that world. Therefore, since whatever is living is nobler than that which is not living, that world is nobler than this lifeless world.

Just as vitality and life are signs of pre-eminence, so is knowledge. That world itself is both alive and knowing, whereas this world is neither. In this world, the noblest creature is the living, knowing human being. Superior to any other creature, human beings are also closer to their creator than any other creature, juxtaposed at the pinnacle of a hierarchy of creatures. Through their ability to gain knowledge, human beings can come to apprehend the pervasiveness of this dual *zahir/batin* structure, seeing that everything in that world is mirrored in this world. Indeed, anything must exist first and primarily in that world before it can be manifest in this. Conversely, patterns and structures in this world are clues and signs of that world. Nasir Khusraw brings examples from politics, biology, physics and everyday occurrences to prove such spiritual and metaphysical points. For example, each person has an individual soul (*nafs-i juz'i*) which is living, knowing and eternal. This individual soul is the part of the person which makes moral decisions, and which increases in knowledge and wisdom as the person matures. It is also the same soul which will suffer in Hell or be rewarded in Paradise as a result of the actions it takes while embodied in the person. Nasir wants to show that this individual soul is connected to the Universal Soul (*nafs-i kulli*), just as a piece of iron is connected to its source, fire. The Universal Soul, being the parent of individual souls (indeed, he often likens it to a mother), is primary and superior. It is much like Plato's World Soul in that it is the force and governor of physical creation, making the heavens revolve and the elements mix and multiply. Nasir wants us to know further that there is a very special relationship between the individual soul and the Universal Soul. To this end, he strikes the simile of a millwheel.

Go inside a mill, Nasir suggests, and you see the millstone turning round and round, grinding the grain. The millstone is very powerful and efficient and accomplishes a difficult task. Go outside and you see that it is powered by something else – the force of running water constantly lifting itself up and throwing itself down. You realise that the running water is the ultimate source of power, and indeed has the more difficult task of both moving itself through the stream and around the wheel, as well as powering the millwheel and the grindstone. With this model, Nasir shows that water's movement of itself is essential (*jawhari*) and in its nature (*tabi'i*), while the movement of the millstone is derivative and secondary (*'arazi*, 'accidental,' is the technical term). The essential movement of water is its own primary, and more difficult, task; the fact that it also moves the millstone is a side effect, a secondary activity, an 'accident.' And the essential movement is stronger than the accidental one. It follows then that the greatest, preeminent, and most difficult task of the Universal Soul is its movement 'in its own species' (*andar naw'-i khwish*) – not what it is most credited with, its work of moving planets and stars in the heavens and all the elements of life on earth. Since its most noble task is moving its own species, and in this world there is 'nothing nobler' than human beings (because each has an individual soul), then the whole movement of the Universal Soul in this world is directed toward human beings and their souls, specifically the increase of knowledge within each human soul (*WD*, 50–1).

### BRINGING KNOWLEDGE INTO LIFE

Having made the decision to change his life, Nasir Khusraw had to find out how to fulfil his resolution. On what intellectual or spiritual principles should he live his life? As mentioned in both the *Safarnama* and the confessional poem cited above, probing into alternate theologies left him unsatisfied until he found out more about the Ismaili interpretation of Islam. Ismaili doctrine appealed to him on many levels, most particularly in what he interpreted as its promotion of intellect and knowledge. In contrast, he says, to those schools which admonish believers to accept doctrine without asking questions, without probing into the 'how and why,' Ismaili precepts championed human intellect as God's finest creation. Below the heavenly or noumenal realm, the realm of phenomenon moves from the lowest to the highest degree, beginning with the four elements (of medieval scientific thought) which combined to make everything else, in a systematic progression from mineral to plant to animal. Human beings are the crown of the animal kingdom and the intellect is the crown of the human being. In such a system, proper respect for God requires energetic use of one's intellect. If the attainment of Paradise depends on doing good and, even more, on striving to perfect one's moral conduct, then human beings must make use of that distinguishing feature, the intellect, which separates them from all other creatures. Nasir Khusraw took hold of this idea and never let it go. In the life he lived – travelling to Multan, Lahore, Jerusalem, Cairo, Mecca and Isfahan, seeking out scholars in every city, continuing a prolific amount of writing even while in exile in Yumgan – he exemplifies the search for knowledge. In poem after poem, and in all his prose writings, he hammers home the necessity and virtue of the pursuit of knowledge and the attainment of wisdom.

> What did God give us alone of all the other creatures?
> The intellect, by which we lord o'er all the beasts.

> But note, that virtue and intellect which makes us lords of
>     donkeys,
> Are the very same trait which binds us as slaves of the Lord.

> With intellect, we can seek out all the hows and the whys,
> Without it, we are but trees without fruit.
>                                   (*Divan*, 33: 28–30)

In another poem our poet is more blunt:

> Why do you suppose God gave you a mind?
> For eating and sleeping like donkeys?
>                                   (*Divan*, 22:3)

Indeed, knowledge is of such critical importance for Nasir that, in this world, the believer can experience a foretaste of Heaven

or Hell through knowledge or ignorance. Hell in this world, he
says, is 'fear of the sword,' that is, dying a painful death (*WD*, 5).
For Nasir, the believer experiences a little piece of that Hell
whenever he or she acts in ignorance. Conversely, in this world
Heaven is experienced in the optimistic and upward-looking feeling of hope based on true knowledge. When one advances, acting
on true knowledge, and when knowledge drives and directs one's
actions, free of doubt and falsehood, one experiences a portion
of Heaven on earth.

When this primacy of knowledge is combined with the notion
of *zahir* and *batin*, the search for knowledge becomes the search
for the inner meaning of things, the esoteric dimension:

> Knowing the hidden meanings of exoteric (*zahir*) things is compara-
> ble to hidden knowledge (*danish-i ghayb*). Hidden knowledge belongs
> to God, as He says [in the Qur'an, 11:123], 'To God belongs the
> unseen [secrets] of the heavens and the earth.' So whoever knows
> more hidden knowledge (*danish-i pushida*) is closer to God (*WD*, 30).

The Qur'anic verse quoted here provides the proof-text for
the Ismaili doctrine of the existence of a distinct realm of unseen
things and activities existing here in this world as in the heavens.
Nasir also finds justification for this doctrine of esoteric knowledge located in several other Qur'anic verses. For instance, he
quotes 62:2, that God sent a Messenger 'to teach them the Book
and the Wisdom,' in which the Book is understood to be the
Qur'an and the Wisdom the *batin*, the inner meaning of the manifest book. Without knowing the hidden meaning of the sacred
book a believer's faith is rendered sentimental and wishful at best.
The superiority of those who have esoteric knowledge over those
who do not is founded on the direct relationship of knowledge to
the fear of God; the more knowledge one has of God and His
Power and Mercy, the more one will fear Him, as in the verse:
'Only those of His servants fear God who have knowledge' (35:28).
Nasir Khusraw argues from this verse to another, 'Surely the noblest among you in the sight of God is the most Godfearing of
you' (49:13), to prove that the noblest in the sight of God are
those who have knowledge. Knowledge is necessary for life in

general, certainly. But Nasir Khusraw has in mind a deeper knowledge, of a kind which transmutes the believer's soul from its base condition to perfection:

What is your soul without knowledge, but lead?
Religion is the alchemy that will make it gold.
(Divan, 45:54)

How shall human beings attain this knowledge, the gold of the alchemists of the spirit? First, what kind of knowledge is this? Even in this world, Nasir explains in his Zad al-musafirin, there are two types of knowledge, physical and spiritual, and human beings possess two corresponding types of senses, external and internal, in order to understand each (ZM, 18–19).[2] Physical knowledge is known through the five external senses and spiritual knowledge through the five internal ones. The theoretical grounding for this argument is based on the connection between zahir and batin. Just as there are traces of that world in this, there are also traces of a higher wisdom (hikmat) in this world (ZM, 191), and human beings obviously have the capacity to fathom this wisdom. We do not call anyone 'heedless' or 'ignorant' (ghafil) who does not have the capacity to discriminate appropriately (ZM, 22); the very use of these words shows that we expect a certain level of understanding. To explain what he means Nasir Khusraw cites the following verse from the Qur'an, which states that humans are endowed with the attributes necessary for them to understand. It is the responsibility of each person to make use of these gifts, but unfortunately not all do.

... They have hearts, but understand not with them;
They have eyes, but perceive not with them;
They have ears, but they hear not with them.
They are like cattle; nay, rather they are further astray.
Those – they are the heedless. (7:179)

Human beings and animals differ in the relative importance of some of these senses, according to Nasir Khusraw. For human beings, the external senses of hearing and seeing are of preeminent importance and act as guides to the other three senses of touch, taste and smell. While in animals, he says, hearing is the least developed sense and smell is the most developed, in humans hearing is more developed than smell (*ZM*, 18–19). In human beings hearing and sight are the two noblest physical senses because when they combine – that is, when a person hears speech and reads writing – that person acquires a knowledge which allows him to move from the rank of the beast to that of the angel. Thus, these two senses are the noblest because they lead humans to knowledge, which is the perfection and fulfilment of the species. Of these two senses, Nasir Khusraw continues, hearing is superior to sight because if a man is born without sight he can still learn from hearing a teacher's voice, even though he would be somewhat deficient by not being able to discern or draw shapes and colours (*ZM*, 20). But on the other hand (based on the science of Nasir's day), if he is born without hearing he can never learn to speak or gain knowledge, no matter how excellent his sight.

The five internal senses – conjecture (*wahm*), thought (*fikr*), imagination (*takhayyul*), memory (*hifz*) and recollection (*dhikr*) – help to clarify meanings and purposes, and to store and withdraw information as necessary. For Nasir Khusraw, the most important use of the internal senses is to comprehend speech and writing. Speech is first perceived through the external sense of hearing, while writing is first perceived through the external sense of sight, seeing the ink of letters and lines. However, sounds and letters are merely external signs; behind those sounds and letters lies the inner meaning.

The internal and external senses are also closely linked, just as the *batin* is closely connected to the *zahir*. For Nasir, the internal senses benefit humankind only through the mediation of the external senses. Thus, while conjecture (*wahm*) is the 'first movement of the intellect,' he declares that conjecture cannot be exercised without sensation (*hiss*) (*ZM*, 23).[3] That is, the person must first have an external, physical sensation to initiate the internal sense of conjecture. As the first movement of intellect, conjecture then moves its contents to the second internal sense, which is a more sustained kind of thought. Imagination, the third internal sense, takes what is seen and heard in the material world and individualises their forms, which it then places in the fourth internal sense, memory. The fifth internal sense, that of recollection, can pull these forms out of memory. Memory must come before recollection because one cannot recall something that is not in the memory. Recollection works because no two forms are alike, and imagination has committed the forms to memory. A person remembers something when what is recollected or recalled matches what is embedded in the memory.

To illustrate this process, Nasir Khusraw explains that when we memorise a piece of writing, both the sounds and the written letters fall away and there remains nothing but their individualised forms in the memory. That which is produced in human memory is a non-material, spiritual writing (*kitabat-i nafsani*), he says, 'written with the pen of imagination on the paper of memory' (*ZM*, 25). This spiritual writing is actually psychic, that is, it takes place in or pertains to the psyche, or soul (*nafs*). As such, the soul can gain direct access to information in the memory without resorting to any of the sounds of language or letters of writing. This is the way we can remember something without repeating it aloud. And there is no limit to the number of forms that can fit in the memory, contrary to the external senses for which only one item can be in one place at one time, 'just as two letters cannot be written in one space.'

An important example of the workings of the internal senses concerns the activities of angels, especially the so-called recording angels and the angel Gabriel. Nasir ridicules the 'unthinking masses' for actually believing that angels are recording their deeds in a ledger which will be placed in their hands on Resurrection Day. These people do not understand the difference between body and spirit (*ruh*), he says. They even think that the angel Gabriel gave the Prophet Muhammad the revelation by physically speaking into the Prophet's ear. 'This is absurd,' he says, 'because a voice is only produced by the expulsion of air between two bodies, and angels are not bodies but spirits. Angels do not take up space, and there is no point that air can enter and escape.' What the ignorant masses think, he says, is exactly the opposite of the meaning of God, for He Himself says that the sending of the Qur'an was by spirit:

> Truly it is the revelation of the Lord of all Being,
> Brought down by the Faithful Spirit
> Upon thy heart, that thou mayest be one of the warners,
> In a clear, Arabic tongue. (26:192–5)

By this Qur'anic verse, according to Nasir Khusraw, a physical voice did not issue from the angel, but rather Gabriel came onto 'the heart' of the Prophet, that is, communicated into his internal, subtle senses.

Thus, the attainment of knowledge, being the highest achievement possible to human beings, should become each person's goal. For Nasir, this knowledge and wisdom is gained through employing the God-given internal and external faculties, in the path of Islam indicated by the *ahl al-bayt*, the Prophet Muhammad and his progeny, especially the Ismaili imams.

### ACTING ON KNOWLEDGE

Just as *batin* cannot exist without *zahir*, or creator without creature, so too knowledge without action is vain. Obversely, action should be undertaken only with knowledge of the meaning of the act. Prayers must be recited with full understanding of the words. Each step of the pilgrimage must be taken with knowledge of the significance of the different stages of the journey. Without the accompanying *batin*, all visible acts are rendered null and void. Performing acts without knowledge of their meaning is what animals do. Angels, on the other hand, possess knowledge without action. The human task is to take the middle road and perfect both knowledge and action, as our author states in the *Wajh-i din*:

Action is the lot of animals without knowledge. Knowledge is the lot of angels without action. Knowledge and action are the lot of humans, for they correspond to animals by virtue of their bodies, but by virtue of their knowledge they do not correspond to animals; they are equivalent to angels. They are midway between beasts and angels so that, with knowledge and action, they can move from the rank of animals to that of angels (*WD*, 75).

Through knowing, humans participate in the act of angels and thus are brought closer to God.

When they learn wisdom and act with knowledge, [then] they rise from Hell and reach Heaven, both in this world potentially and in that world actually (*WD*, 5).

The Heaven attained in this world is only a potential paradise, the forerunner of the true Heaven in that world, but the attainment of both requires wisdom, and action based on that wisdom. This theme is often repeated in his poems, as in these lines:

If you would light a lamp within your heart,
make knowledge and action your wick and oil.
(*Divan*, 78:16)

And these:

If you wish to dwell in the meadow of mercy and blessing,
graze on knowledge and action today.
Moisten the seed of action with knowledge,
for the seed will not grow without moisture.
(*Divan*, 130: 20–1)

In order to gain one's rightful reward in Heaven it is necessary to observe the religious law (*shari'a*), but it is equally necessary to understand the inner meaning of each act. Our poet returns to this theme in another *qasida*:

On the body of blessings, devotion is the head;
on the book of goodness, devotion is the seal.
But obedience without knowledge is not obedience,
a mere wisp of wind in the morning.
Since you are two things, body and soul,
then your obedience is also twofold.

> Exercise both knowledge and action, for on Resurrection Day
> these two shall surely save all humankind from eternal fire.
>
> (*Divan*, 45: 62–5)

The importance which Nasir Khusraw accords to informed action can be seen clearly in his introduction to the *Wajh-i din*, where he states that the reason he wrote this book was so that Muslims could understand the foundations of the *shari'a*, the reasons underlying the required confession of faith, ablutions, prayers, almsgiving, pilgrimage to Mecca, *jihad*, *wilayat* (belief in the viceregency of 'Ali), and the various commands and prohibitions of the law. This way people would know the true 'face of religion' (which is the translation of the title of the book, *Wajh-i din*), that is, what lies underneath the veil, and those who are wise and discerning (*khiradmand*), when reading his book, would then practise the faith with full knowledge, and thereby earn a reward through pleasing God (*WD*, 6). In order to make the work accessible to ordinary people, he adds that he has even placed a list of contents at the beginning of the book. Here are the tools of learning, he implies, use them to acquire a proper understanding of your faith.

The Prophet Muhammad's religion is adorned with two things, Nasir maintains, which are knowledge and action (*WD*, 69). Proof for each of these is found in the word of God, the Qur'an, in verses showing the high expectations that God has for His people. In propounding this argument, Nasir Khusraw quotes segments of several Qur'anic verses, including the following:

[Those who] perform the prayer, and expend of that We have provided them (*zakat*) (2:4).

Say: Work, and God will surely see your work, and His Messenger (9:106).

And know that your wealth and your children are a trial (8:28).

So know you that God is All-forgiving, All-compassionate (5:38).

In his argument, the first two examples illustrate the Qur'anic injunction to be active and perform pious deeds, while the second two illustrate Nasir's point that God commands believers to use their faculties of knowledge, even if it should prove difficult and they might be prone to error.

Besides using Qur'anic exegesis to prove his point that knowledge and action must go hand in hand, Nasir provides an esoteric perspective to show the parallel between the written words themselves in both Arabic (*'ilm* and *'amal*) and Persian (*danish* and *kar*). His argument can be paraphrased as follows (*WD*, 70):

Just as the word for action (*'amal*) in Arabic is one word with three letters and the Persian word *kar* is one word with three letters, so too is action within religion one whole with three parts: the task of the ear, the task of the tongue and the task of the whole body. The task of the ear is to listen to the words of truth; the task of the tongue is to speak the language of truth with words of devotion; and the task of the body is to perform the required acts of prayer, pilgrimage and so on. Furthermore, the word for knowledge in Arabic (*'ilm*) is one word with three letters, and the Persian *danish* is knowledge activated through three human faculties. The sensory faculty (*quwwat-i hissi*) allows the believer to know the sensible dimension of the legal aspect of religion, such as how to perform the prescribed prayers, or what the different rituals of the pilgrimage are. With the faculty of speech (*quwwat-i halq*), human beings produce words and cause them to be heard. The faculty of intellect (*quwwat-i 'aql*) is a gift by which humankind is able to strip away both likeness (*tashbih*) and negation (*ta'til*) from the Divine Oneness (*tawhid*), leaving it single and alone. Through the intellectual faculty a person also comes to know that the human intellect has the potential to encompass all things.[4]

The argument continues that, thus, all things have two sides, knowledge and action, or theory and practice. When both are combined in one person, we call him religious (*din-dar*), just as when a being is made up of body and soul combined we call that entity a person. The practice of religion is like the body and its knowledge is like the soul. The religion of someone who practises its rites without understanding is dead (*jan na-bashad*) like a corpse.

Likewise, whoever has knowledge but does not practise it has no religion. However, if asked to choose between them, Nasir holds that practice without knowledge is better than knowledge without practice, just as a corpse is better than nothing (*WD*, 71). He seems to be saying that, while the spiritual is indeed superior, in the physical world at least some form of existence is better than non-existence. But perhaps he is also saying that it is better to have lived than not to have lived at all.

For the conduct of one's life, Nasir Khusraw offers other lessons as well. One of the most beautifully and succinctly expressed is found in his famous 'Eagle' poem, well-known and committed to memory by generations of Persian speakers for the poignancy of the tale it tells:

> One day an eagle rose up from a craggy perch,
> Stretched wide his wings and feathers in search of food.
> Admiring his graceful feathers, he grew proud and boasted loud:
> 'Today, the world entire lies beneath my wings!
> When I soar over the ocean, I can see with eagle eye
> Even a tiny speck deep at the bottom of the sea!
> And if on land a gnat should move along a twig,
> I catch that movement too, sharp within my sight!'
> And so he boasted proudly, never fearing divine decree.
> Look now, what the cruel Wheel of Fortune rolled out for him!
> Suddenly, from a hidden spot, a mighty bow let loose
> An arrow of disaster hurling straight to its mark.
> That searing, tearing arrow struck deep within the eagle's wing
> And brought him crashing down from high to low.
> Down he thudded, that helpless bird, flipping like a fish,
> Ripping out his feathers, right and left.
> 'How strange!' he cried, 'It's naught but wood and iron.
> Only when he spied the arrow's eagle feather did he comprehend
>     at last:
> 'How can I complain?' he cried, 'What comes from us, returns
>     to us!'
> O Hujjat! Cast all your arrogance and conceit aside,
> And see what befell that eagle full of selfish pride![5]

Incredulous that something made of wood and iron could stop his awesome flight, the eagle only realises the power of the arrow when he sees its eagle feather, the very thing he had been exulting in just moments before. On the one hand, this poem can be viewed simply as an allegory warning against excessive pride in any accomplishment or possession. However, what makes the poem so palpable and apt is found in the climaxing cry of comprehension on the part of the eagle. The fact that the line, 'What comes from us, returns to us' (much more pithy in the original Persian, '*az ma-st ki bar ma-st*') is uttered still today to signify personal responsibility for one's actions and disasters indicates that this is the real lesson learned. Not simply pride in something, but the object of pride itself carries the potential for success or failure. The poet's point is that the very thing that can bring human beings up to their highest heights can also bring them crashing down. If we are the doers of our acts, then we are responsible for them. Therefore, the poem also carries an uplifting message, not just 'it's our own fault,' but that retribution and just reward are the result of individual responsibility and the power that comes when that responsibility is given, and taken.

We have seen that for Nasir Khusraw happiness for human beings lies in a life lived with each act founded on true knowledge of the meaning and purpose of that act. In this way the believer will be able to live a righteous life in this world and attain Heaven in the next world. In fact, with knowledge it is possible to know and experience that other spiritual world, even in this world before death. And for such a person eternal reward is guaranteed.

Whoever truly knows that world, his soul (*jan*) will reach that world, even today while he is in his body. And when he also observes the *shari'at* he will reach that world and will remain forever in eternal favour (*na'im*) (*WD*, 42).

But why would one not want to 'reach that world, even today' while in the body, he asks? The instruments have been supplied by God, the message has been delivered, the ability to connect with the higher realm has been established, and the rewards are clear enough:

God calls you to the heavens;
     why have you thrown yourself into the pit?
To ascend to the highest heavens, craft for yourself
     feet out of knowledge and wings out of devotion.

                                        (*Divan*, 22:39–40)

# CHAPTER SIX

# The Journey Begins

I ... renounced everything worldly, except for a few necessities.

*Safarnama,* 2

Nasir Khusraw has now entered a new phase in his life, one that will lift him out of his position at court, propel him across a continent, and raise him to the highest levels of the Fatimid Ismaili religious hierarchy. He has resolved his religious doubts, accepted the message of Ismailism and committed himself fully to its cause. His seven-year journey to Mecca and Cairo and his subsequent return home as head of the Ismaili *da'wa* activities in eastern Iran stand as vivid confirmation of the force of his commitment. This commitment will play out on two levels, the public and the private.

On the public stage, Nasir makes dramatic changes. He leaves his job, his home and his family. After announcing his decision to set off for the pilgrimage to Mecca, he settles his debts and renounces everything else, 'except for a few necessities.' Of his family, we know only of two brothers. One of them, Abu Sa'id, accompanies him on the journey and the other stays behind continuing his employment with the Saljuqs. We know of no wife or children, which does not mean that they did not exist; and we cannot know the domestic scene he left behind.[1]

In the private realm, Nasir will plunge himself into learning all he can of Ismaili theology and philosophy from books and teachers. He will reside for months at a time in Mecca passing his time in prayer and discussion. He will live in Cairo for three years studying advanced points of Ismaili theology to such a degree that eventually he is entrusted with the responsibilities of a *hujjat*, the chief *da'i* in one of the twelve regions of the Ismaili *da'wa*. Wherever he goes in his travels he will look for the causes and motivations for what he sees, not being content to report (as he does so well) only on the externals.

### EAST TO WEST, ACROSS THE NORTH

It took Nasir Khusraw exactly one year to travel from his home in Marv to Jerusalem, from 23 Sha'ban 437/5 March 1046 to 5 Ramadan 438/5 March 1047, a distance he reckons at 876 parasangs, which is approximately 2,800 miles or 4,500 kilometres.[2] He reflected later on this speedy progress: 'It had been one solar year from the time we left home, and throughout our travels we had not stopped anywhere long enough to have rested completely.' They had been moving quickly.

He covers this momentous year in fewer than twenty pages of the English translation. But even with his succinct language he manages to pack in an enormous amount of detail. In these first few pages he establishes local political and economic contexts, tells a joke, records several meetings with local men (including one who said he had studied under Ibn Sina), describes the technologies for extracting ammonia and for making roads passable in winter, expresses surprise at some Christian practices in Armenia, measures city walls by pacing them out, and makes comparisons of calendars, weights, prices and water supply sources.

His quick survey of the first year of his journey covers his passage through northern Iran. His contemporary readers would have been familiar at least with the city names and general histories and descriptions of the places (he is writing in Persian and years later, back in Iranian territory). Compared with his lavish descriptions of Jerusalem, Cairo and Mecca further on in the book, the northern cities themselves barely receive a mention. What we have instead are some of his best stories of people: jokes, quips, sarcastic barbs and (almost) tender reflections on friendship.

Nasir first stops in Nishapur, crossroad of cultures dating from pre-Islamic times, a major stop on the Silk Road and home to significant populations of Buddhists, Christians, Jews and Zoroastrians, besides all the schools of thought in Islam, some from the local Persian population and others having settled there. Of this great city, the only thing Nasir notes is that the current prince of the city, Tughril Beg (brother of Chagri Beg), was not present at the time, having 'gone to Isfahan for his first conquest of that city,' and that a school currently under construction near the Saddlers' Bazaar was the result of Tughril's orders. Not only does this short account provide proof that he compiled the *Safarnama* at a later date ('first conquest'), but it gives the first example of one of the items he consistently notices in city after city – the construction of civic buildings. Here we have Nasir Khusraw, certainly no fan of the Saljuq rulers, juxtaposing two actions by the ruling prince: building a school and embarking on a conquest. Very careful, Nasir neither praises the one nor condemns the other.

In Nishapur, Nasir obviously met with local dignitaries. For when he left the city a few weeks later, he rode in the company of the 'sultan's agent,' Khwaja Muwaffaq, all the way to the region of Qumis in northern Iran. While there, he went to the town of Bistam where he paid a visit to the tomb of the famous Sufi shaykh, Bayazid Bistami (d. 261/874). That is all he says, and again he is too terse; he tells us nothing of what the visit meant to him. Nasir Khusraw was not a Sufi, though certainly he was devout and a spiritually pious person. Therefore, while this visit to Bayazid's tomb can be seen as a traveller's excursion (it may well have been the only site worth seeing in the town), with definite historical and cultural significance for Nasir, it also displays his consistent personality as a traveller – genuinely curious, always learning, always placing himself near those who might have a touch of wisdom to offer.

On 1 Dhu'l-Hijja 437/9 June 1046 he arrived in Simnan which would be the site of his first human story, where he 'stayed for a period of time, seeking out the learned.' Here, he heard of a certain Master 'Ali Nasa'i and one day went to see this teacher, 'a young man who spoke Persian with a Daylamite accent and wore his hair uncovered.' He found him with his students around him, one group 'reading Euclid, while another group read medicine and yet another mathematics.' When Nasir spoke with him, the teacher tried to show off by saying 'I read this with Ibn Sina' and

'I heard this from Ibn Sina.' Nasir is on to him and observes dryly,
'His object of this was, of course, for me to know that he had been
a student of Ibn Sina.' Then when Nasir himself became involved
in conversation with some of the students, the teacher said, 'I know
nothing of arithmetic (*siyaq*) and would like to learn something
of the arithmetic art.' Nasir took his leave of this learned one,
puzzled, 'wondering how, if he himself knew nothing, he could
teach others.'

What an insight this episode gives of Nasir Khusraw himself!
The foundation of his life, the very purpose of his journey, is to
learn enough to be worthy of teaching others. This is the whole
gist of the anecdote, sandwiched as it is between calendar dates
and reckoning of mileage from city to city, but full in its personal
application to Nasir's ethics for living. In this search for knowledge to be able to impart it to others, Nasir thus went beyond the
widely accepted ethos of the Muslim societies, that of *talab al-'ilm*
(quest for knowledge), an ethos encapsulated and fuelled by the
Prophet Muhammad's injunction to believers, 'to seek knowledge
even unto China.'[3]

Continuing westward, on his way to Rayy, an important city since
ancient times and the foundation of the modern city of Tehran,
Nasir followed the southern fringe of the range of mountains
which separates the central desert of Iran from the Caspian Sea
to the north. He passed by mighty Mount Damavand, snow-clad
year round and visible for great distances from the plains below, a
feature found both in ancient myth and national epic. But the
traveller is more interested in the industrial activity there:

They say that on the top of the mountain is a pit from which ammonia is extracted, and also sulphur. Leather skins are hauled up and
filled with ammonia, and when full they are rolled down the
mountainside, there being no road over which they can be transported
(*S*, 3).

In the middle of July he arrived in Qazvin, where he was amazed
to see that the many orchards around the city were not protected
by walls or hedges, 'nothing to prevent access.' Of the city itself
he writes, 'I thought Qazvin a nice city: its walls were well fortified

and furnished with crenellations, and the bazaars were well kept, only water was scarce and limited to subterranean channels.' Here we have the civil engineer's observations – in town after town, he will write of the walls and the water, that which protects people from invasion and that which gives life itself. These are the fundamental elements of a healthy society. The subterranean channels he describes, called *qanat* today, are a specialised water system where water flows in underground tunnels, making it less subject to evaporation. Archaeological evidence records such tunnels even in ancient times and many are still maintained in Iran to this day. Keeping them free of silt and other debris required a highly organised society.

Nasir continues on his journey and tells us the joke about the grocer of Kharzavil. He is travelling with his brother and the Indian boy servant. Kharzavil is a small village outside of Qazvin where they stop to pick up some supplies. Nasir's brother approaches the self-proclaimed grocer ('I'm the grocer'), who asks him what he would like. 'Whatever you have will be all right with us,' Nasir's brother responds openly, 'for we are strangers passing through.' When the grocer asks him to be more specific, Nasir's brother suggests something to eat, probably quite ordinary. But the grocer replies that he does not have it. When the brother asks for something else, the grocer again does not have the item. This goes on for a while until the brother gives up. He then must have had to return empty-handed to the waiting Nasir. They not only laughed about it but, 'From then on, wherever we saw anyone like this man, we would say, "He's the grocer from Kharzavil!"'

We can be sure that the travellers procured their supplies more profitably elsewhere, for they went on from there, shifting further north, towards Azerbaijan. They paid a toll on the Shahrud River for one of the Daylamite kings, and continued along to Shamiran and the city of Taram in the province of Gilan. In his description of Taram, Nasir combines his admiration for fortified structures and concern for the water supply with praise for its ruling prince:

Beside the city is a high fortress, the foundation of which is laid on solid granite. It is surrounded by three walls, and in the middle of the fortress is a water channel connected to the river, the water of which is drawn up into the fortress. There are a thousand sons of the aristocracy kept inside that fortress so that no one can rise up in rebellion. It is said that the prince has many such fortresses in Daylam and that he rules with such complete justice and order that no one is able to take anything from anyone else. When the men go to the mosque on Fridays, they all leave their shoes outside, and no one steals them (S, 4).

In Shamiran Nasir made the acquaintance of a fine man whose personal qualities touched him. His telling of their conversation is, in keeping with his unadorned style, short and crisp. But their conversation, which Nasir records as a dialogue, comes across as one of those bittersweet meetings where two people realise they could be friends, if only one of them were not on the road to somewhere else.

In Shamiran I saw a good man from Darband whose name was Abu Fadl Khalifa, son of 'Ali the Philosopher. He was a worthy fellow and displayed much generosity and nobility of character to us. We discoursed together, and a friendship sprang up between us.
'Where do you intend to go from here?' he asked me.
'My intention is to make the Pilgrimage,' I said.
'What I desire,' he replied, 'is that on your return journey you pass through here so I may see you again' (S, 4–5).

On 26 Muharram/2 August the pilgrims left Shamiran and twenty days later arrived in Tabriz. Nasır Khusraw took his time in Tabriz, staying nearly a month in 'the principal town of Azerbaijan' which was 'in a flourishing state.' He actually paced the length and breadth of the town himself, recording it as a square of 1,400 paces on each side.

While in Tabriz, Nasir visited the major poet Qatran, 'who wrote decent poetry, but he could not speak Persian very well.' This odd statement on Nasir's part may be explained by Qatran's accent, perhaps affected by the local Turkic influences in Tabriz. Even though he wrote in official court style New Persian, perhaps he actually spoke a local Azeri dialect rather than the eastern Persian familiar to Nasir. As part of their meeting, Qatran recited some of his own poetry to Nasir. In addition, Qatran brought along the works of other Persian poets, Manjik and Daqiqi, which he read aloud to the visiting poet. They discussed the poems and 'Whenever he came across a meaning too subtle for him, he asked me. I explained it to him and he wrote it down.' Nasir acknowledges that Qatran's poetry was decent, but is not shy about showing that he was better at interpreting poetry than Qatran. Maybe Nasir is simply boasting, or the host being merely polite, or this interchange is evidence to support the respect accorded Nasir Khusraw's abilities with languages and ideas.

Nasir also leaves one of the few historical records of the great earthquake of Tabriz which had occurred four years earlier, a catastrophe that would still certainly have been vivid in conversation and most likely evident in the state of the city's buildings. Qatran in fact wrote an ode on the earthquake which is considered a masterful combination of emotional forms. Nasir writes that after the night prayer on Wednesday night, the 17th of the month Rabi' I, 434/4 November 1042, the earthquake struck and part of the city was totally destroyed while other parts were unharmed. He was told that an estimated 40,000 people lost their lives.

When the travellers left Tabriz, they were accompanied by one of Prince Vahsudan's soldiers. This indicates that, even far from his eastern homeland, Nasir had access to the local courts and administration. In fact, Prince Vahsudan, a member of the Musafarid dynasty, was an Ismaili, though belonging to the dissident Qarmati faction.

They continued northward, up toward Lake Van, now in eastern Turkey, taking two months to arrive on the northwestern shore of the lake at the town of Akhlat, 'the border town between the Muslims and the Armenians.' Nasir is slightly taken aback at the Christian customs he witnessed there. 'They sell pork in the bazaar as well as lamb.' But more than this, 'men and women sit drinking wine in the shops without the slightest inhibition.'

Having passed their highest point north, the travellers continue west and south, still in what is today's Turkey. When they leave on 20 Jumada/22 November, it was snowing and extremely cold, Nasir writes. But the extreme weather does not interfere with his appreciation of the local engineering solution to travelling in heavy snow. The people had laid planks on the ground 'so that on snowy and blizzardy days people can find their way over the wood.' A little further on, the travellers bought some honey for what appears to be a reasonable price ('at the rate they sold to us' which was one dinar for 100 maunds), being told that some men in the town produce three to four hundred jars of honey a year.

Nasir goes on to mention that he came upon a place with a mosque 'said to have been built by Uways Qarani,' a contemporary of the Prophet Muhammad from Yemen and later regarded as a precursor of Sufism. His quick notation about the Sufi is followed by another local industry report. Nasir writes that he 'saw men who roamed about the mountainsides and cut a wood something like cypress.' His curiosity leads him to inquire what they did with this wood. They explained that they place one end of the wood in the fire and collect pitch from the other end in pits, which is then put into containers and exported abroad for sale. While Nasir moves quickly from a report on a mystic to the production of pitch, we may pause to reflect on how these contrasting topics reveal not only the breadth of his interests, but also exhibit in themselves the intimate juxtaposition of the spiritual and material worlds that remained a lifelong concern of his, both in theory and practice.

When they reached Amid, in the region near the northern sources of the Tigris River, Nasir was overwhelmed by its grandeur:

I have seen many a city and fortress around the world in the lands of the Arabs, Persians, Hindus, and Turks, but never have I seen the likes of Amid on the face of the earth or have I heard anyone else say that he had seen its equal (S, 9).

Nasir the engineer is so fascinated by the town that he walks all over it (2,000 paces in length and breadth), exclaiming over the remarkable monolithic rocks on which the town is founded and the wall of black rock surrounding it ('each slab weighing between a hundred and a thousand maunds'), the fittings of the rocks ('so expert that they fit together exactly, needing no mud or plaster in between'), the formidable quality of the defensive walls (on which is 'a passageway wide enough for a totally armed man to pass and to stop and fight with ease'), the four gates (all cast in iron without wood) and the water supply (a spring inside the town flowing from 'a granite rock about the size of five millstones').

The city's large congregational mosque is made of the same black stone as its city walls, 'and a more perfect, stronger construction cannot be imagined.'

Inside the mosque stand two-hundred-odd stone columns, all of which are monolithic. Above the columns are stone arches, and above the arches is another colonnade shorter than the first. Above that is yet another row of arches. All the roofs are peaked, and all the masonry is carved and painted with designs. In the courtyard of the mosque is placed a large stone atop which is a large, round pool of stone. It is as high as a man, and the circumference is ten ells. From the middle of the pool protrudes a brass waterspout from which shoots clean water; it is constructed so that the entrance and the drain for the water are not visible. The enormous ablution pool is the most beautiful thing imaginable (*S*, 9).

The Christian church nearby also receives his praise. It is made of the same stone and the floor is laid out with marble designs. Beneath the dome, he writes, is a latticed iron door, 'the likes of which I had never seen before.'

They left Amid by caravan for Harran (in present-day Iraq), choosing the settled route of sixty parasangs instead of the shorter route of forty parasangs along a road with no settlements. It would take them longer, but safety had to be considered. After Harran, they came to a town where they were invited to someone's home. A 6o-year-old bedouin Arab came in, sat down next to Nasir, and asked him to teach him the Qur'an. This was the man, mentioned previously (in Chapter 3), who surprised Nasir Khusraw with his inadequate knowledge of Arabic.

After entering Syria and spending a few days in Aleppo ('a nice city. It has a huge rampart, twenty-five cubits high, I estimated, and an enormous fortress, as large as the one at Balkh, set on rock'), they entered the town of Ma'arrat al-Nu'man, 'quite

populous' and with a stone wall. Water for this town comes from
both rain and wells. The main agriculture, he notes, is wheat which
is quite abundant, as well as other produce including figs, olives,
pistachios, almonds and grapes. While the town is most famous
for one of its poets, whom Nasir will discuss, something attracts
the traveller's eye even before he passes through the city gates.

Next to the city gates he notices a tall cylindrical column of
stone about ten ells high, according to his estimation. On it something is written in a foreign and unfamiliar script. Curious as ever,
he asks someone what it is. He is told that it is a talisman against
scorpions and very effective; for if a scorpion was ever brought
into the town and turned loose, 'it would run away and not stay in
the town.'

The town of Ma'arra was home to the famous blind poet, Abu'l-
'Ala al-Ma'arri (363/973–449/1057). Although 'he was the head
of the city and very wealthy, with many slaves and servants,' he
lived a frugal and ascetic life. Nasir Khusraw does not state that
they actually met, but his admiration for the poet's talent, prestige and personal character comes through in the details of his
entry, as also his pride in having been in the town when this illus-
trious personage was alive.

In the city was a man named Abu'l-'Ala of Ma'arra. Although blind,
he was the head of the city and very wealthy, with many slaves and
servants. Everyone in the city, in fact, was like a slave to him, but he
himself had chosen the ascetic life. He wore coarse garments and
stayed at home. Half a maund of barley bread he would divide into
nine pieces and content himself with only one piece throughout the
entire day and night. Besides that, he ate nothing. I heard it said that
the door to his house was always open and that his agents and depu-
ties did all the work of the city, except for the overall supervision,
which he saw to himself. He denied his wealth to no one, although
he himself was constantly fasting and vigilant at night, taking no part
in the affairs of the world. This man has attained such a rank in poetry
and literature that all the learned of Syria, the Maghreb, and Iraq
confess that in this age there is no one of comparable stature. He has
composed a book called *al-Fusul wa'l-ghayat*, in which he speaks in
enigmatic parables. Although eloquent and amazing, the book can

be understood only by a very few and by those who have read it with him. He has even been accused of trying to rival the Qur'an. There are always more than two hundred persons from all over gathered about him reading literature and poetry. I have heard that he him-self has composed more than a hundred thousand lines of poetry. Someone once asked him why, since God had given him all this wealth and property, he gave it away to the people and hardly ate anything himself. His answer was, 'I own nothing more than what I eat.' When I passed through that place he was still alive (*S*, 11–12).

Given his direct writing style up to this point, where Nasir care-fully notes whether he heard something from others or conversations in which he took part, there is no evidence in this passage that he actually met al-Ma'arri. But the likelihood of a meeting between these two intellectuals is increased when we con-sider that al-Ma'arri corresponded with Nasir's teacher, al-Mu'ayyad, on the subject of vegetarianism.[4] Nasir may have read the book of parables he mentions and most surely some of the poetry. Their poetic temperaments are similar – al-Ma'arri talks often of the importance of attending to the spiritual life and shed-ding the need for the temporal things of this world, themes which will recur in Nasir Khusraw's later poetry composed in exile.

But for now, he is on the road again, moving south, through the mountains, past a spring which flows only three days a year, continuing on until his party is drawn up short and stands amazed by a field so completely 'covered with narcissus in bloom' that 'the entire place looked white because of all the flowers.' Here is our bureaucrat, engineer, philosopher, poet, and exile of later times, stopped in wonder by a thousand tiny flowers.

## TO THE SHORES OF TRIPOLI

A few more parasangs and they reach the sea. Nasir speaks very highly of Tripoli. He admires its outskirts filled with agricul-tural plots ('lots of sugar cane and many groves of oranges, citron, bananas, lemons and dates,' and they were making molas-ses at the time), its physical layout (three sides of the city face the sea, 'and when the water is rough, some of the waves lap against

the city walls') and its defences with walls of hewn stone, battlements and embrasures, and balistae on top of the walls ('they live
in constant dread of naval attack by the Byzantines'). In one of
the streets of the bazaar 'water spills out from five spouts for people to draw water. The excess runs down over the ground and
down into the sea.' The excess does not need to be conserved or
used for some other human consumption; it can be let loose to
return to the source.

The city itself, which he reckons to be 1,000 cubits square in
area, is home to 20,000 people in the city proper, with many villages and dependencies. He writes that the people are all Shi'is.
The buildings of the city are generally four or five stories high,
with some as high as six stories. It appears very well kept: 'The
lanes and bazaars are so nice and clean you would think each was
a king's palace.' For his readers back in Khurasan, he includes
two comparative items: 'Every type of food, fruit, and other edible I ever saw in Persia was to be found there, but a hundred
times more plentiful,' and 'they make very good paper there, like
the paper of Samarqand, only better.'

In Tripoli, Nasir Khusraw is already within the sovereignty of
the Fatimid state based in Cairo. Once, he writes, a Byzantine army
came and attacked the city, but was defeated by the Fatimid caliph, who rewarded the allegiance of the city by lifting the land
tax. 'There are now always soldiers garrisoned there and a commander over the soldiers to protect the city from its enemies.'
Military might also secured the commercial base of the city, a major
port of call for ships from throughout the Mediterranean – 'from
Byzantium, Europe, Andalusia, and the Maghreb.' Each ship paid
a customs duty of 10 per cent into the Fatimid coffers, income
which Nasir reports was used to pay for the upkeep of the soldiers. The Fatimid caliph kept his own fleet of merchant vessels
docked in Tripoli, which would sail to 'Byzantium, Sicily, and the
Maghreb to trade.'

'We continued south along the shore.' On the way to Beirut,
they passed the 'triangular' town of Byblos, 'with one angle to
the sea.' Byblos has 'a very high, fortified wall' and around the
city are date palms and 'other tropical trees.' Nasir's amazement
at the effects of the warmer climate is crystallised again for his

Khurasan audience in yet another of his snapshot-like comments:

I saw a child holding both a red and a white rose, both in bloom, and that was on the 5th of the last Persian month, Esfandarmadh, old reckoning, of the year 415 of the Persian calendar (*S*, 13).

Since in the Persian calendar, the last month of the year is followed by the first day of spring (21 March), the sight of roses blooming in early February presents a pleasant surprise for someone from a more northerly climate.

In Beirut, the traveller was most concerned with the ancient stone ruins, particularly a stone arch so large 'the road ran right through it.'

I estimated the arch to be fifty ells high, and on all sides were slabs of white stone, each of which weighed over a thousand maunds. This edifice was made of bricks up to a height of twenty ells, and on top were set up marble cylinders, each eight ells tall and so thick that two men could scarcely reach around (*S*, 15).

Knowing Nasir and his habit of measuring things out, we can surmise that the two men he is referring to are his brother and himself who tried to reach their arms around the stone column.

On top of these columns were more arches on both sides, of such exactly fitted masonry that there was neither plaster nor mud in between. Above this was a great arch right in the middle, fifty cubits high. I estimated that each stone in that arch was eight cubits long and four wide, so that each one must have weighed approximately seven thousand maunds. All these stones had designs carved in relief – better in fact than one usually sees executed in wood. Except for this arch, no other edifice remains in that area (*S*, 15).

Amazed at this phenomenon of engineering standing alone in an out of the way place, he asks what it was. He is told that it was the gate to the Pharaoh's garden, and extremely old. But even this response does not satisfy him. He notices that the whole plain is strewn with the wreckage of old stone buildings: 'marble columns, capitals, and bases, all of carved marble – round, square, hexagonal, and octagonal – and of a kind of stone so hard that iron makes no impression on it.' But at the same time, as he looks around trying to figure out how these buildings were constructed, he is even more perplexed because 'there is no mountainous terrain nearby from which the stone might have been quarried, and all other stone there is soft enough to be hewn with iron.' He inquires about the source of the broken columns, but 'no one knows what they were or from where they were brought.'

They continued down the coast to Sidon, whose bazaars were so ornately decorated that Nasir supposed some important event or celebration was taking place, but was told that the city was usually arrayed that way. His pleasure continued outside: 'The gardens and orchards were such that one would think an emperor had laid out a pleasure garden with belvederes, and most of the trees were laden with fruit' (S, 15).

Five parasangs away, they arrive at the city of Tyre, 'renowned among the cities of the Syrian coast for its wealth and riches.' It sits partly in the sea, on a spit of land near the shore. 'It is such that the walls are not more than a hundred yards on dry land, the rest being in the sea. The ramparts are all masonry, and the joints are plugged with pitch so that the seawater cannot seep through' (S, 16). Water is brought to the city from the mountains in aqueducts built on top of stone arches. He reports that even though the city's people are mostly Shi'is, 'there was a judge there, however, who was Sunni by sect, named Ibn Abi 'Aqil; he was of a pleasant countenance and rich.'

### ON TO JERUSALEM

By now Nasir Khusraw is becoming an expert on coastal towns. 'Along the coast, they only build towns where there is elevated ground for fear of being inundated by seawater when the waves strike the shore.'

The city of Acre is located on an elevated spot near the shore, and the main mosque 'is in the middle of the town and is on the highest spot.' The central courtyard of the mosque is not completely paved, as is usually the case, but some parts are planted with grass. Nasir explains: 'They say that Adam cultivated that very spot.' Adam's legacy is also found nearby, to the left of the eastern gate, where a spring is located beneath the ground, which requires climbing down twenty-six steps (he counted) to reach it. 'They say,' the traveller explains, 'that Adam discovered it and watered his own cattle from it,' and so it is called Cow Spring (S, 17).

Also, 'most of these coastal towns have a *mina*, which is like a stable for ships.' Acre's *mina* is situated to the south of the city. It is constructed with walls extending out into the water, forming an enclosure, but with an opening left for ships to go in and out. A chain is stretched across this opening from one wall to the other to block the passage of ships. 'When a ship is about to enter the *mina*, they loosen the chain so that it goes beneath the surface of the water, allowing the ship to pass over; afterwards the chain is raised again lest strangers make untoward attempts on the ships.'

But Acre is an exciting stopping place for Nasir because at a slight distance away, off the main road, 'is a mountain where various prophets' shrines are located.' Nasir was strongly discouraged by the people in Acre from attempting to make these pilgrimages because 'there were evil people along the way who would set upon a stranger and take whatever he might have.' He ignored their warnings but, as a precaution, left all his valuables in the mosque for safekeeping.

He first visited the tomb of 'Akk, the founder of the town, 'a great and pious man.' But then, after a time, Nasir realised he was a little lost. 'Since I had no guide with me to show me the way, I had become confused.' With the warnings of the townsfolk in his ears, we can imagine his enormous relief when suddenly, 'thanks to God's great goodness,' he came upon a Persian man from Azerbaijan who was familiar with the area from a previous visit. In his gratitude, Nasir Khusraw 'prayed two *rak'at*s in thanks to God and rendered thanks to Him for giving me a companion so that I could fulfil the intention I had made' (S, 17).

From his use of the word 'companion,' perhaps they travelled on together. The first stop was the village of al-Birwa, where he visited the tombs of Esau and Simeon. Then a small cave, 'since

they say it is the tomb of Dhu'l-Kifl.' In another village he visited
a shrine 'where they claim is the tomb of [the prophet] Hud,' as
well as the tomb of the prophet Ezra. In the village of Hazira is a
shrine with 'a door so small that it was difficult to enter,' with two
tombs side by side, one of Jethro and the other of his daughter,
Moses' wife. Nasir Khusraw noticed that 'the people of this village
keep up the mosque and shrine very well, cleaning them and
maintaining the lamps.' Continuing on to the village of Irbid, he
visited the tombs of four sons of Jacob, brothers of Joseph. Farther
on was a cave with the tomb of Moses' mother, which he also visited.

Having made a tour of these holy sites, he proceeded to the
shore of a small sea and the city of Tiberias. This may be the one
city in his entire travelogue for which he has more to say about its
waters than the walls. And startling things they are, as for example, 'all the bath and sewage water empties into the sea, yet the
people of the town and shore district all drink from the water of
the sea.' It seems this practice was distasteful, not only to him but
also to a former prince of the city Nasir heard about who decided
to plug up all the sewage drains which emptied into the sea. But
the results were not as expected. For when the drains were all
stopped up, 'the water turned so foul it wasn't fit to drink. He
then ordered the drains reopened, and the water became good
again.' 'The lake is full of fish,' Nasir reports further, as if to un-
derline the unaccountable freshness of its water (S, 18).

On visiting the Friday mosque of the town, Nasir comes across
a hot spring near its gate, with a bathhouse which, so he heard,
was built by Solomon. Nasir 'went inside to try it out,' this bath
with the water 'so hot that unless it is mixed with cold water you
cannot stand it.'

Further south lies the Dead Sea, 'the water of which is salty,
although it is south of Tiberias and the fresh water of the Sea of
Galilee flows into it.' Nasir mentions that 'Lot's city was on the
shore of this sea, but no trace of it remains.' Of the Dead Sea,
the traveller learns of something so strange that he ends his report of it with a careful disclaimer:

I heard from someone that in the bitter waters of the Dead Sea is
something shaped like a cow that grows up from the bottom and

resembles stone, but not so hard. It is gathered, broken into pieces, and peddled around in the towns because one piece of it planted at the base of a tree will keep worms from attacking the roots and will repel underground vermin from a whole orchard. This, at any rate, is what I was told (*S*, 18–19).

It seems 'druggists also buy it because a worm called *noqra* that gets into medicines is repelled by this substance.'

Before heading back to Acre, Nasir Khusraw wanted to stop at the tomb of Abu Hurayra, one of the companions of the Prophet and a prolific narrator of his Traditions. But he was unable to, because the local people did not want anyone revering this man. 'No one can go there because the people are Shi'i and whenever anyone does go, the children make a racket, attack, and harass and throw stones.'⁵ Undaunted, Nasir went on to visit another shrine, 'said to be the tomb of the prophet Jonah,' with an immovable door.

After leaving Acre, they arrived at Haifa, at that time a village 'with many palm groves and orchards.' Along the way, they noticed a great quantity of a type of sand used by Persian goldsmiths, called Meccan sand. A short comment like this reveals not just Nasir Khusraw's curiosity and powers of observation, but supports the impression of him as an experienced and knowledgeable administrator attentive to the tools required for various trades. He must have watched goldsmiths very carefully. Also in Haifa, he mentions that the shipbuilders 'make large seagoing vessels they call *judi.*' Thereafter, they stopped in the town of Caesarea, 'a nice place with running water, palm groves, orange and citron groves, and a fortified rampart with an iron gate.'

The next major town before Jerusalem is Ramla, 'said to belong to Syria and western Palestine.' Ramla is 'a large town with a fortified rampart of stone and mortar, tall and strong, with iron gates … . Their water supply is rainwater, and inside every building are pools to collect it so that there will be a constant supply.' True to his habit, Nasir remained in town to measure the courtyard of the Friday mosque by pacing it out; it came to 300 paces by 200. A main industry is the production of marble, and 'most of the buildings and houses are made of sculpted marble.' He explains the technique of cutting marble: 'They cut the marble with toothless saws and Meccan sand. The saw is drawn along the length of the shaft, not across the grain, as with wood. From the stone they make slabs.' And before leaving Ramla, he reports on another export, 'a kind of grape there that is better than grapes elsewhere and is exported all over.'

They left Ramla and came to one village, and then another. This is where he noticed fields filled with rue growing wild all along the way. They stopped at a spring with 'very good fresh water.' The traveller continues, 'From there we started up a hill as though ascending a mountain, on the other side of which one would expect to come down to a city.' But there is no city in the valley. 'Once we had gone up a way, however, a vast plain came into view, partially rocky and partially soil. Atop the hill is the city of Jerusalem.'

# CHAPTER SEVEN

# Jerusalem, the Holy

Blind they are and deaf who neither see nor hear
the writing of God upon the earth,
or the sermons sent from heaven.

*Divan*, 96:10

'It is a large city, there being some twenty thousand men there
when I saw it. The bazaars are nice, the buildings tall, and the
ground paved with stone. Wherever there was a rise or hill it has
been graded down level so that when it rains the whole ground is
washed clean' (*S*, 22).

Jerusalem, which the 'people of Syria and that region'[1] call the
Holy, the Pure (*al-Quds*), is a city 'situated on top of a hill.' The
outlying areas support the extensive cultivation of olives, figs and
other produce, 'totally without irrigation, yet prosperity is widespread and prices cheap.' However, since there are no springs
within the walls, all water for the city depends upon either rainfall
or a canal bringing mountain water collected in a reservoir three
parasangs outside. Inside the city, each house also has pools and
pipes for collecting rainwater from its own roof. 'And everything
else,' including the public baths and the ablution pools in the
mosques, runs on rainwater. As for the wall around the city, it is a
'fortified rampart of stone and mortar with iron gates.' Nasir
Khusraw adds the engineering detail that it is built at a constant
height, so that 'wherever the ground goes down, the wall becomes
correspondingly somewhat taller, rather than having the top of

the wall follow the rising and falling of the ground.'

When he arrived in Jerusalem on 5 Ramadan 438/5 March 1047, Nasir Khusraw spent considerable time examining the sanctuary of the Dome of the Rock and al-Aqsa Mosque. 'I wanted to measure the dimensions of this sanctuary, but I thought that first I should get a general idea of the plan and layout, after which I could make my measurements. For a long time I wandered about the area, looking at it from different vantages.' Finally, on the northern side, he discovered an inscription in stone near the Dome of Jacob which gave the precise dimensions of the sanctuary. From his tone, we gain the impression that he appreciated not only the fact that someone had saved him the trouble of recording the measurements, but also that this person had shared his interest in such things. From his subsequent details, we can see that Nasir Khusraw was deeply impressed by Jerusalem's sacred history. He describes carefully its shrines and other holy places, enumerating the hallowed local references to Abraham, Sarah, Isaac, Moses, Jacob, Jacob's wife, Joseph son of Jacob, Solomon, David, Zachariah, Mary, Jesus and Muhammad, all of whom are part of the Christian and Jewish legacy also revered by Muslims as proof that God cared enough for human beings to repeatedly send guidance. A core tenet of Muslim faith is that God has been sending guidance through prophets, messengers and warners to the world since the time of Adam. These messages of ultimate meaning and directions to people on how they should conduct their lives are found in the sacred texts and traditions, among others, of Judaism, Christianity and Islam. For Muslims, the message given to the Prophet Muhammad marks God's final revelation. In Jerusalem, Nasir Khusraw intended to experience every trace of this sacred legacy and steep himself in the city's climate of piety.

While visiting some of the sites in this holy city, he also followed the custom of offering prayers there, adding that 'everyone knows' a prayer said in Jerusalem is worth 25,000 regular prayers, one in Medina worth 50,000, and one in Mecca worth 100,000. He is at times content merely to observe and watch other pilgrims at prayer, but at other times he is moved to follow popular custom and pray also. At the double gates of Repentance and Mercy – so called, 'they say,' because David repented on that spot and

God accepted his repentance and forgave him – the traveller joined those who were praying, 'hopeful to be forgiven their sins as well.' 'I, Nasir, prayed there and asked God for grace in piety and to be cleansed of the sin of disobedience.' And since Muslims believe that Jesus was a prophet of God, born miraculously of the virgin Mary, this pilgrim also prayed in Jesus' cradle, which, he reports, 'is made of stone and is large enough for men to pray in.'

For Nasir, Jerusalem is filled with sacred places of prayer and meditation, and he prays in many of them. Indeed, so moved is he by these visits that, years later, when writing those passages in the *Safaranama* on the city and its shrines, he frequently breaks into his own prayer. That is, he not only reports that he prayed in a certain place, but utters a spontaneous prayer within the narrative. For example, after recording that he prayed for forgiveness at the double gates of Repentance and Mercy, he inserts another prayer: 'May God the Exalted grant grace to all his servants in accordance with his pleasure and grant repentance of sin, through the sanctity of Muhammad and his pure offspring!'

Nasir was also inspired to pray when he writes of the plain called Sahera, where 'they say' the Resurrection will take place, all people being gathered together for the great event. He writes that many people have come here to live and to die, so that they will already be present at that time. Then he exclaims, 'O God! On that day wilt Thou be Thine own servants' protector and Thy mercy. Amen. O Lord of the universe!'

Also, at the edge of the plain lies a large cemetery 'where there are many spots in which men pray and make special requests, which are granted by God.' Nasir Khusraw himself offers this prayer: 'O God, receive our supplications and forgive our sins and evil deeds. Have mercy upon us, O Most Merciful!'

Because Muslims should face Mecca during the ritual prayer, *salat*, each mosque is built with one entire wall facing Mecca exactly, according to a careful calculation of latitude and longitude. That wall is marked with an indentation, or niche, called a *mihrab*, carved into the wall to indicate clearly that it is the *qibla* wall which points the direction to Mecca. While the *qibla* is an abstract concept – the direction of prayer, the aim, the goal to which one orients oneself – the *mihrab* is quite physical and often gloriously decorated with colourful tiles, carved stone, ornate calligraphy and metalwork. As Nasir observes, many of the mosques in Jerusalem have multiple *mihrabs* commemorating famous people. This is the case in the mosque of Jesus' Cradle, where the large stone cradle takes the place of the *mihrab*, he says, but there is also a *mihrab* of Mary and one of Zachariah, inscribed with verses from the Qur'an about them. He explains what he has learned: 'it is said that this was Jesus' birthplace. One of the columns has the imprint of two fingers and looks as though someone had grasped it. They say that when Mary was in labour, she held onto this very column.'

In the early years of Islam, when the Prophet Muhammad commenced his preachings in Mecca, Jerusalem was the direction of prayer for all Muslims. Nasir explains that the sanctuary area of Jerusalem 'was built in that place because it is the site of the very rock which God commanded Moses to make the direction of prayer.' Moses followed God's commandment. Then, Nasir continues, in the time of Solomon the holy area for prayer was built around the rock, with the rock in the centre. The custom continued, and Muhammad and his followers themselves faced Jerusalem during prayer until the time when the divine commandment came to henceforth turn and face the Ka'ba in Mecca.

The English word 'mosque' derives from the Arabic word *masjid*, literally a place to pray, from the root verb *s-j-d*, meaning to bow down, to worship. Thus a mosque can be a very humble place, just large enough for one person or a very grand space for thousands, especially for services on Fridays. Friday is the holiest day of the week in Islam, and mosques built for the large public crowds are often known as *al-masjid al-jum'a*, the Friday mosque. Thus, Nasir refers to the entire sanctuary area of Jerusalem as 'the mosque,' a sacred place to worship God.

Within the larger sanctuary area, 'you see another very beautiful mosque.' This is al-Aqsa, 'a skilfully constructed edifice' with 280 columns supporting a stone arcade, with the caulking done in lead to make the construction very tight.

There is a large *mihrab* inlaid with tile; on either side of the niche are

two marble pillars the colour of red carnelian. ... To the right is
Mu'awiya's *mihrab*, and that of 'Umar to the left. The ceiling is covered with wood carved in elaborate designs. ... One of these [15]
gates in particular is done in such beautifully ornate brass that one
would think it was made of gold burnished with silver (*S*, 27).

Al-Masjid al-Aqsa, which means 'the Farthest Mosque,' holds a
pivotal place in Muslim piety due to an event which occurred to
the Prophet Muhammad in the early part of his career. The miracle is known as the *mi'raj*, the Night Journey.

According to popular Muslim tradition, of which there are several versions, one night while the Prophet was sleeping, God sent
the angel Gabriel to him with a bright, glittering steed. Mounted
on this unearthly winged creature named Buraq (often depicted
in paintings with a human face and a peacock tail), and accompanied by Gabriel, Muhammad was carried quickly, in flashes,
through the sky to Jerusalem to pray at the Temple of Solomon
with the prophets Abraham, Moses, Jesus and others. While there,
Muhammad was offered a variety of drinks to choose from. When
he chose milk instead of wine, he was lifted from the rock and
carried by Gabriel to Heaven. He passed through the seven heavens, meeting each previous prophet along the way. At the very
highest point, he approached 'the Lote Tree of the Uttermost
Limit' where he received the command from God that his people
should pray fifty times a day. When he returned down through
the levels and reported this, the prophets advised him to request
that the number be reduced. Muhammad made several trips up
and down until the number of prayers came to a more humanly
manageable five. On his return journey to Mecca, again through
the night sky mounted on Buraq, Muhammad noticed caravans
down below in the desert also making their way steadily towards
the city. When he reported this event to the Meccans, many
mocked his tale of night travel to 'the Farthest Mosque,' but the
arrival of the caravans a few days later supported his account.

Al-Aqsa Mosque, Nasir Khusraw reports, 'marks the spot to
which God transported Muhammad from Mecca on the night of
his heavenly ascent, and thence to heaven, as is mentioned in the

Qur'an: 'Glory be to Him who carried His servant by night from the Holy Mosque to the Further Mosque' (17:1). Thus, in addition to its stature as God's first direction for prayer, Jerusalem also represents the place where Muhammad's legitimacy as a prophet was confirmed by the previous prophets during the Night Journey, the place which marks his successful intercession for his followers, and the place from which the religious prescription for prayer was definitively established. Within the Ismaili tradition this journey is interpreted as a spiritual event, marking a pivotal moment in the Prophet's experience of the divine presence.

### IN THE PRESENCE OF GOD

From the living prayers which suffuse his statements that he prayed somewhere or other in the city, and which adorn his narrative of Jerusalem's water pipes and walls, we see that for Nasir Khusraw, God is a very real, living presence. Nasir actively seeks mercy from God and gives thanks for His blessing.

Nasir did not perceive this personal relationship with God to be in any way in conflict with the absolute transcendence of God which he espouses in his philosophical writings. To speak of a God beyond being means to acknowledge the absolute otherness of God, a reality so great, so immense, so all-encompassing, that all words fall far short of circumscribing Him. Words are limiting because language is only human. In addition, as the ultimate source, the infinite ground of being itself, God cannot be part of the class of 'beings' at all. He cannot be a 'being,' for in Ismaili thought God transcends altogether the categories of being and non-being. Thus, while Nasir the poet could write the lines heading this chapter, confirming that the signs of God are writ large and small throughout the created world, and that God's power and wisdom can be understood by contemplating this creation, Nasir the philosopher could write in one of his doctrinal works, the *Shish fasl*, that God 'Himself, in His essence (*huwiyyat*) is above everything, and nothing can have a relation to Him' (*SF*, 34). Not only is this God absolutely unique, incomparable and indescribable, He is actually beyond everything, including human conception and knowledge.

The seeming contradictions between these two approaches to God (one affirming God's presence even in the things of this world and the second declaring His absolute otherness) can be seen as the product of different levels of interpretation, depending on the expected audience of the text. While in his doctrinal treatises Nasir may take hundreds of pages to present complex and nuanced positions to those with a philosophical training, for readers of his poetry he telescopes these ideas into a key word or phrase, or veils them with metaphor or allegory, and in the *Safarnama* he shows his faith in God as he lived it, from the very first page with its auspicious beginnings and life-changing dream to the prayers of thanks and adoration he offers when visiting holy places throughout his journey.

But, besides the different possible audiences for these three different genres, the variation in literary style also derives from the human attempt to distinguish between the two modes of understanding God, the transcendent and the immanent. Reflections on God generally situate themselves between one or the other. The first mode sees God as totally beyond all human estimation and attribution, acknowledging that since human beings cannot comprehend all that exists, including such ideas as infinite time, space and number, how can they understand the absolute grandeur and mercy of God? But the problem of transcendence is not only one of human comprehension; a transcendent God actually *is* higher and greater than all that exists, even all that exists infinitely. Nasir Khusraw argues that, 'it is impossible to attribute to God either the notion of being a cause or the result of causation because both these categories have been produced by Him' (*SF*, 33). That is, God so transcends being that He cannot even be connected to it as its cause. Furthermore, in Ismaili thought 'God beyond being' transcends not only being but also its opposite, non-being; even the nothing (*na-chiz*) out of which God is said to have created everything cannot be attributed to Him.[2] Muslim thinkers found ample proof for the transcendence of God in verses of the Qur'an, such as: 'Like Him there is naught; He is the All-hearing, the All-seeing' (42:11); 'The eyes attain Him not, but He attains the eyes; He is the All-subtle, the All-aware' (6:103); and 'Say, He is God, One, God the Everlasting Refuge, who has not begotten, and has not been begotten, and equal to Him is not any one' (112:1–4).

The second mode of understanding sees God as immanent, pervading the entire universe, suffused somehow within each being, interpenetrating and sustaining each atom of creation. The immanent God not only resides inherently within each creature, aware of all that it does and all that befalls it, but also actively guides and directs the existence of each being. In Islam, this nurturing presence is reflected in doctrines such as God's mercy (*rahman*), compassion (*rahim*) and generosity (*ikram*). It is expressed frequently, as in the famous invocation with which each chapter of the Qur'an begins *'Bismillah al-rahman al-rahim,'* meaning 'In the name of God, the Merciful, the Compassionate.' Muslim thinkers found ample proof also for the doctrine of the immanence of God in verses of the Qur'an, such as: 'We indeed created man; and We know what his soul whispers within him, and We are nearer to him than the jugular vein' (50:15), 'And when My servants question thee concerning Me – I am near to answer the call of the caller, when he calls to Me' (2:186). For several centuries in medieval Islam, theological debates between rival schools of thought raged precisely on this point, confirming or denying God's active care for human beings, as well as showing this providential regard for something so seemingly insignificant as 'the wing of a gnat.' So fundamental are these two modes of understanding God, the transcendent and the immanent, that each religion, indeed each person of faith, must come to some level of accommodation between the two.

One solution to this theological problem is to distinguish between God's essence and His actions. That is, God can create a thing, a whole universe in fact, without affecting His essence. According to this argument, God's essence is not increased by creating the world (that is, He is not greater after He creates a new galaxy), nor is He decreased by any change or diminution in the created world (He is not diminished if a galaxy disappears). Our author takes this position in his *Gushayish wa rahayish*:

Creator, creation and creature, lord and lordship, are always in the effect (*athar*) of God without that effect having any connection with His essence (*huwiyyat*) (*GR*, 4:12, 5–6).

Nasir Khusraw explains that everything created in this world, including plants and animals, comes forth from the mixing of the elements, with the help of time and space. That is, things do not come directly from God's essence but are His effects, or traces, through intermediate entities like time, space and the elements. But God is in no way enhanced, diminished, or otherwise changed by this constant coming into being and passing away of things.

One good analogy of this, Nasir suggests in the *Gushayish wa rahayish*,[3] is that of a writer who cannot achieve an effect without first 'asking Nature to help him' in providing all the necessities of writing such as paper, inkwell, pen, place, time and motion. And just as the state of being of a writer remains complete within him, even after he has authored a text into which he has poured his knowledge, so too does the essence of God remain untouched by the creation of a thing. In the *Shish fasl*, Nasir gives another example, that of a man who at one moment is holding a handful of dates or straw and who subsequently tosses them aside. The man is still the same man whether he is holding these things or not. He is not enhanced or enlarged by holding them, nor lessened as a human being by relinquishing them. This is, he argues, because there is no similarity (*manandagi*) between the man and the dates or straw. One can only speak of similarity between like things, such as two human beings, but one cannot cross fundamental lines and try to compare, say, humans and plants. For even though plant and man share one quality, that of being alive,[4] there is such fundamental dissimilarity between them that it is an error to assert that the man is bigger or smaller whether or not he is holding dates or straw in his hands (*SF*, 32–3).

This philosophical position allows God in His transcendence to maintain His uniqueness and status of perfection uncompromised and unsullied by direct contact with the material world. In short, the creation of the universe with its spiritual and material worlds neither enhances nor detracts from God's essence.

And yet, in his daily living Nasir keeps God very close. His personal conviction in the divine immanence cannot be explained away merely as the duties of a preacher. Nor does it appear only later in his life after his conversion, for we saw it even during an official trip recounted in the *Safarnama*, where his first reaction on having his prayer answered was to thank God. A few days later, he received the dream which changed his life precisely because he understood it to mean that God had communicated with him. And indeed his response to the dream – to get up and leave and turn his life around spiritually – is that of an already deeply committed man, one who is convinced of God having intervened in his personal life. Nasir Khusraw does not question God's existence; for him the world is proof enough of that. Nor does he question God's justice; even at his most miserable, he knows that the injustices of the world are caused by human beings and not God. His awareness of God as Creator, as all-powerful in bringing the spiritual and material worlds into existence, and of God as Judge, as all-knowing in rulership over the future bliss or damnation of human beings, runs like a thread throughout his writings and forms the foundation of the ethics by which he lives his life. God has been generous in making the physical creation and in placing human beings in charge of it, and He has been merciful in sending His revelation to help guide humanity in ethical modes of conduct. For Nasir Khusraw, the appropriate response to God's power, generosity and mercy is to obey and worship God, to be devoted to the Prophet Muhammad and his family, and to persevere ceaselessly in the search for knowledge.

### GRATITUDE, THE HUMAN DEBT

One of the first acts of worshipping God is the acknowledgement of His abundant generosity and mercy. For Nasir Khusraw, the entire creation is laid out like a feast for human beings to partake of, not in gluttonous abandon but in judicious pleasure. The world itself provides proof of God's powers to create and provide all the things that humans need, which is a great gift deserving of thanks. The believer should be grateful for many things, but foremost and most certainly for God's creation of the physical world itself, and this gratitude should take the form of both word and action:

> With this creation, God has performed a real kindness for you.
> In word and deed, give thanks for this kindness.
>
> (*Divan*, 52:39)

The orderly progression of material creation from the lowest to the highest ranks exists in all its hierarchical stages to serve the human race. First, the four original elements of earth, air, fire and water combine to formulate all the minerals, then the next higher level of existence, plants, comes forth, and finally animals. At the top of the hierarchy are human beings, who contain, or rather subsume within themselves, all the qualities of the lower ranks, but with one added aspect: their reason or intellect. It is precisely through their intelligence that human beings can comprehend the good manifest within God's creation, the order inherent in the world, and the function of each creature. Since the human intellect is thus the supreme creation of God, it must be respected and nurtured as such. To do otherwise – to only concentrate on the needs of the body – is to misuse a gift from God, indeed to raise the body to the level of the idol, as our author so often makes clear:

> Whoever, like an ass, struggles only to sleep and eat
> is indeed an ass, though his form declares him a man.
> O you with your stomach full of blessings, but soul vacant,
> how can you commit such a crime, with God as the Judge?
> If you yourself worship none but idols,
> why do you curse the idol-worshippers?
> A real Azar[5] you are, for dressed in silk and linen
> your body itself seems a richly decorated idol.
>
> (*Divan*, 16: 1–4)

For Nasir Khusraw, the human intellect is to be used for the pursuit of knowledge and devotion to God; its function is not only to avoid sin, but to learn and understand the meanings of God's rules, signs and messages. Consequently, Judgement Day always looms large in Nasir Khusraw's mind. In the *Khwan al-ikhwan*, he warns that the proper use of the intellect has eternal implications, in that whoever employs the intellect in worshipping God and obeys Him with understanding will gain an eternal reward, but whosoever forsakes the intellect and acts unthinkingly, without any knowledge, will face eternal doom (*KI*, 91). He echoes this point in the following verses:

> Your body was made for worship, but you ruined it with sin.
>     What excuse will you bring, if called to account tomorrow?
> If, like a jackass, you are occupied with eating and not worship,
>     then cast off your pious robes; a donkey pack would suit you
>     better than a hundred robes.
> It was so you might worship, which you, a jackass, don't do;
>     why else would God have created the whole of the heavens,
>     the stars, the elements, for you?
> Just because the donkey rejoices in the springtime
>     does not mean the desert blooms for the donkey.
>                                         (*Divan*, 136:23, 27–9)

The last line exemplifies the poet's tendency to coin proverbs. He means that the joys of the material world have their own purposes and do not necessarily exist only in and of themselves. For Nasir Khusraw, the pleasures as well as the pains of the material world serve the sole purpose of pointing to their real counterparts in the spiritual world.

True worship and gratitude to God must be evidenced in action, not only in statements, no matter how deeply heartfelt. Nasir likens the act of promising to take certain actions but then not following through in deed to fraud, like something gilded on the outside which gives the appearance of superior quality, but whose inside is really only copper – base, cheap, and unworthy to be ranked with gold.

> Come to know God and to give thanks unto Him;
>     for we will not be held responsible for other than these.
> Make your words and deeds one, your heart not opposed
>     to your speech, like a copper coin covered in gold.
>                                         (*Divan*, 15:7–8)

The 'deeds' to which the poet exhorts the reader do not refer simply to one's everyday relations with other people, but also to the religious practices showing one's relation to God. For Nasir, there are two types of worship, exoteric (fulfilling the exterior obligations, such as the five ritual prayers a day) and esoteric (understanding the spiritual meaning behind these observances and gaining more knowledge of the oneness of God). Prayer is beneficial, but only when accompanied by an understanding of its inner meanings. In the *Khwan al-ikhwan*, he makes an analogy with gathering firewood, saying that whoever spends more time and energy on reading the Qur'an, studying the religious law of the Prophet and carrying out acts of worship, will gain a clearer understanding of what is meant by the oneness of God, 'just as whoever gathers more firewood will have more heat and light from the natural fire' (*KI*, 77). The accumulation of good deeds is as effective, he is saying, in the spiritual realm as it is in the realm of nature. This teaching found in his philosophical works also appears in his poetry, as in these two verses from two different poems. The second verse maintains that this truth applies even to our enemies, bad as they may be:

> My son, by prayers shall your incomplete soul become whole,
>     by carrying them out wholly.
>
> > (*Divan*, 27:32)
>
> Everyone benefits from sugar – both the sick and the healthy
>     and all their enemies and friends also benefit.
>
> > (*Divan*, 31:36)

Nasir's expressions of thanksgiving are often deeply personal. He thanks God for creating the heavens and earth, for helping him when he is lost, for answering his prayers, for sending the guidance of the Prophet and the imams, for leading him along the right path:

> Thanks be to that God who showed me the path to His religion
>     and knowledge, who opened for me the very door of mercy.
>
> > (*Divan*, 6:16)

While Nasir ends many poems with a finale of gratitude, he opens one with a prayer of praise and thanksgiving, so grateful is he for the opportunity to serve God through the teachings of the Prophet and his family.

> O Lord of this cerulean sky,
>     a hundred thousand thanks from me to You,
> That, out of this barbarous flock,
>     You give me as proof of the family of the Prophet.
> So that I might follow Your Prophet obediently,
>     I shall not follow my own desires or thoughts.
> And though, day in and day out, I surely fall short,
>     with every breath I take, I thank You.
>
> (*Divan*, 209:1–4)

Nasir uses this exordium to the poem to further elaborate on his commitment to faith and knowledge, rising to a declaration that it is precisely through his gratitude to God, expressed through the deeds of his body, that he protects and guards himself against the evil and demonic forces in the world.

### THE ONENESS OF GOD

Nasir Khusraw holds that the key to salvation lies in understanding the oneness (*tawhid*) of God. In fact, he opens his book *Shish fasl* with the statement, 'eternal bliss (*baqa*) may be attained by the human soul (only) through the recognition of the oneness of God' (*SF*, 29). The first step, he says, in understanding what is meant by the oneness of God is to disassociate God from all anthropomorphic attributes (*tashbih*), such as thinking literally that God has hands or eyes or a mind distinct from other parts of Himself, or sits on a throne with another part of Himself. But the other, hyper-transcendentalist extreme, such as that advanced by the Mu'tazila, must also be avoided, namely denying God any attributes whatsoever so that He is thereby emptied (*ta'til*) of anything meaningful (*SF*, 29). Both extremes must be firmly rejected.

The problem can be expressed as follows: given the Qur'anic revelation that speaks of God as seeing, hearing, knowing, and as having a face and hands, Muslim theologians and philosophers were challenged to explain the relation of such attributes to God's essence. Is there one 'part' of God which sees and another which hears? Does He see and know with different parts? Does He know the past and present simultaneously? Does He know the future? Is His hand different from His foot? What part of Him 'sits' on the throne? One response was to take these attributes literally since they are recorded in God's word, but to qualify this by saying that humans cannot understand 'how' God actually 'has' any of these attributes. Another response was to regard such anthropomorphism as constituting mere metaphor or allegory, as being God's way of communicating in order to be comprehensible to finite human intelligence.

In Islam, this issue crystallised in the 2nd/8th and 3rd/9th centuries when the Mu'tazila school of rationalist theologians insisted on maintaining an absolute sense of divine unity and transcendence, denying any shred of anthropomorphism: '... eyes do not see Him, sight does not attain Him, imagination does not comprehend Him; He is not heard by hearing; [He is] a thing, not as the things [of this world]; knowing, powerful, living, not as [men are] knowing, powerful, living; He is eternal, alone.'[6] The Mu'tazila argued against any attribution to God of time ('no time passes over Him') or space ('He is not subject to directions, left, right, in front of, behind, above, below'). So great was their desire to preserve God's unity and eternity ('there is no eternal except Him'), that they also denied that the word of God was eternal, and maintained therefore that the Qur'an must be created and not eternal. The effect of this was to disallow any positive description of God and to deny the more generally accepted understanding of the status of the Qur'an as co-eternal with God. Their opponents, mostly of the Ash'arite school, later clarified their counter-arguments and crafted a logic which, while declaring that God is one, legitimised His being endowed with attributes, in order not to diminish God's omniscience. The Ash'arites also defended the doctrine that God's word (and therefore the Qur'an) is eternal.

For Nasir Khusraw, a proper understanding of the true oneness of God dissolves the problems posed by the two theological extremes (*tashbih* and *ta'til*), annulling and subsuming them into *tawhid*. To prove this, in the *Shish fasl* he builds his own argument, rejecting the position that God is one through His being perfect in might or wisdom, for this would imply that God's oneness somehow depends on His might or wisdom, and such dependency is invalid for God (*SF,* 29). Nasir also rejects the idea that God is unique (*yakanagi*) of His kind, arguing that there is no 'kind,' or genus (for example, of 'gods') and no pair (as in dualistic religions), of which God is an example. Rather, 'He is one in that He is the One who brought into existence all the creations, both spiritual and material, which are subject to counting' (*SF,* 30). In other words, since God is responsible for all creation, not just the physical, material realm, but also the entire spiritual, intelligible realm, His oneness is not even 'one of a kind' because there is no kind, category, or class by which He can be recognised, for that 'kind' would have to be larger than He. Further proof of this argument for Nasir Khusraw is found in the underlying correspondence between opposites. He holds that whatever exists, both spiritual and physical, 'matches' another thing. Even things which on first glance seem utterly unconnected (such as the profound opposites of being and nothingness) naturally form into pairs and are thereby related. This analogical polarity 'forms a proof that God has created them to be like one another, while oneness belongs to Him' (*SF,* 37). Thus, God is not caused, is not dependent on any thing, and does not correspond to any thing.

In his *Jami' al-hikmatayn,* Nasir devotes an entire chapter to the issue of the oneness of God. Centring his argument mostly on the relation of God to the world, he divides people into two groups, those who say the world is eternal and has no creator, the materialists (*dahriyya,* also known as *ahl-i ta'til*), and those who profess there is a creator (*sani'*) of the world. He dismisses both the Dahriyya and those among the second group who acknowledge more than one creator, such as idolaters (with many gods), Zoroastrians (with two gods) and Christians (with their belief in the Trinity). He also discards those philosophers who say that creatures should not adore God, but only seek to know Him, an important statement from one so celebrated for his advocation of knowledge, learning and intellect. For him, there is only one group worth discussing oneness with, that is, the monotheists who say God is one and He is the only one to be worshipped and adored.

But even the monotheists can be further divided into three smaller groups. For example, the literalists (*ahl-i taqlid*) follow the letter of the law (most of the common people fall into this group, he says), ascribing attributes to God but then saying that only God understands their meaning. By the same token, he continues, the rationalist theologians (*mutakallimun*), including the Mu'tazilis and the followers of Ibn Karram, claim to follow logical arguments, but these arguments lead them to deny all anthropomorphic language. Then there are those Shi'is who use an esoteric hermeneutic to deny creaturely attributes to the Creator, and claim that *tawhid* occupies a station between *tashbih* and *ta'til.* Nasir Khusraw notes that all three groups say 'the truth of *tawhid* is what we claim' (*JH*, 32–3).

Against the first group, the literalists, he complains that they say nothing is like God, but then proceed to declare that God is knowing, seeing and hearing. With only an exoteric interpretation (*tafsir-i zahir*), the first part of their assertion contradicts the second, for humans can see and hear also. And yet, since God's word cannot be deficient, an esoteric hermeneutic (*ta'wil*) is required. In the end, the literalist is left with no logical ground on which to stand and 'has no defence or proof' and can only declare, 'God sees us and we see Him not' (*JH*, 36). What an ironic admission for a literalist this is, that in the end he cannot know how to understand the word of God!

Our author also rails against the literalists for their interpretation of the famous Qur'anic verse, 'Whithersoever you turn, there is the Face of God; God is All-embracing, All-knowing' (2:115). Nasir Khusraw declares that the only proper interpretation of this verse is that no matter in which direction one turns, the power and wisdom of God are manifest everywhere. But according to the exoteric understanding of this verse, he says, the world is literally encircled by or contained in the 'face' of God; that this immense sky and the supreme sphere which englobes the totality of the universe, is literally the 'face' of God. The literalists, according to Nasir, also interpret this verse to mean that God was referring to the *qibla*, the Ka'ba, the sanctuary of Mecca, when He used the word 'face.' Nasir rejects the latter interpretation as absurd for several reasons. First, a position that he considers heretical (*kufr*), would mean that the Ka'ba, a building constructed by men with wood and stones, is the 'face' of God. Second, whoever said his prayers with his back to the Ka'ba would be facing the *qibla*, which is erroneous. Furthermore, he says, they also misinterpret another verse, 'All things perish, except His Face' (28:88). The most 'stubborn' of them, he says, hold this to mean that the words 'face of God' signify here the 'essence of God' (*huwiyyat*) and not the *qibla*, direction. Nasir Khusraw declares this second interpretation to be as absurd as the first because the word 'face' in Arabic means the countenance of something and not the essence (*dhat*) or the direction of a thing. He dismisses these arguments vehemently, saying they do not 'even amount to an exegesis, but constitute rather an alteration of the divine word' (*JH*, 40–1).

Verses about the 'hand' of God are equally misinterpreted, especially 39:67: 'The earth altogether shall be His handful on the Day of Resurrection, and the heavens shall be rolled up in His right hand. Glory be to Him! High be He exalted above that they associate!' Since the literalists do not recognise an esoteric dimension in the word of God, they take this verse at its outward level. Nasir ridicules their understanding of these lines, especially the notion that God literally has two hands, with one actually 'specified as right and one as left!' Nor in his conclusion does he try to temper his disdain for the literalists' unprobing approach to God's message. 'This group which claims to be monotheist,' he writes, 'is really polytheist because they qualify God with attributes of a creature: knowledge, hearing, sight and organs for moving.' He concludes the discussion almost with a sigh of weariness, observing that 'most people, who are the common ignorant folk, fit into this category. ... First they affirm that nothing is really like God and then they proceed to qualify Him with attributes' (*JH*, 44).

Another group who felt the power of Nasir's pen were the followers of Ibn Karram, who had achieved a noticeable following in Khurasan during the 2nd/8th and 3rd/9th centuries,[7] and were reportedly influential in encouraging Mahmud of Ghazna's violent persecution of the Ismailis in the region. But the

Karramiyya did not get along well with the local Sunni authorities either. The historian Ibn al-Athir records a civil war in Nishapur in 488/1095 between the Karramiyya and a combined force of two Sunni schools, the Hanafis and Shafi'is. It seems that in their attempts to address the issue of the substance (*jawhar*) of God, many Karramiyya understood this literally to mean that God has a 'body' (*jism*) in physical contact with the 'throne' of God.

In his refutation of the Karramiyya doctrine of the oneness of God, Nasir Khusraw criticises their reasoning. First, 'they say God is one, nothing resembles Him;' but then they proceed to assert things like 'He is a body not like bodies,' just as His knowledge is not like other knowledges, His power not like other powers, nor His life like other lives. Nasir declares this to be nonsense, exemplifying not monotheism but polytheism (*shirk*). He accuses the Karramiyya of seeing each of these attributes as a separate, eternal and infinite thing, which he equates with polytheism (*JH*, 45).

Our philosopher tackles this 'nonsense' from several directions. First, he counters with the argument that body is a substance with three dimensions – length, width and height – and that God cannot be limited by such dimensions. Even the four elements are bodies. So to say that God is 'body not like bodies' would be as sensible as saying 'It is a fire, not fire.' Then he says that their phrase, 'God is knowing not like the wise; powerful not like the powerful; living not like the living,' is equally ridiculous in its attempt to describe God by human characteristics. Take the first one, wisdom, he suggests. What does it mean to say, 'God is knowing not like the wise?' God Himself has designated one group of the sons of Israel as the wise ones (26:197). So what is it that they know, Nasir Khusraw argues, that is contrary to the knowledge of God? This would be the case if God were 'knowing not like the wise.' Since God has already designated these people as wise, it would be a lie to qualify them as ignorant, and in this case God's words would be lies, which is absurd. Similarly with power, an attribute in which both God and human beings participate. When God commands men to pray and give alms, does He know or not know that man has the power to pray and obey? If God is 'powerful not like the powerful,' has He commanded something which is not in the power of man? If a Karramiyya answers that God knows that man does not have the power (following their assertion of the absolute difference between the two types of power), then he is admitting that God ordered the impossible. However, this conclusion is refuted by God's own words: 'God charges no soul save to its capacity' (2:286). Nasir Khusraw cautions, however, that 'just because I say that we cannot say God is knowing, this does not mean I am saying that God is ignorant – such impiety and absurdity!' Thus, he will not allow either attribute – knowledge or ignorance – to be ascribed to God.

The significant point for him here is that those who want to ascribe qualities to God only ascribe positive qualities, not negative ones. They only want to ascribe knowledge to God, not ignorance:

You qualify God as knowing but do not want to qualify Him as ignorant, just because knowing is a good label and ignorant is a terrible label. But you are mistaken. The reason one cannot call God ignorant, poor, mortal, and so on, is not because they are bad, but because these attributes, good or bad, apply to human beings. By the same logic, you cannot apply good attributes to God. Both knowledge and ignorance, the one as much as the other, are attributes which apply to human beings (*JH*, 50).

He then warns the Karramiyya that 'Whoever worships something which has an attribute belonging to a creature is actually worshipping the creature, not the Creator.' For him, such a person is in reality a polytheist, not a monotheist.

### FROM PRACTICE TO UNDERSTANDING

In introducing the Mu'tazili doctrine of *tawhid*, Nasir Khusraw states, 'Of all the different schools within Islam, there is no stronger school (*tariqat*) on the subject of *tawhid* than this' (*JH*, 58). Indeed, he has no quarrel with their position that the first duty of the believer is to know God, and that by this knowledge the person is led to do good and to shun evil, a doctrine entirely in line with his own philosophy. The man who realises that he is the work of a wise creator and understands the reason for performing the requirements of his faith will aspire to the good and avoid the bad. But, when the Mu'tazilis add that such knowledge of God is obtained neither by necessity nor by blind imitation (*taqlid*), Nasir Khusraw challenges them and inserts a subtlety into the discussions surrounding the term *taqlid* (*JH*, 52–3).

He agrees with the Mu'tazilis that human beings cannot know God by necessity (for if we acquired knowledge of God by necessity, then all would know God equally, just as everyone knows to satisfy thirst with water), but he disagrees about the role of imitation, even questioning their understanding of the word itself. They assert, Nasir says, that since any belief can be proclaimed and then imitated by others, even erroneous doctrines such as that of the eternity of the world, it is invalid to obtain knowledge of the One by imitating, that is by blindly following the opinion of someone else. Nasir declares that the Mu'tazilis are confusing 'imitation' (*taqlid*) with 'habit' (*'adat*), and that anyone who holds that the world is eternal is thereby not practising *taqlid* but rather acting according to habit, by merely believing 'that which his father and those among whom he grew up believe' (*JH*, 59). Such a person merely accepts the beliefs held by those amongst whom he lives 'to the point where his animal soul takes on this brutish habit and becomes lazy in the acceptance of the religious law' (*JH*, 59). He thus remains at the level of animal habits and does not transcend this primitive mode of existence. Hence, this habitual nature of the animal soul leads to one of two extremes: either the abandonment of religious law or the blind acceptance of religion. In this sense, *taqlid* means 'unthinking imitation,' a popular connotation of the term also reflected in the following verse from his *Divan*:

> I never accepted *taqlid*, nor ever opened the ear of my heart or
>     the cap of my inkwell to all the traditional 'He related to us.'[8]
> (*Divan*, 59: 66)

However, Nasir Khusraw argues that *taqlid* must in fact mean something more like 'following religious practice,' for there has never been a prophet who told his followers to stop the practices of religion. 'We say that such an absence of practice would be equal to a denial of religious practice.' Religious practice is a necessary part of religion, in fact it is the foundation of the divine religions themselves, brought by the prophets Noah, Abraham, Moses, Jesus and Muhammad (*JH*, 59–60). The religion of Islam is practice, he asserts, placed in the hearts of Muslims. Those who oppose practice are equating it with habit and blind imitation, that is, just following the practices of others without thinking about them or feeling them.

Therefore, for Nasir Khusraw the term *taqlid* takes on a richer meaning than mere blind imitation: it means to carry out the visible religious practice as a first step toward understanding *ta'wil*, the esoteric understanding of religious rituals. As proof of this, he invokes the 'contradictory verses' of the Qur'an, so-called by Muslim theologians and jurists because certain verses in one part appear to be contradicted by a verse somewhere else in the book. He gives an example of one such verse which appears to counter the doctrine of the oneness of God, the verse which states that God was angry with Pharaoh and so took vengeance on his people (43:55). Nasir observes that in this verse it appears that God is acting like a human being, seeking vengeance out of anger, just as when a man is irritated at another he strikes or kills him. But, he continues, while God may appear in this verse to reflect human behaviour, that is not in fact the case because God cannot resemble human beings, as the Qur'an elsewhere says (42:11): 'Nothing resembles Him!' Therefore, the outer sense of this passage cannot be taken literally, since such contradiction is not possible within the unity of God. Indeed, the fact that some verses seem to contradict each other proves that a true understanding of the oneness of God can only be found through *ta'wil*, in the hermeneutic interpretation of the scriptures. Only through the esoteric exegesis of *ta'wil* can the underlying harmony among these apparently contradictory verses be discerned. It is possible that the words differ by their letters, as indeed the theologians admit, but the words of God cannot truly be contradictory (*JH*, 62). The underlying truth of all God's words must be as constant and unified as is the essence of God Himself. In short, only through the hermeneutical process can we come to understand the real underlying meaning, the eternal truth of the scriptures.

## UNDERSTANDING THE NAME OF GOD

The names of God hold a special meaning for Muslims, from the ninety-nine names mentioned in the Qur'an to the well-known 'Allahu Akbar,' the invocation calling on 'God Almighty' and uttered most commonly before embarking on any serious or difficult venture. The ninety-nine names are favourite names for boys, as for instance, Jabbar (the Irresistible), Jalil (the Majestic), Karim (the Generous, the Noble), Hamid (the Praiseworthy), 'Aziz (the Precious), Sami' (the Hearer), Malik (the King) and Nasir (the Helper); girls are given the feminine forms of these names by the addition of the letter 'a' at the end of the name, as in 'Aziza and Malika. Names of God are inscribed in stone, painted on tiles, embroidered into amulets, wall hangings and banners, and used as decoration in mosques and other public and private spaces. In Sufi circles, the rhythmic repetition of a name of God, sometimes rarefied to repeating the one-syllable 'Hu' (meaning 'He'), often lasting for hours, forms an integral part of the mystic's religious practice. Ismaili esoteric interpretation, based essentially on the principle of a symbolic correspondence between the physical and spiritual worlds, offers the opportunity for determining the inner significance of a name through an examination of the letters themselves and their relative positions.

In two different works (*Shish fasl* and *Khwan al-ikhwan*), Nasir presents the *ta'wil* of the written form of the Arabic name of God, 'Allah.' In the Arabic alphabet, Allah is written with four letters: one *Alif* ('A'), two *Lam*s ('L'), and one *Ha* ('H'). Reading from right to left, the four letters are arranged as such:

الله

In the *Shish fasl*, Nasir Khusraw derives his esoteric interpretation from both the shapes of the letters themselves and their positions in the word, and demonstrates the correspondence that these physical structures have to various levels of the spiritual world (*SF*, 34–6).

The fact that there are four letters is in itself significant for Nasir. He writes that the four letters are intended as symbols for the four primary levels (*hadd*), two spiritual and two corporeal. All spiritual entities fall under the aegis of Universal Intellect and Universal Soul (represented by the first two letters). All corporeal entities are under the governance of the *natiq* and the *asas*, respectively the prophet-messenger and the imam who succeeds him (represented by the second two letters). The *natiq* organises and controls the world of religion and the *asas* teaches the faithful the connection between the world of religion and the spiritual world, thus completing the circle. In this way, the letters of God's name encompass all levels of reality. He is all-in-all, and the all-encompassing oneness of God is found even in His name.

Nasir then takes each letter individually and shows how its orthographic form also demonstrates this correspondence. The first letter (*Alif*) is written as a vertical line which stands alone. *Alif* does not join any subsequent letter, but other letters can attach themselves to it. All letters other than *Alif* are thus of a class which form curved (*junbanida*) lines, distinct from *Alif*'s straightness. *Alif* symbolises the first originated being in Ismaili cosmogony, the Universal Intellect ('*aql-i kulli*), from which all spiritual and material entities receive existence and to which some are directly connected, while it in itself depends on nothing other than God. Further on, Nasir will explain these distinctions in human terms: through reason or intellect one can understand things, but there is nothing by which one can understand intellect itself (*SF*, 42–3).

The next letter (*Lam*) consists of a line, 'the lower part of which is drawn forward' to the left, and connects with the following letter. *Lam* resembles *Alif* somewhat in being straight, but differs in that all letters can attach to *Lam* from either side. This first *Lam* will provide support for the second *Lam*. Thus, as second in position and function, *Lam* corresponds to Universal Soul (*nafs-i kulli*), the second originated being in Ismaili cosmogony, which is connected to Universal Intellect on one side and to Nature on the other.

The third letter is also a *Lam*, similar to the preceding one, but not exactly like it. Following the rules of Arabic orthography, a second *Lam* is written at half the height of an *Alif*. Connected on one side to the first *Lam* (which represents Universal Soul), the second *Lam* symbolises the *natiq*, the prophet-messenger who, in his effort to organise (*ta'lif*) the world of religion, receives support from Universal Soul. We can understand this better, Nasir elaborates, if we speak of three worlds – the world of spiritual entities (governed by Universal Intellect), the material world (governed by Universal Soul) and the world of religion (governed by the prophet-messenger).

The fourth letter of God's name is *Ha*, which symbolises the material world in that its shape possesses length, width and breadth, whereas the other letters are mere line. Its physical complexity corresponds to the material world's abundant variety of minerals, plants and animals, providing bounties and food for human beings. Written as a circle in which one end of the line is brought down to meet the other end, it represents the *asas*, the imam who is charged with explaining the *ta'wil* of religious law to the believers. The *asas* is connected in this effort to the *natiq* who provides the support he receives from the power of Universal Soul. The *asas* brings the souls of the faithful back to the higher world through the recognition of the oneness of God and the interpretation of religious law, so that ultimately creation may rejoin its source, just as the little line in the letter *Ha* rejoins its beginning in a circle.

The second interpretation which Nasir Khusraw presents to explain the esoteric meaning of the name of God occurs in Chapter 24 of his *Khwan al-ikhwan*. While much of the correspondence between the letters and the different worlds is similar to the *ta'wil* given in the *Shish fasl*, in this work Nasir also highlights the connection of the four letters to the four elements of the material world. Briefly, *Alif* corresponds to Universal Intellect, which is the source of confirmation (*ta'yid*). The first *Lam* corresponds to Universal Soul, which is the source of composition (*tarkib*). The second *Lam* corresponds to the *natiq*, who is the source of organisation (*ta'lif*). The fourth letter *Ha* corresponds to the explanations of the *asas*, who is the source of esoteric interpretation (*ta'wil*).

Nasir Khusraw continues that the four letters of the name of God thus correspond to the four sources of Good in the two worlds – Universal Intellect, Universal Soul, *natiq* and *asas*. These four spiritual sources correspond, in turn, to the four material sources created from Universal Nature. These are, moving downward from the most subtle to the most gross: fire, the source of warmth and making things subtle; air, the source of bringing out and composing things; water, the source of assembling and mixing; and earth, the source of preservation, increase and growth. Nasir holds that if an intelligent person examines these elements of nature and the manner in which these 'four corners of the world' are placed in the name of God, he will see God's name, Allah, written over all creation. For example, he will see that fire always goes up without any deviation or hesitation, just as the letter *Alif* does. The first *Lam* he sees corresponds to air which has two sides, one facing fire and the other facing water. The second *Lam* is like water in that it possesses length and breadth. The letter *Ha* is circular like the earth, the appropriate and secure place for living creatures.

Having shown how the letters of God's name correspond to the spiritual and physical elements, Nasir Khusraw continues his *ta'wil* in the *Khwan al-ikhwan*, explaining how the four sources correspond to the four elements, thus showing how the spiritual world is reflected in the material. The significance of this hermeneutic exegesis of the name of God lies both in the hidden inferences and meanings he draws out from the letters of the name, and their relationships to the spiritual and material worlds, as well as in his demonstration of the principle of *tawhid*, the fundamental unity of all in God.

### THE SHRINES OF JERUSALEM

Nasir Khusraw's philosophic effort to apprehend the oneness of God finds a parallel expression in his acts of devotion, including the visitation of shrines and the offering of the appropriate prayers in each one. The diary of his days in Jerusalem is replete with the many places to pray. Jacob's Dome is a place of prayer because, he notes, it is supposedly the very place where

Jacob himself prayed. On the other side of a wall are the cloisters of the Sufis, where many of them are always at prayer, 'except on Fridays when they go inside the mosque to hear the sermon.' At another dome, described as the *mihrab* of Zachariah, Nasir explains that people congregate there because 'they say he used to pray constantly in this place.' He remarks that even at the double gates of David's repentance, what was once a hall has now been turned into a mosque for prayer decorated with many carpets of all sorts.

He gives a very detailed 'walking tour' of the Dome of the Rock, counting its pillars, steps and gates, measuring its walls, even the Rock itself (100 ells in circumference), describing its internal furnishing: doors made of teak, roofs of lead, columns of marble, carpets of silk, candles of ambergris and lamps of silver.

The pillars and arches are covered with gold and enamel designs and are too beautiful to describe. The balustrades around the platform are all of a flecked green marble that looks like a meadow with flowers in bloom (*S*, 34).

Nasir then decides to visit the tomb of Abraham, the founding prophet of the three 'Abrahamic' religions whose message, Muslims believe, is encapsulated and epitomised in the scripture revealed to Muhammad. The Prophet Abraham (Ibrahim) is known to Muslims as Khalil, 'the friend of God.' His tomb, located at the town of Hebron, more than a day's journey south of Jerusalem, is also known as 'Khalil' to all the 'people of Syria and Jerusalem,' even though, Nasir notes, 'the proper name of the village, which they do not use, is Matlun.'

Along the way to visit Abraham's shrine, Nasir stayed overnight in a place the Christians 'hold in great veneration, and there are always many pilgrims and people holding retreat there. It is called Bethlehem.' He reports that Bethlehem is a site of sacrifice for the Christians, many of whom come all the way from Byzantium. We have to wonder why the traveller is so brief about Bethlehem, to the point of not even mentioning the Christian belief that Jesus was born there, and not in Jerusalem. Did he really not inquire why the Christians hold this place in great veneration? Was he reluctant to enter into religious polemic? This would be entirely consistent with the tenor of the rest of his travelogue, one of the significant features of which is Nasir's scrupulous avoidance of giving offence to any of the religious traditions he encounters on his journey.

The shrine of Abraham contains more than the tomb of Abraham, as Nasir soon discovers: 'Altogether there are six tombs in this shrine.' The pilgrims also visit the tombs of Abraham's wife Sarah and his son Isaac, as well as the tombs of Jacob and his wife and their son Joseph. As usual, Nasir goes on to measure the walls and learns how water is supplied. The area is surrounded by 'four masonry walls, eighty cubits longs, forty cubits wide, and twenty cubits high. The top of each wall is two cubits thick.' Within this enclosure are a number of structures housing the tombs. The village of Matlun, which along with many other villages is endowed to the shrine for its perpetual upkeep, has a small spring. 'Not much water comes from it, and it is a long way off, but a channel has been dug to bring the water to just outside the village, where a covered cistern has been constructed to store the water lest it go to waste and so that there will be enough for the people of the village and for the pilgrims who come there.' Within the walls of the shrine, inside the structure with the tombs of Isaac and his wife, 'the floor and walls are decorated with costly rugs and Maghrebi carpets even finer than brocade.' By way of example, he writes:

I saw a prayer carpet said to have been sent by a prince of the army who was a slave of the [caliph] of Egypt. He was supposed to have bought it in Egypt for thirty gold dinars, which is more than he would have paid for Byzantine brocade. I never saw its equal anywhere (S, 36).

The tombs of Sarah and Abraham are in separate buildings. The one which contains the tomb of Abraham has another structure inside which 'you cannot walk all the way around, but it has four small windows through which visitors can look and see the tomb as they walk about.'

The tomb of Joseph is situated outside the walled enclosure, on a nearby hillside, and described as being covered with 'a nicely built dome.' Beyond Joseph's Dome lies a large cemetery, with bodies 'brought from all parts.' This shrine also 'is heavily endowed with villages and freeholding in Jerusalem.' These endowments allow the income from properties and agriculture to ensure the continued care and upkeep of the shrines. The visitor learns that the major crop is barley, 'wheat being less cultivated,' and 'there are, of course, many olives.' He reports that 'there are also many gristmills where oxen and mules grind flour all day long. There are also young girls who bake bread every day, each loaf weighing one maund.' From this local production, each pilgrim is given food:

Everyone who goes there is given a daily ration of one loaf of bread, a bowl of lentils cooked with olive oil and raisins, a custom that has been maintained from the time of Abraham himself down to the present. On some days there are five hundred people present, all of whom receive this hospitality (S, 36–7).

Nasir also learns that for some time the shrine of Joseph had fallen into disrepair until the time 'when the Mahdi was established in the land of Egypt' (referring to the first Fatimid Caliph-Imam, 'Abd Allah al-Mahdi) and he ordered the repair and improvement of the place.

The last item Nasir mentions before leaving Jerusalem is a description of the grand and 'very ornate' Christian church, the Church of the Resurrection, to which he says 'every year many people come from Byzantium to visit,' and even 'the Byzantine king himself comes in disguise so that no one will recognise him.' In this connection, he reports quite frankly the destruction of the church ordered by the sixth Fatimid Caliph-Imam al-Hakim, providing another instance in which he is not afraid to speak the truth, even if it should reflect poorly on himself or, as in this case, the Fatimids. In his customary manner he refrains from describing the political circumstances which led to this event.

In the days when the ruler of Egypt was al-Hakim bi-Amr Allah, the Byzantine emperor came. Al-Hakim found out about it and said to one of his equerries, 'In the [church] of Jerusalem a man of such-and-such a description wearing such-and-such clothes will be seated. Go to him and say that al-Hakim has sent you. Tell him not to imagine that I have no knowledge of his presence and not to fear, for I have no ill intent with regard to him.' It was this very al-Hakim who ordered this church plundered and pulled down, and it remained in this state of ruination for a time. Afterwards the emperor sent emissaries with many gifts to seek a reconciliation and to intercede for permission to rebuild the church (S, 37–8).[9]

In Nasir's time, the church was large enough, he figures, to hold 8,000 people inside. He is impressed with its elaborate decorations of coloured marble, paintings and Byzantine brocades. 'Much gold has been used.' A Muslim accustomed to the proscription against visible images of the prophets and other holy individuals, he studies the Byzantine paintings, carefully observing the subject matter and also, true to his interest in technology, the methods of art preservation:

… in several places there are pictures of Jesus riding on an ass and also pictures of other prophets such as Abraham, Ishmael, Isaac, and Jacob and his sons, which are varnished in oil of sandarac and covered with fine, transparent glass that does not block any of the painting. This they have done so that dust and dirt cannot harm the pictures, and every day servants clean the glass. … There is one place in this church painted in two parts to represent heaven and hell and their inhabitants; in all the world there is nothing to equal it (S, 38).

He continues his admiration of the Church of the Resurrection: 'many priests and monks remain here to read the Gospel, pray, and occupy themselves with acts of devotion all day and night.' Thus, even Nasir's last line about his sojourn in Jerusalem, before he sets off for Egypt, focuses on the spiritual life of piety, prayer and devotion.

In all, Nasir Khusraw stayed three months in Jerusalem, from March to May, before setting off for his first pilgrimage to Mecca, the holiest city in Islam. But, he declines to write about Mecca in too much detail at this point, explaining that he will write about it when giving an account of his last pilgrimage. Indeed, his party did not linger long in Arabia because, whether from drought or other trouble, there was little food to be had anywhere. His group was back in Jerusalem by the beginning of July. Within a month, he was in Cairo.

# CHAPTER EIGHT

# The Splendour of Fatimid Cairo

> The people are so secure under the [caliph's] reign that no one fears his agents, and they rely on him neither to inflict injustice nor to have designs on anyone's property.
>
> *Safarnama*, 55

Nasir Khusraw can hardly praise Cairo enough. Whether he is there in the city itself, participating in the daily pulse of this imperial capital, or whether he is far away, exiled in the Pamir mountains of Badakhshan, he extols the glories of the Caliph-Imam al-Mustansir and the good government which gives people the freedom to prosper and flourish. The Fatimid rule reaches far into many lands, and the abundant signs of its worldly power testify, in his mind, to its profound attachment to the realm of spiritual values and divine power.

He lived in Cairo for three years, studying and training with other Fatimid intellectuals and, from what we can gather from his own statements, enjoyed a privileged and trusted relationship with the court. The Fatimids were also the caretakers of the holy cities of Mecca and Medina, and thus responsible for preparing and supplying many necessities for the annual pilgrimage (*hajj*) to Mecca, particularly the lavishly embroidered draperies to cover the Ka'ba. Several times, Nasir was selected to accompany the royal caravan from Cairo to Mecca which carried the cloths and provided protection and transport for great numbers of pilgrims. Even in years of drought and famine so severe that pilgrims were warned not to attempt the pilgrimage, the caliph still had to make sure the new cloths arrived. Given the hardships of the journey, he viewed it as a pious adventure for himself and the noble fulfilment of a public trust undertaken by the Fatimid state authorities. He found many such examples to admire in Fatimid governance.

### THE FATIMID CALIPHS

The Fatimid caliphs claimed both genealogical and spiritual descent from the Prophet Muhammad. Ruling over the twin realms of faith and politics, just as the Prophet had, these Ismaili caliphs represented for their followers the earthly summit of all temporal and spiritual matters. The caliph was therefore also the supreme Imam, the highest prince of the faithful. Nasir Khusraw devotes many pages of his *Divan* to praise of the Ismaili imams, especially al-Mustansir, the eighth Fatimid caliph.

> The Prophet's descendant has taken up the seat of his ancestor
>     in majestic glory, the tip of his crown stretching all the way
>     to Saturn.
> The Chosen One is the one whom God has chosen;
>     what foolishness do you keep babbling on about?
> There, where the Prophet sat by God's command,
>     his descendant sits today by the same command.
>
> (*Divan*, 232:70–2)

These lines express not just praise for a prince, but a core tenet of Ismaili theology. For according to Shi'i Islam, the rightful successor (*khalifa*) to the Prophet Muhammad, 'Ali, was appointed by divine mandate from God; it was God who commanded Muhammad to appoint 'Ali, the first Shi'i imam. Nasir Khusraw thus professes that the Fatimid caliph, a blood descendant of the Prophet through his daughter Fatima and her husband 'Ali, to be the legitimate spiritual descendant of 'Ali in his role as rightful interpreter of the Holy Qur'an. According to Shi'i doctrine, the mission of the Prophet was to deliver to people the divine revelation (*tanzil*) given in the words of the Qur'an; after the Prophet only 'Ali was entrusted by God with the function of conveying the true interpretation (*ta'wil*) of the book. Referring to the well-known saying of the Prophet, 'I am the City of Knowledge and 'Ali is its Gate,' Nasir exhorts his readers to seek out this city of wisdom that can only be entered through allegiance to 'Ali:

> If my words should please you,
> Take leave of the desert and hasten to the City,
> The City of Knowledge whose door is 'Ali,
> Abode of the poor, home of the rewarded.
> All that exists outside the city is wasteland –
> No water, no fruit, wretched desert.
>
> (*Divan*, 63:41–3)

For Nasir Khusraw, the inheritors and guardians of that City of Knowledge are the Prophet's family (*ahl al-bayt*), specifically his descendants from 'Ali and Fatima, the Ismaili imams who, for a while, ruled as the Fatimid caliphs:

> A tree of wisdom was our Prophet, and from him
>     each member of his family is a tree with the same fruit.
> Today, the worthy sons of 'Ali
>     have sons, just as the Prophet's daughter had sons.
> The sons of 'Ali are those who are the Imams of truth,
>     as famed as their father for their greatness.
> Their father spread justice throughout the land;
>     why be surprised that his sons follow their father's wisdom?
>
> (*Divan*, 31:25–7; 32)

Besides employing the metaphor of trees bearing fruit, Nasir also likens the Prophet's religion (*shari'at*) to a complete garden itself, with fruits for the wise and thorns for the ignorant. Every aspect of the garden image shimmers with layers of other meanings for the poet. The gateway to enter signifies 'Ali, as we have seen, but there is more. For example, Mount Sinai stands for the Prophet (*natiq*), who has brought the message (*WD*, 99). Like all mountains, this one appears hard and rough on the surface, and only by mining one's way into its depths are the riches discovered, such as rubies, emeralds, gold, silver and copper.

In the garden of the way of the Prophet,
There is no one but his family to act as the Guardians.
To the wild and the lost, the Guardian never gave away
But sticks and leaves from this garden,
For they are asses, and asses cannot differentiate
The scent of ambergris and aloe from that of dung.
Hasten to find the pathway to this garden,
Even unto China and Ma-chin.[1]
See the figs and olives of this garden,
That city of safety and Mount of Sinai.[2]
O soul! Adorn yourself with knowledge and action
From the garden of the Guardian!
Enter into the garden and pluck up the berries
And fruits and fragrant herbs.
Set the thorns and leaves and sticks before the asses,
Keep the box-tree, jasmine and wild roses for yourself.

(*Divan*, 24: 27–34)

As much as 'Ali was reputed for wisdom and justice in govern-
ing during his lifetime, he also acquired fame for his physical
prowess and valour in battle, especially as the heroic champion of
the Battle of Khaybar (7/628), thus earning renown for his apti-
tude in ruling over the physical world as well as his proficiency in
spiritual matters. For Nasir Khusraw, the Fatimid Caliph-Imam
mirrors 'Ali's fame in both wisdom and politics, and thus inherits
his double sovereignty over religion and society. The poet basks
in the glow of both successes, drawing on well-known medieval
Islamic images of wise Luqman[3] and powerful Caesar:

And today a fruit-filled branch from that tree sits in his place
      with the wisdom of Luqman and the might of Caesar.

(*Divan*, 59:52)

As the embodiment of all excellences, the Fatimid Caliph-Imam
stands as the pole, the pivot, of all God's creation and plan, our
author declares:

Dominion and the imamate befit such a person who already
    possesses
The dominion of Solomon and the knowledge and wisdom of
    Luqman,
And whom all the world's kings do serve at his court
As mere chamberlains, servants or beggars and guests.
Heaven itself received grandeur and stature by his kingdom,
And the world found peace and repose through him.
The names of Muhammad and 'Ali have come alive through him,
The gracious king of the world, the ultimate of ultimates.
The wise one who knows to whom I speak, even if I haven't said:
'The deputy of God, the sun of the generous ones!'

(Divan, 215:27–31)

Nasir expresses his gratitude to God for his new-found faith, and
for the Imam, for together they show him an eternal constancy
lacking in the otherwise fickle and faithless world:

All praise to God, who has imposed no burden on me
But this that bends my back in obligation to His grace.
Praise be to God that by generosity of the true Imam of God,
I have come to know him in truth, certainty and in his reality.
He is that prince without peer in all the world,
Whose realm is free of any trace of the demon realm.
By the rising of his blessed, auspicious countenance,
Even Jupiter is bereft of justice in Sagittarius' rising.
O Lord, by Your grace, grant me success
That, day and night, I may keep myself devoted to him.

(Divan, 82:51–5)

### 'SO THAT THE PEOPLE NEED NOT FEAR'

Nasir Khusraw finds evidence of the rightness of the Caliph al-
Mustansir's rule in his broad state policies and individual legal
decisions. For example, a basic policy of paying people fairly and
liberally for their work marks him as a wise ruler, according to the
traveller from Khurasan, for they then work more willingly, which
leads to them working more productively. Nasir's familiarity with

the administrative policies and practices of the Ghaznavid and Saljuq courts in eastern Iranian lands influences what he notices and comments on. His experience in the Saljuq revenue office comes out clearly in his particularly keen appreciation of Fatimid fiscal practices. He notes that, except for houses, practically all buildings are owned by the caliph, who then leases them out as people need them. Nasir emphasises that there is no sort of coercion used by the state in this arrangement.

But for Nasir, even more critical than such fair decisions on personal property issues is the Fatimid ruler's regular payment of the military in order to ensure the security of the larger population and the general peace of the realm. If an army depends on looting for its pay, citizens in the countryside and the city cannot be safe and will resent the government for its failure to protect them. Nasir illustrates the links that exist between the Fatimid tax collection system, the satisfaction of the military and social calm. Once a year, he writes, the tax collectors in each province send their assigned taxes to the central treasury and the army's pay is then distributed at a predetermined schedule from this common fund. Soldiers are paid from the caliph's treasury and each one receives a fixed salary depending on his rank. Nasir observes that, due to the well-managed tax collection and payment system under the caliph, 'no governmental agent or peasant is ever troubled by demands from the army,' because he knows it stands in stark contrast to systems elsewhere. He is concerned explicitly with the security of the individual 'agent or peasant,' and nowhere even hints that a satisfied military is essential for the continued rule of the sovereign, but rather that they should be fairly compensated so that the populace can live in peace. He sees al-Mustansir's rule as just and for the sake of the greater good of society, rather than merely efficient to ensure its own survival.

Besides the tax collection system and the army, the legal system also must be free from employees who expect to receive extra income from the normal administration of their duties, such as judges. That is, one's guilt or innocence before the law should not be determined by how much payment a judge receives. Nasir Khusraw explicitly states that a hierarchical pay scale was established by the Fatimids, 'so that people need not fear venality from the bench.' He describes how the chief justice receives a monthly stipend of 2,000 dinars, and a proportionate amount is paid to every judge down the ranks. This former court clerk has certainly seen different systems, ones where justice could be bought and sold. He admires the Fatimids for regulating their judiciary system and purposely giving generous salaries to forestall such abuse of law, so that the people need not fear corruption or injustice.

Many other types of people are paid by the caliph for the stability and splendour of the state. The Fatimid court supported an extensive array of intellectuals and writers, including Nasir himself. 'Besides soldiers, there are also many contingents of princes and their families and retinues from far away, as well as people of other ranks and stations, such as scholars, literati, poets and jurisprudents, all of whom have fixed stipends.' Even with his extensive court experience, Nasir opens his eyes wide at the sums the caliph gives out for seemingly minor responsibilities in the court:

No aristocrat receives less than five hundred dinars, some drawing stipends of up to two thousand dinars. The only function they have to perform is to make a salaam to the grand vizier, when he sits in state, and then withdraw to their places (S, 50).

All states need an audience, a populace to acknowledge the sovereignty of the ruler. The practice of paying princes 'from far away' to publicly make obeisance during official ceremonies allowed the Fatimids to exercise control over them and demonstrate at home the far-flung political reach of their empire.

Fatimid central authority not only asserted its authority in the provinces by having local aristocrats brought to the capital, but exerted its ultimate suzerainty, in matters of religion, deep into every town and village directly under its control. This was accomplished by the government itself paying for all expenses incurred by mosques (at least from Syria to Tunisia, an area under direct Fatimid control and the extent of Nasir's record of this issue). The royal treasury paid for all the carpets and rugs, all the salaries for those tending the mosques such as watchmen, cleaners and muezzins, and all the oil used to light the considerable number of lamps. As an example of state authority over religious affairs, Nasir relates that one year the governor of Syria wrote to ask if he could substitute a less expensive type of oil than the one officially approved for use in the mosque. 'He was told that he was to obey orders, that he was not a vizier, and that furthermore it was not licit to institute change in things pertaining to the House of God.' Beyond the confines of the court, our traveller noticed how state benevolence can actually strengthen the financial and civil foundations of the state itself.

Fabrics were an important commodity in Egypt and their production highly regulated by the state then in control, whether Greek, Roman, Byzantine, or Arab.[4] Just as today academic degrees and other honours are symbolised with the placement of a ribbon, stole, or other fabric on the honoured person, it was even more so in Fatimid times. Ceremonial 'robes of honour' (khil'a) were one of the most common official presents with which to show esteem to guests and employees of the state. One source records that nearly seventy-five years after Nasir Khusraw's visit, in the year 516/1122, a total of 14,305 pieces of clothing were distributed, the most desirable being something that came directly off the back of the caliph. Since these articles were worn publicly, both the honoured person and the bestower earned public credit and acknowledgement for excellence, a more effective tribute in this regard, perhaps, than today's practice of giving a 'key to the city,' for example. The Fatimids also excelled in producing fabrics with ornate embroideries (tiraz),[5] often using gold or silver thread to embroider verses from the Qur'an and prayers into clothing for individual wear, as well as draperies and banners for decorating entire buildings at state occasions. Also woven into the bands of tiraz would be the name of the caliph, that of the prince who ordered its manufacture, and sometimes the name of the administrative officer, the official in charge of tiraz, the city of production, the date and the name of the artist.

Nasir paid attention to fabrics wherever he went. In Asyut, in southern Egypt, for instance, he commented that he saw a shawl made from sheep's wool finer than anything from Lahore or Multan (in today's Pakistan), 'so fine you would think it was silk.'

Along the way to Cairo, he stopped at Tinnis, a factory island in the Nile Delta region, 'where they weave multicoloured linen for turbans, bandages, and women's clothing. The coloured linen of Tinnis is unequalled anywhere except by the white linen woven in Damietta.' Tinnis was famous throughout the Mediterranean region for its production of fine fabrics with intricate patterns, supple weaving, finely stitched embroidery and creative colour combinations. So exquisite was its workmanship that Tinnis had the honour and the responsibility to produce the great veil of the Ka'ba in Mecca, delivered twice a year. The colour of the veil changed over time: when the Sunni Abbasids controlled Tinnis the veil was black (as it is today); under the Fatimids it became their official colour, white.[6] Nasir Khusraw gives several examples to illustrate how coveted Tinnis fabrics were, such as the following anecdote about a king from the southern province of Iran:

I heard that the king of Fars once sent twenty thousand dinars to Tinnis to buy one suit of clothing of their special material. [His agents] stayed there for several years but were unsuccessful in obtaining any (S, 39).

The island of Tinnis housed the official Fatimid looms for many types of linens and damasks (whose name comes from the nearby city of Damascus), as well as an iridescent fabric known as *buqalamun*,[7] meaning 'chameleon,' due to its shimmering, change-able colour. Made of purple, red and green interwoven threads, *buqalamun*'s main hue would change dramatically as it moved. This exquisite fabric struck Nasir's fancy, not only as an object of beauty made by human skill and design; he saw it as a brilliant metaphor for the changeable, fickle, physical world:

Like *buqalamun*, the world does not show just one face.
Now your friend, now your enemy, just like a shining Indian
     sword.

(*Divan*, 164:8)

Tinnis was such an important source of income and interna-tional commercial status for the Fatimids that the king of

Byzantium, Nasir Khusraw relates, once offered to exchange a hundred cities of his for Tinnis alone. He was turned down by the Fatimid caliph who knew, of course, 'that what he wanted with this city was its linen and *buqalamun*.' But probably the most remarkable thing about Tinnis, according to Nasir Khusraw, who had seen plenty of state-run industries, was that 'nothing is taken from anyone by force.' Moreover,

The full price is paid for all the linen and *buqalamun* woven for the [caliph], so that the people work willingly – not as in some other countries, where the artisans are forced to labour for the vizier and caliph! (*S*, 40)

Again, we see his acknowledgement that compulsion generally works against creativity and civil satisfaction. He repeats his point that people should be paid fairly for their work. Nasir thus holds up the Fatimid administration as an exemplar of wise governance. Paying artisans for their labour leads to a willing work force and one that demonstrably produces better quality items. Paying soldiers regularly makes them less likely to molest the peasants. Paying judges a good salary helps to keep jurisprudence fair and saves the citizens from unjust judgements.

Further proof, according to Nasir, that the Fatimids exercised wise administrative decisions lies in the safety with which the people conduct their daily living. He remarks that the security and welfare of the people of Egypt are such that the shopkeepers do not need to lock their shops. This includes even the money changers, jewellers and drapers. When they wish to leave they only lower a net across the front of the shop, 'and no one tampers with anything.' Nasir notes that while generally the merchants of Cairo are honest, if one is in fact caught cheating a customer,

he is mounted on a camel with a bell in his hand and paraded about the city, ringing the bell and crying out, 'I have committed a misdemeanour and am suffering reproach. Whosoever tells a lie is rewarded with public disgrace.' (*S*, 55).

During his time in Cairo, Nasir witnessed two crises in which all the players recognised a threat to the Fatimid throne and its authority. The first involved a local altercation between some government soldiers and the Jewish businessman in charge of buying all the jewels for the caliph. In this capacity, the businessman had become very rich himself. Without supplying any further background information of the crisis, Nasir writes that one day some soldiers rose up and killed this businessman. Since he had been so close to the Caliph al-Mustansir, the whole army realised its loyalty was now in question. They gathered 'twenty thousand' soldiers on horseback and stationed them in the main square. 'When the army appeared thus in the field, the populace was in great fear.' The army's intentions were at this point unclear: would it stage a coup, commit another assassination, or run rampant? The horsemen remained mounted in the square all morning, with those inside the palace wondering, along with the people of the city, what their next step would be.

In the middle of the day, after hours of this standstill, a servant was sent out from the palace to determine the soldiers' plans.

'The caliph asks whether you are in obeisance or not.'

The soldiers all cried out at once, 'We are his slaves and obedient, but we have committed a crime.'

The servant answered, 'Then the caliph commands you to disperse immediately.'

The military demonstration had, in fact, been a show of allegiance to the throne. With this immediate crisis dissipated, the caliph's sovereignty was thus assured. But the jeweller's family still remained concerned for their own safety from reprisals or further attacks from the army. The jeweller's brother wrote a note to the caliph asking for protection and saying that he was willing to pay for the protection himself, some 200,000 dinars on the spot. (The proportions of the crisis are now apparent, remembering that the annual salary of the chief judge of the city was 2,000 dinars.)

Nasir records how justly the caliph resolved this conflict. He ordered the brother's note to be torn up in public and assured him, 'You rest secure and return to your home. No one will harm you.' The caliph also refused the offer of payment from the family, saying, 'We have no need of anyone's money.' On the contrary, the Jewish family was compensated for the killing of the businessman.

The second crisis reached into international concerns. In the year 442/1050, 'while I was in Egypt,' Nasir writes, the news arrived that the king of Aleppo (in today's northern Syria) had rebelled against the Fatimid caliph. To put down this rebellion, the caliph dispatched a tremendous force, outfitted 'with all the trappings of kings, such as canopies, pavilions, and so on.' At the head of this force, he placed a very wealthy and propertied man by the name of 'Umdat al-Dawla. Here Nasir interrupts his narrative to explain that this 'Umdat al-Dawla had grown wealthy as the head of the Matalibis, 'what they call the people who dig for buried treasure in the graves of Egypt.' Nasir reports that people would come from throughout the empire to search for the treasure of the pharaohs. 'Often much outlay is made without anything being found,' but when treasure was found, the finder would give one-fifth to the caliph and keep the rest. Obviously the head of the Matalibis also took a share. 'At any rate,' Nasir continues his story, when 'Umdat al-Dawla reached Aleppo, he led the war against the rebel and was killed. Two problems now arose: what to do about the rebel king, still alive, and what to do about 'Umdat al-Dawla's property?

Nasir Khusraw relates that 'Umdat al-Dawla's wealth was so considerable that it took two months to have it transferred to the caliph's treasury. The traveller does not consider it odd or unfair that the state should appropriate this man's wealth. He does, however, comment on the hundreds of slave girls who made up part of the dead man's wealth. He writes that of his properties, for instance, 'he had three hundred slave girls, most of them beauties, a few of whom were of the type taken to concubinage.' The caliph did not simply leave their fate to be decided by his treasury, but declared that they should each be given a choice. Either they could take a husband, or 'if such was not their choice,' they could share in the remainder of the man's estate 'so that they might remain in their own house, no command or force being exerted upon any of them.' Nasir provides no hint of what choices the slave girls made. One can only wonder which they would have preferred. From his tone the reader gathers that Nasir sees the caliph's decision as unusually generous, yet strangely just.

Meanwhile, the rebel king realised he was in serious trouble and, fearing an even greater show of force by the caliph, sent messages of great apology and contrition. He also despatched camel loads of presents and gifts, including 'his seven-year-old son along with his wife.' Of course, the son and not the wife was the main gesture of peace, as an absolute show of the king's servitude. But when the caravan with the son, his wife and gifts arrived at Cairo's gates, they were kept outside waiting for nearly two months. As the crisis wore on, the Fatimid caliph and his vizier within the palace had to listen to many arguments interceding for those outside the gates. By extension, of course, the interceders were also begging forgiveness for the king of Aleppo himself, and as long as the caliph did not open the gates he showed his power over his subject states. Only after intense lobbying by 'all the judges of the city' were the gifts accepted and the son and his wife allowed into the city; indeed, they were admitted with great honours.

Nasir's affection for the Caliph-Imam al-Mustansir and his reign becomes apparent in one of his poetic celebrations of springtime, composed during his exile in Yumgan. In this *qasida*, here translated in full, he uses the metaphor of seasonal change and renewal to describe the triumph of the Fatimids over the Abbasids. The black banners of the Sunni Abbasids in Baghdad are likened to the crow and the raven, while the Fatimids are shown by their royal colour with emblems of whiteness and light, including 'Ali's white steed and shining sword, Zulfiqar. The brilliant sun transforms the mud of earth into fiery flower jewels of ruby and ambergris. The arrival of spring marks the victory of the sun over darkness and becomes a metaphor for the triumph of knowledge over ignorance, which the poet turns into a challenge to engage in reasoned debate, directed especially at the religious judges of Balkh and Bukhara:

Spring arrived and the season of ice has fled.
Once again, this ancient world turns young.

Ice-blue water now turns dark like wine,[8]
Silvery fields turn a verdant green.

January's harsh wind, whipping like flags,
Has turned soft like mildest mist of incense.

The poor willow, stripped naked all winter,
Now drips heavy with earrings of silk.

The faces of all the fields and plains are dewy fresh
And the eyes of all the blossoms, open wide, can see.

All the land is now alive and open-eyed.
The east wind is touched by the charm of the Messiah.

Bursting with blossoms, the orchard becomes
Like the starry sky, the flower garden like the Pleiades.

If these clouds are not the miracle of Joseph,
Then why does the desert become like Zulaykha?[9]

The tulips have blossomed, like blushing lovers' cheeks
And like love-struck eyes, the narcissus opened wide.

If, from the snow, the little violet is now secure,
Why does it turn purple like the Christian's cloak?

Dark became the water and light the air;
Mute the raven, yet the nightingale sang.

The garden became like heaven and tulips began
To shine like the faces of *houris.*

Like a darksome slave, the jet-black raven
Is turned to the lowest minion before the rose and nightingale.

That flowering bush whose curve was covered in white
Now sparkles like a dome of stained glass and enamel.

Like 'Amr 'As before 'Ali, January before Spring
Is reduced to weakness and shame.[10]

Cast aside was the raven, shunned and removed,
For the foe it became of Fatima's sons;

Like the Abbasids, its treachery and enmity
Clearly apparent from its cloak of black.

The sun became Fatimid and returned in full strength,
Ascending from the depths to on high,

'Til its light shone bright like the sword of 'Ali
And the rosebush grew strong like Duldul, the mount of 'Ali.

When the sun reached the level of the equinox
It turned into the enemy of the season of ice.

Daylight blossomed like faith, while
night crumpled like heresy, dark in melancholy.

Dark night like the enemies of 'Ali, the hypocrites,
Bright day like the lovers of 'Ali.

The world became like the mind without forgetfulness,
Brimming with light and joy and abundance.

Why was the world dark before, like an ignorant mind,
Yet now appears like the heart of one who is wise?

Because the sun, the *sayyid* of all the stars, now in Aries,
Has found the power to establish justice in the world.

Justice is the core of good things, that's why
Anushirvan became famous, through justice.

See how, when the sun raised its head in the equinox,
Such a wild variety of things was made manifest.

See how this old rotten mud
Has become like red rubies and yellow amber.

Virtue is aught but knowledge and justice;
Saved are they conversant in these two tongues.

Act as intelligence demands, for it is thus
That the world was prepared for intellect and justice.

Become beautiful from learning, for one is not beautiful
Who has become beautiful to the world.

Follow not the world, but seek after learning because
So many people has the world deceived.

Do not become impressed when you hear that
So-and-so has become a judge in Balkh or Bukhara,

Because true knowledge of religion disappeared from view
When the work of religion and learning fell into vulgar hands.

Do not accept the word of the ignorant imitators,
Though they be famed throughout the world.

Seek the answers to 'how' and 'why,' because for the ignorant
The world has become a constricting ring.

Speak knowledge to your opponent, for without a foe
Knowledge is neither sharpened nor polished.

Since the person who goes alone to see the judge
Is sure to come out happy,[11]

Adopt the manners of the good and be humble
Before the sage who's great from knowledge.

Look how the black soil, by obedience and submission,
To the palm tree became a date, bit by bit.

Choose knowledge and seek to be patient, for it was
Through patience and knowing that Darius became king.

Take on the manners of the generous, for the free man
Adopts the habit of the noble as his alpha and omega.

(*Divan*, 161)

## THE INTELLECTUAL DEBATE

In the 4th–5th/10th–11th centuries, the Fatimid court at Cairo
engendered some of the liveliest theological and intellectual debates in the Muslim world. Astronomers, poets, grammarians,
physicians, legal experts, theologians and other members of the

intelligentsia were brought to the capital and given generous stipends and materials for their creative work.

In the century before Nasir arrived in Cairo, the famous jurist, al-Qadi al-Nu'man (d. 363/974), was consolidating the scope and structure of Ismaili law in many books, especially his two major works, the *Da'a'im al-Islam* (*The Pillars of Islam*) which detailed the *zahir* or externals of the religious law, and the *Ta'wil da'a'im al-Islam* (*Interpretation of the Pillars of Islam*) which explained the esoteric, *batin* meaning of the exoteric doctrine contained in the *Da'a'im*.[12] By the year 378/988, or perhaps earlier, public lectures on Ismaili law were held in al-Azhar Mosque.[13] In 396/1005, the sixth Fatimid caliph, al-Hakim (386–411/996–1021), founded the Dar al-'Ilm (House of Knowledge), an academy where a variety of subjects were taught; this academy was also equipped with a major library. A text survives which describes the marvellous opening of this institution:

Into this house they brought all the books that the Commander of the Faithful al-Hakim bi-Amr Allah ordered to bring there, that is, the manuscripts in all the domains of science and culture, to an extent to which they had never been brought together for a prince. He allowed access to all this to people of all walks of life, whether they wanted to read books or dip into them. One of the already mentioned blessings, the likes of which had been unheard of, was also that he granted substantial salaries to all those who were appointed by him there to do service – jurists and others. People from all walks of life visited the House; some came to read books, others to copy them, and yet others to study. He also donated what people needed: ink, writing reeds, paper, and inkstands.[14]

In light of this tradition of active state support of education and learning, al-Mustansir's generosity toward the intellectual elite of his day, as Nasir described it, is less surprising, though no less grand an achievement. The state would surely benefit if the finest minds of the day were occupied in advancing their specialities, even 'people from all walks of life.' For example, during the few years Nasir was in Cairo, al-Mu'ayyad fi'l-Din al-Shirazi, the administrative head of the Ismaili *da'wa*, was also there. This is the same person Nasir Khusraw credits, in the confessional poem we examined earlier, with his conversion to Ismailism.[15] In their invitations to creative thinkers, however, it appears that the Fatimids were not successful in attracting the blind poet, Abu'l-'Ala al-Ma'arri, whose pious asceticism and profound spiritual leadership Nasir had described with admiration when recounting his time in the town of Ma'arra in Syria.

In Fatimid Cairo, quite a number of influential intellectuals and missionaries hailed from eastern Iran. It was this group of Persians who set Ismaili theology on a strong doctrinal foundation, articulated within the framework of Islamic and Greek, particularly Neoplatonic, philosophy. Five individuals are significant in this group, including Nasir Khusraw himself. The first, Muhammad b. Ahmad al-Nasafi (executed in Bukhara in 332/ 943 for his Ismaili teachings), is the one generally credited with adapting Neoplatonic philosophy into Ismaili theology. While it appears we no longer have a complete volume of his work, major portions of his *al-Mahsul (The Yield)* are recorded in works by his critics as well as his defenders. Al-Nasafi was criticised by his fellow Ismaili, Abu Hatim al-Razi (d. 322/934), who wrote a book called *al-Islah (The Correction)* precisely to correct al-Nasafi's positions on many topics, including the order of creation, on the nature of the intelligibles and on the salvation of the soul (*nafs*).[16] Al-Nasafi was defended by one of his disciples, Abu Ya'qub al-Sijistani (d. ca. 361/971), in the latter's *al-Nusra (The Defence)*, a work also aptly named because he took Abu Hatim al-Razi to task for errors and weaknesses in his arguments, and presented new proofs to defend his teacher's positions. To bring some order to these debates, a fourth Ismaili scholar, Hamid al-Din al-Kirmani (d. ca. 411/1020), set all these various arguments side by side and commented on them in his book, *al-Riyad (The Meadows)*, the work which is in fact the main textual source for this entire debate.[17] For the most part, al-Kirmani seems to side with Abu Hatim, whereas Nasir Khusraw, whose Ismaili writings come at least fifty years after al-Kirmani's death, clearly favours al-Sijistani.[18]

Sijistani's interpretation of Ismaili thought maintains that all 'being' comes from the God beyond being and non-being through His command (*amr*), which originates the Universal Intellect (*'aql-i kulli*), from which in turn issues the Universal Soul (*nafs-i kulli*). From the Universal Soul comes Nature and the formation of the physical realm, which the Soul is intimately involved in sustaining. Therefore, the intelligible realm of the Sijistani model of creation, and subsequently that of Nasir, can be seen to follow closely that of the Neoplatonic philosopher Plotinus (d. 270 CE), that is, in the 'descending order' of God, Intellect, Soul and Nature. In the material world, the progression then moves in an ascending hierarchy from the four elements (earth, air, fire, water), up through minerals, plants and animals, until the pinnacle of the animal kingdom is reached – human beings, who are endowed with a rational soul. Nasir Khusraw refers directly to this model when he writes in one poem:

> Know, it was from substance and not by an increase in being,
>     for none but the One was the cause of creation.
> Know, Intellect was the first created being, then Soul, then body,
>     then plants, species of beasts, and then the rational animal.
>
> (*Divan* 1: 17–18)

However, al-Kirmani introduced in his most ambitious work, *Rahat al-'aql* (*The Peace of the Intellect*), another model of a descending creation from God to the world, a model which instead of the Neoplatonic intellect-soul construct of al-Sijistani, placed ten separate intellects between God and the world.[19] The ten-intellect model, where each intellect is a sort of 'mind' or 'spirit' ruling over its particular level of being, derives from Aristotle and had been first expounded in the Islamic world by the philosopher al-Farabi before it was later adopted by Ibn Sina (Avicenna). In this model, the lowest level of intellect is the Active Intellect, which is generally accessible only to prophets, and through which they receive inspiration from God. Therefore, al-Kirmani was interpreting Ismaili cosmology from an alternative model based on an Aristotelian adaptation. What is noteworthy for our study is that Nasir Khusraw does not adopt al-Kirmani's ten-intellect model to explain the process of creation. Instead, he consistently adheres to the earlier system in which the creation of the material world flows from God through Intellect and Soul.

### THE INTELLECT

In the previous chapter on Jerusalem, we examined Nasir's theology of God. Now that he has arrived in Cairo, the seat of Fatimid intellectual flowering, it is fitting to follow Nasir's theory of creation and examine the characteristics of what he considers the first entity in the intelligible world, namely, the Intellect (*'aql*).

The Intellect merits close review both for its philosophical import and because it is perhaps the most difficult notion in his entire system. It is difficult to comprehend because what we understand today as the 'mind,' 'intellect,' or 'reason' is not exactly or always what Nasir and the other Ismaili thinkers meant when they spoke of the Intellect philosophically, no matter how much they valued rationality and intellectual activity. Human intellect or reason (*'aql* or *khirad*, Nasir uses both the Arabic and the Persian terms interchangeably) differs in fact from Universal Intellect (which is why we capitalise the latter).

Nasir Khusraw discussed Intellect in all his philosophical works. Generally speaking, the Universal Intellect for Nasir is the first being to issue (*padid amad*) from God after the divine command 'Be!' But as the first originated being (*mubda'*), the first caused, the Intellect is not separate from God in any temporal or spatial sense, just as the thoughts of a person's mind are not separate from the mind itself, to use a human analogy. The Intellect is complete and perfect. It knows all things, and knows them all at once; there is nothing for it to know later or better. There is no motion or time within the Intellect or within which the Intellect functions, for time and motion have not yet come into existence in the realm of the Intellect. Not only does the Intellect know all things; it encompasses all beings, material and spiritual. In fact, following the command 'Be!' the Intellect *is* all being; there is nothing outside of itself. Nothing new will come to be that is not already within the Intellect. The Intellect also lacks nothing and needs nothing, because there is nothing other than its actual perfection. In his *Shish fasl*, Nasir Khusraw thus writes:

The first cause is the Word (*kalima*), and what it has caused, the *'aql*, came into existence through it. ... For this reason we say that the *'aql* is both the cause and the caused, both the reasoner (*'aqil*) and the result of reasoning (*ma'qul*), because its original cause is inherent in it, without separation' (*SF*, 38–9).

Ismaili thinkers differed over which entity actually was the first caused, part of the problem stemming from their uncompromising view of divine unity (*tawhid*), which negated all attributes to God, even that of the first cause. So in some Ismaili works God features as the cause, through His Word, and the Intellect is therefore the first caused. In other works, the Word is considered the first cause and the Intellect is, therefore, in this case also the first caused. But in other works the Intellect is the first cause, and the Universal Soul becomes the first caused. Nasir Khusraw's works exhibit this diversity of interpretation. For example, as we see in the passage from *Shish fasl* cited above, he is making the case that Intellect is both cause and caused. But in his *Zad al-musafirin* he holds that Intellect is clearly the first cause, the cause of all causes, and Soul is caused by Intellect (*ZM*, 193, 196).[20]

Even Nasir himself seems to admit at one place the difficulty of defining the Intellect's status by saying, 'Since we have shown that Intellect is the first being which has been caused to be produced by God, it would not be fitting to try to determine its individual nature (*hasti*)' (*SF*, 40). By so doing, Nasir gives expression to the human incapacity to explain, through merely linguistic tools, one of the most intractable problems in philosophical theology, that of the relationship between God and the creation.

Regarding the Intellect's relation to the second originated being, namely the Universal Soul, Nasir emphasises the distinction between perfection in actuality and in potentiality. Plotinus had written that 'because Soul has an element of potentiality and changeability in it,' it must have an eternally actual cause to account for its existence, and 'this cause is Intellect (*nous*).'[21] In the *Khwan al-ikhwan*, Nasir adheres to this position, holding that the Intellect is the stronger, more perfect of the two because it is closer to the Word and 'whatever is closer to its cause is stronger than that which is farther from its cause' (*KI*, 88–9). Nasir echoes this in his shorter work, *Gushayish wa rahayish*, where he maintains that the First Intellect (*'aql-i awwal*), as the first originated being with 'whom the command of God Almighty became one, without intermediary,' is 'perfect in act and potentiality' (*GR*, 4). This is in contrast to the Universal Soul, the perfection of which lies only in potentiality, not in actuality.

Since the physical world is a reflection of the spiritual, according to Ismaili doctrine, the position of the Intellect between God and the Soul has earthly parallels. In the *Wajh-i din*, Nasir provides an in-depth *ta'wil* of the letters which spell out the *shahada*, the Islamic confession of faith, *La ilaha 'ill-Allah* (There is no god but God) (*WD*, 93–4). The first two letters, he writes, correspond to the two highest entities in the spiritual realm, namely Intellect and Soul, as well as to the two highest beings in the physical world, namely the *natiq* (meaning the Prophet-messenger Muhammad) and the *asas* (meaning the first Shi'i Imam 'Ali, the Prophet's deputy charged with the mission of expounding the esoteric meaning of the divine message). Thus the Fatimid ruler, the descendant of Muhammad and 'Ali, is shown to fit into, indeed embody, an essential component of the hierarchy of the spiritual world.

On an individual level, the relationship between a person's soul and intellect must also mirror that between the Universal Soul and Universal Intellect. In the *Khwan al-ikhwan*, Nasir explains how each person has a soul (*nafs*) which seeks knowledge and requires careful watching and nurturing. The human soul's watcher and teacher is its intellect. That this is indeed the case is proven, he says, by the fact that when the soul of an individual starts to control itself and shuns the perilous path of ignorance, we call that person wise, that is, one with intellect. Furthermore, 'since the soul of man is incomplete and wretched without intellect, we know that in the spiritual world the same occurs and thus the Soul needs the Intellect' (*KI*, 89–90).

For Ismaili intellectuals, as for most other Muslim thinkers, it was obvious that human beings were superior to other creatures of God, mainly because of their capacity for rational speech. God Himself communicates through the Word and it is His word 'Be!' which eternally suffuses itself through the creation that ensued from His command. The Universal Intellect, as we have seen, knows all things perfectly. The ability of humans to rationally articulate and understand words is indicative of their active connection between the physical and spiritual worlds. God selects some individuals as prophets and gives them the ability to grasp truths and concepts in their entirety perfectly, all at once. But most humans are bound by their humanity; they do not have any complete or perfect understanding of either grand truths or minute concepts. Instead, humans use discursive reasoning, that is, one thought following another, made up of words coming one after another. This unique power demonstrates the human potential to seek knowledge and to understand. For his part, Nasir never advocates a non-rational route to attaining wisdom. He never suggests a purely mystical or self-negating approach to seeking knowledge; rather, in Nasir's philosophy, reason and revelation, intellectuality and spirituality, are harnessed together for a common purpose.

In one poem, Nasir employs imagery of the ocean, with a pearl and a diver, to illustrate the importance of the human intellect and the high standing of speech in the entire creation. In these few verses with several layers of microcosms within macrocosms, he refers directly to the Active Intellect, understood to be the highest level of intellect attainable by a human being, one found only in prophets:

> The universe is like a rolling sea,
>> the planet a little boat, with nature as the anchor,
> Its water like the plants, its stones the animals.
>> But the pearl, like finest carnelian, is you endowed with speech.
> Who is the diver for this pearl? The Active Intellect
>> which was worthy to be the mind of the Prophet himself.
> At the end, what? Whatever was at the beginning.
>> And the goal, what? Whatever is the best.
>
> (*Divan*, 113: 14–18)

It is through the intellect, then, and actually only through the intellect, that a person may aim to achieve 'whatever is the best.'

The goal that humans need to strive for, according to Nasir Khusraw, is wisdom (*hikmat*), true understanding of God's plan and purpose. For ordinary people such wisdom can only be attained by a conscious and repeated use of reason and intelligence. For Nasir, the human intellect is the crucial gift from God, accessible in varying degrees to each human being. It is a powerful weapon to be used by human beings to defend and arm themselves against the endemic ignorance and corruption of the physical world. It is thus an indispensable tool for the attainment of truth and salvation.

### CELEBRATING THE RHYTHM OF LIFE

Besides the government policies of Fatimid Egypt, our traveller takes careful notice of many local customs of daily life, including shopping, the slave trade and the celebration of major holidays.

Probably one of the most charming shopping details we have from the 5th/11th century occurs in Nasir's travelogue where he records the wonders of Cairo's bazaars. He observes that the merchants, including grocers, druggists and peddlers, 'all furnish sacks for the items they sell, whether glass, pottery, or paper; so there is no need for shoppers to take their own bags with them.' His outsider's eye is constantly delighted at social innovations that solve problems and make life easier for the people to be both efficient and enjoy the things of life. In the following anecdote on urban gardening, he notices that the Egyptians have devised an ingenious system of moving fresh trees into someone's home, and then removing them when desired:

Among other things, if any one wants to make a garden in Egypt it can be done during any season at all, since any tree, fruit-bearing or other, can be obtained and planted. There are special people, called *dallals*, who can obtain immediately any kind of fruit you desire, because they have trees planted in tubs on rooftops. Many roofs are gardens and most of what is grown is fruit-producing, such as oranges, pomegranates, apples, quince, roses, herbs, and vegetables. When a customer wishes, porters will go and tie the tubs to poles and carry the trees wherever desired. They will also make a hole in the ground and sink the tubs if wished. Then, when someone so desires, they will dig the tubs up and carry their fragments away, and the trees will not know the difference. I have never seen or heard of such a thing anywhere else in the world, and it is truly clever! (*S*, 62–3)

Another marvellous product one can purchase in Fatimid Egypt is a porcelain so fine you can see the shadow of your hand when you hold it up to the light, a porcelain which is often painted to resemble the iridescent fabric *buqalamun*, 'so that different colours show depending on how the article is held.' They also make clear glass, 'so pure and flawless that it resembles chrysolite, and it is sold by weight.'

The price of thread also draws the traveller's thoughtful attention. In conversation with 'a reputable draper,' Nasir was able to compare the prices of thread in Cairo and Nishapur. In Nishapur, he writes, 'I priced the very best thread available there and was told that one-dirham weight of the finest was sold for five [silver] dirhams.' In Cairo the same weight was selling for the equivalent of three-and-a-half gold dinars, that is, at a considerably higher price.

Even water had to be purchased, although with the buildings situated as they were, it was possible for people to draw their own water from the Nile. All drinking water was sold by water carriers, some selling from pitchers on camels and some with the pitchers on their backs. He says the brass pitchers were kept so well, meaning not tarnished, that they looked like gold. Water selling was big business: 'I was told that there is a woman who leases out no less than five thousand of these pitchers' at the cost of one dirham a month and with the stipulation that they be returned in perfect condition, a comment that also reveals the role of women in Cairo's commercial life and tells us that business was more than just the sale of water.

Cairo was such a major commercial centre for ships coming from all the ports in the Mediterranean as well as along the Nile River and its many canals and tributaries in the Delta, that 'there are more ships and boats in Old Cairo than in Baghdad and Basra combined.'

Nasir has a few things to say about slavery. Although the Qur'an prohibits slavery among Muslims, the trade in slaves became an important aspect of medieval Muslim societies as it was in many parts of Europe and Asia at the time. Coming from Khurasan, our author was certainly accustomed to the raids which regularly brought new supplies of slaves from Central Asia, who were then kept for local use or passed along the caravan routes through Iran, Syria, Palestine, Arabia, Egypt, or further on to Byzantium or North Africa. He was also familiar with the strength of slave armies; indeed the founders of both the Ghaznavid and Saljuq empires had been Central Asian military slaves who had risen in rank and then succeeded in wresting power for themselves and their dynasties. So the enslavement of individuals and sometimes of whole villages and regions was part of his understanding of contemporary society. In his travels he notices the differences. In Egypt, he sees that the slaves come either from Greece, meaning Byzantium (including today's Turkey) or Nubia (in present-day Sudan):

Farther upriver to the south is the province of Nubia, which is ruled by another king. The people there are black and their religion is Christianity. Traders go there taking beads, combs, and trinkets and bring back slaves to Egypt, where the slaves are either Nubian or Greek (*S*, 41).

In another passage, he remarks that the king of Nubia 'continually sends gifts to the [caliph] of Egypt and makes treaties so that Egyptian soldiers will not enter his land and molest the populace.'

When Nasir made his three pilgrimages from Cairo to Mecca, the journeys of course took him south, toward Nubia. On one journey, he waited for twenty-one days in Aswan, just four parasangs from Nubia, for the caravan to arrive to take him across the desert to the Red Sea. After inspecting and hiring a camel, he joined the caravan and made the fifteen-day journey across the desert. When he finally arrived at the port town of 'Aydhab on the Red Sea (with a population of 500, he notes), he had to spend more time, three months actually, waiting for a ship to sail to Arabia. 'Aydhab belonged to Egypt and was an official trade and customs port for ships coming from Abyssinia, Zanzibar and the Yemen. Some of the goods were of course slaves.

While in the port, he noticed a local community known as the Bajawis, who performed a critical function in the economy of this transit city. Since there was no water from wells or springs, but only the infrequent rainwater, keeping a steady supply of drinking water for the traders and pilgrims passing through was essential. This task fell to the Bajawis who, as residents, collected the rainwater and sold it. Nasir records that he and his travelling companions bought water at the rate of one or two dirhams a jug. He was impressed by the Bajawis, who were neither Muslim nor Christian. In fact, he says, they have 'no religion and [have] had no prophet or spiritual leader because they are so far from civilisation.' Their territory covered a broad expanse of desert, 1,000 parasangs long and 300 wide he reckons, running from the Nubian River to the Red Sea, but contained only two small villages. In buying water from them over three months, Nasir would have come into personal contact with a good number of Bajawis. They are not a bad people, he says, they do not steal or make raids on other tribes, and they keep to themselves, tending their flocks. And with the frankness with which we have seen him point out his own failings, he adds 'Muslims and others, however, kidnap their children and take them to sell in the cities of Islam.' His sympathy is evident for these people 'so far from civilisation,' who want to live out their lives simply and gainfully. The traveller who saw that textile workers in Tinnis worked far more productively and happily when paid fairly sensed also that it was wrong to kidnap children and sell them, whatever their background.

During his three years in Cairo, Nasir personally witnessed some of the grandest state ceremonies and processions of the time.[22] We have already seen how the traveller from Khurasan arranged to view the banquet hall the day before one of the two annual feasts. He also tells us of another annual ritual he took part in, 'one of the biggest festivals of the year,' which was centred around the annual flood of the Nile River, the lifeblood of Egypt (S, 48–51). In order to regulate the annual flood season, the practice had been developed to close all the canals during the months when the Nile was rising, and to measure the water level each day. When the backed-up water level was high enough, they would announce the Festival of the Opening of the Canal, when the caliph would ceremoniously throw a spear at the main dam to release the flow of water for the whole nation. Helped along by men with shovels, the dam was opened and the water rushed dramatically to fill all the canals and water channels throughout the countryside.

Preparations for the festival began with the setting up of an enormous pavilion, 'large enough for a hundred horsemen to stand in its shade,' made of Byzantine brocade spun with gold and studded with jewels. (Here we see again Nasir's habit of observing fabrics.) One essential preparation was to accustom thousands of horses for what would certainly be overwhelming noise and commotion; so for three days before the celebration the musicians would beat drums and blast trumpets in the royal stables. For the parade, 10,000 horses (he repeats this number two pages later) were lavishly decorated, not for riding but to be led by special servants whose job it was to hold their bridles. (True to his style, Nasir tells us their pay, which was three dirhams each.) These 10,000 horses had to be ready for tremendous noise, for they walked – by the hundreds, he says – right behind the bugles, drums and clarions. Behind these horses came the camels, many with howdahs and litters (most likely to transport the royal women, since these public festivals were attended not only by men), as well as other horses and mules. The parade of animals was followed by the army battalions. He tells us that each of the 10,000 horses wore a gold saddle and bridle, with the reins studded with jewels. Under the saddles were placed specially designed saddle cloths of Byzantine brocade and *buqalamun* woven seamlessly, with beautiful inscriptions containing the name of the caliph woven into the corner of each saddle cloth. Each horse was also outfitted with some piece of weapon or armour, such as a spear or a helmet hanging from the pommel. Ten thousand riderless horses, ready for battle, thus proclaimed the power and authority of the Fatimid throne.

The parade of the caliph from his palace to the dam presented a major show of his rule over many lands (contingents from each region would march together) and his power over the very sustenance of their lives. In the parade, rank and honour were displayed through elaborate protocol regulating clothing, position in the procession, and whether one walked or rode. Nasir Khusraw himself was probably included in the contingent of 'people of other ranks and stations, such as scholars, literati, poets, and jurisprudents.' The figures he records for the numbers of soldiers are staggering: 20,000 Kutami Berber horsemen, 15,000

Batilis from the Maghreb region of North Africa, 20,000 black Masmudis, 10,000 'powerfully built men' of Turkish and Persian descent, 30,000 slaves who had been purchased, 50,000 spear-carrying bedouins from the Hijaz, 30,000 Ustazi horsemen purchased for military service and 30,000 black Zanj footsoldiers carrying swords. These are some of the soldiers, Nasir Khusraw had noted earlier, who received a fixed salary from the caliph according to rank so that they would not have to steal or raid villages to support themselves. Even though the traveller has proven himself a fastidious chronicler of details, it is difficult to imagine how nearly 200,000 soldiers and animals of war could march down the streets. Could the text be saying that these numbers represent the total number of these contingents present in Cairo in service to the caliph, or are these the numbers who actually marched in the parade?

'But let us return to our account of the opening of the canal.' Following behind the horses, howdahs and the military groups, walk 300 Daylamites (Persians from just south of the Caspian Sea) 'wearing Byzantine goldspun cloth with cummerbunds and wide sleeves, as is the fashion in Egypt.' Right behind the Daylamites rides the caliph himself, mounted on a camel and dressed in pristine white. The caliph's camel, however, is unadorned: it has a plain saddle and a bridle and reins with no gold, silver, or studded jewels. The caliph does wear a wide cummerbund with matching turban, the cummerbund so fabulous that it alone is valued at 10,000 dinars. Only one other rider accompanies the caliph, bearing the royal parasol over the caliph's head. The parasol-bearer wears a gold turban with jewels and suit of clothing worth 10,000 dinars. The parasol itself 'is extremely ornate and studded with jewels and pearls.' To the right and left of the caliph march thurifers, wafting incense of ambergris and aloe. As the caliph passes, 'it is the custom here,' the Persian writes, 'for the people to prostrate themselves and say a prayer.' Behind the caliph follow the grand vizier and the chief justice, accompanied by 'a large contingent of religious and government officials.'

When the caliph arrives at the top of the canal, he remains seated on his camel for some time (one can only imagine how

1. al-Aqsa Mosque, Dome of the Rock, exterior, Jerusalem (Creswell Photographic
Archive, Ashmolean Museum, Oxford, neg. C.1406)

2. The world's oldest university, the Mosque of al-Azhar, founded by the Fatimids, Cairo (H. Halm Collection)

3. The Mosque of al-Hakim, Cairo (J. Bloom Collection)

4. Bab al-Futuh, the Gate of Victories, one of three Fatimid gates, Cairo (Creswell Photographic Archive, Ashmolean Museum, Oxford, neg. C.3623)

5. Bab al-Nasr, the Gate of Victory, one of three Fatimid gates, Cairo (H. Halm collection)

long it takes to settle a crowd like this). When all is ready and the moment decided,

He is then handed a spear, which he throws at the dam. Men quickly set to work with picks and shovels to demolish the dam, and the water, which has built up on the other side, breaks through and floods the canal (*S,* 50).

The day of the Festival of the Opening of the Canal brings the entire city, 'the whole population of Old and New Cairo,' together. The first ship that sails into the canal is filled with deaf-mutes, a custom even he finds unusual; he suggests that the Egyptians must consider the deaf-mutes a lucky token for, besides riding on the first ship into the canal, they also receive alms directly from the caliph on this day.

### THE AZURE WHEEL OF HEAVEN

In Chapter Three we looked at the first section of Nasir Khusraw's poem (*Divan*: 64) which I have entitled 'The Azure Wheel of Heaven,' and saw how he criticised those who blame fate or the stars for their misfortunes. We left that poem with the poet's challenge that if people would gain knowledge they could take the wheel of fortune into their own hands.

In the next lines, the poet launches into a criticism of the demeaning job of court poets, who use their art to weave the praise of unworthy kings, telling beautiful lies for worldly wealth. Court poets in his day were held in high esteem and were often paid handsomely for their ability to, as we would say today, put the spin on delicate or uncomfortable situations, such as advising the king against a foolish course of action or bringing news of the death of a favourite slave. Poets were paid to present truth and lies in a palatable manner. They were especially rewarded for ornate, splendiferous praises of the king. Nasir reserves explicit condemnation of the famous poet 'Unsuri, panegyrist to Mahmud of Ghazna, and praises the pious lives of two companions of the Prophet, 'Ammar and Bu Zar, as more appropriate subjects for panegyric honour.

The panegyrists deceive themselves, the critic from Khurasan declares, in thinking that because they are master wordsmiths they are nearer to the knowledge and wisdom which leads to salvation in the next world. These professional flatterers misuse and abuse words, the very building blocks of poetry, words which should be used instead in the cause of knowledge and truth. He alludes to the Ismaili doctrine that words are merely external expressions, and that just as Moses gave the inner meaning of the scriptures to Aaron, so too did the Prophet Muhammad give esoteric wisdom to 'Ali and his descendants. Samiri, the one who fashioned the golden calf while Moses was away receiving God's messages, but was unable to compete against Moses once the message and its meaning had been delivered, exemplifies the ultimate futility and hollowness of worldly prizes. Nasir likens the court poets to slaves, in contrast to their own exalted view of themselves, and points out that even musicians (who were looked down upon) were allowed to sit in court while the orating poet would have to stand. Nasir Khusraw also ridicules the ornate vocabulary of the court poets, with its tulips and roses, beloveds as beautiful as the moon, fragrant curling tresses, and so on. He finishes his bombardment with a personal flourish against the poet laureate 'Unsuri and a declaration of not only his refusal to debase himself in this genuflection of art but also his refusal to debase the Persian language.

> O brother, do not count too heavily as knowledge
>     the arts of writing and poetry,
>
> Which are professions well placed
>     for acquiring worldly wealth and fame.
>
> But it is something else entirely, another road, another science,
>     to acquire the comfort of the other world.
>
> True, both of these use words and speech,
>     but every magic spell is not a revelation.
>
> Even though the partridge and the falcon both are birds,
>     the partridge holds no danger for the falcon.
>
> The Prophet gave the knowledge of truth
>     to the one most deserving of this honour,

Just as Moses gave our Aaron the Qur'an
    and Samiri had no power to tamper with it.[23]

You have the script, which captures and enchains the
    sciences,[24] your mind is strong, like chains on army horses.

But, rope in hand, you go on foot before the riders,
    suited for nothing more than being a slave.

Know that by this slavish act you have become the slave
    of the king of Shughnan and the prince of Mazandaran.

You may indeed have chosen the life of a professional poet
    but another has chosen to be a musician.

Yet he gets to sit, while you have to stand;
    better to cut out your slithering tongue.

How many more times will you describe a box-tree or tulip,
    or a moon-like face, or fragrant, curly locks?

With knowledge and worth you compose praises for
    one who personifies ignorance and corruption.

You embellish lies into poems, all in your greed for money,
    but lies are the financial capital of heresy.

With such saints around like 'Ammar and Bu Zar,
    is it right to sing the praises of Mahmud as 'Unsuri does?

Well, I, for one, refuse to throw at the feet of swine
    this precious pearl – the Persian language.

As the poem now moves toward the finale, Nasir offers advice
for living properly and for gaining the knowledge that will per-
mit taking the wheel of Heaven into one's hand. This repetition
of theme gives the poem a cohesiveness and reminds the reader
of the consistent message of the poem. Having separated himself
morally from professional poets who write for money by praising
kings and princes great only in worldly affairs, he now describes
how one should choose a suitable master, one who is truly worthy
of praise. For Nasir that could only be the Imam of the Time, the
Caliph al-Mustansir, descendant of the Prophet Muhammad and

'Ali, the hero of Khaybar. The poet's reference to rings, amulets and armbands in this section can be taken both literally and metaphorically. Possibly he gives clues here about the items that were worn to declare one's allegiance to the Fatimids or to seek protection in battle. Rings, armbands, yokes and shackles all depict round-shaped items which bind one to another. The poem ends with the signature in the conventional praise of the poet's own skill and talent.

I shall guide you – whose yoke to put on,
    to whom to bow like the swaying cypress tree.

A wise man will only bow before the one whom
    God has chosen of all creatures to be the Guide;

Someone whose works of justice have wiped out
    all forms of oppression from the face of the earth.

That is, the Imam of the Time, whose followers
    are never deceived, even by the sorcery of Samiri.

There is no doubt that his wisdom for all mankind
    bears no fault but that his magnanimity surpasses all!

If you wish to sit in the highest seat of honour by dint of intellect,
    you must have Mars in your signet ring.

Go to the Imam whose father's writing is like an amulet
    for the good of the people of Khaybar.

Look, if you need, how you can see in his outward form
    the inner essence and character of 'Ali, Haydar.

But the exoterist cannot possibly regard it,
    for the light of his knowledge sorely wounds his eyes.

If the exoterist were truly searching to become human,
    he would rid himself of such asinine ideas through prayer.

But no one wise would consider you a cow
    if you're searching after the wisdom of Baqir.[25]

How can he think me a donkey just like himself,
    that my ring resembles a heavy yoke?

He doesn't see all my poetry and prose before him,
    how it transforms everyday paper into brocade.

Read each of my two *Divans*, and you will see
    'Unsuri made one with Buhturi.[26]

# CHAPTER NINE

# Mecca, City of Pilgrimage

There is a correlation between pilgrimage and prayer.

*Wajh-i din*, 262

Pilgrimages to Mecca had been going on long before the Prophet Muhammad brought the message of Islam to the Arabian peninsula in the seventh century CE. Here in Mecca could be found the first sanctuary, built by Abraham, to worship the one God. Here were the two hills between which Abraham's outcast wife Hagar ran desperately seeking water for their son Ishmael (Ismail). Here was the well of Zamzam that miraculously sprang forth to save her and the child, a well so celebrated it is mentioned in Psalm 84: 'How amiable are thy tabernacles, O Lord of hosts! Blessed are they that dwell in Thy house ... who passing through the valley of Baca [the ancient name of Mecca] make it a well ...'

A great economy built up around the steady stream of traffic to these sacred spots in the Hijaz, the region bordering the Red Sea. Once a year, all tribal and clan bickering would cease for the pilgrimage month in order to allow safe passage from all corners of the peninsula to Mecca. They came to conduct rituals centred around the Ka'ba, a large cubic structure erected on the site of Abraham's sanctuary and containing within it a sacred black stone. Over the centuries, the sanctuary became the home to over 365 separate gods, their statues venerated by the polytheistic Arabs. The Prophet Muhammad's reform was to cleanse the sanctuary of these gods and call the people to a clear understanding of the

absolute oneness of God. 'There is no god but God' is the first
article of faith for all Muslims. In his effort to restore religion to
its Abrahamic purity, Muhammad, and especially his immediate
successors, had to press home the point that this re-formation of
God's original religion surpassed all clan gods, all tribal loyalties,
all family allegiances, and transcended even national, cultural and
linguistic differences. Besides removing the gods of the pagan 'days
of ignorance,' Muhammad also called on Christians and Jews to
return to the true root of their religions. In the Qur'an (22:26–
27), God explains how Abraham founded the pilgrimage to this
first sanctuary, the Ka'ba:

> And when We settled for Abraham the place
> of the House: 'Thou shalt not associate
> with Me anything. And do thou purify
> My House for those that shall go about it
> and those that stand, for those that bow
> and prostrate themselves;
> and proclaim among men the Pilgrimage,
> and they shall come unto thee on foot
> and upon every lean beast, they shall come from
> every deep ravine ...'

With this, the pilgrimage to God's House in Mecca was legitimised as a sacred ritual for Muslims, those who would agree to
submit to one God and to accept Muhammad as His prophet and
messenger. Because it was such an arduous and expensive endeav-
our, often taking years of travel, the greater pilgrimage to Mecca,
the *hajj*, is a 'recommended' ritual, obligatory to a Muslim only 'if
he is able to make his way there' (Qur'an, 3:97). Those who are
able to complete the *hajj* are honoured for the rest of their lives
and called 'Hajji,' but no one is penalised or shamed for not being able to go.

The *hajj* itself consists of certain prescribed rites which require
several days to complete in and around Mecca on particular days
during the month of Dhu'l-Hijja. The 'lesser pilgrimage' (*'umra*),
also in Mecca, can be conducted day or night at any time of year,
and its rituals take less than two hours to fulfil.

The *hajj* proper begins with a declaration of intent to complete the pilgrimage and a literal change of clothes to signify the transformation of the pilgrim into a state of consecration. Regular clothes are set aside and the pilgrim's clothing, the *ihram*, consisting of two seamless, white pieces of cloth, is put on. Once in this consecrated state, certain profane acts are forbidden to the pilgrim, such as cutting nails or hair, hunting or killing, or having sexual relations. The pilgrim thus consciously and visibly enters a state of internal and external purity. 'Putting on the *ihram*' is done at various places in the approach to Mecca, ranging anywhere from 30 to over 100 miles away. In the *Wajh-i din*, Nasir says that in his time there were four of these places.

The stages of the greater pilgrimage proceed in basically the following manner, with minor modifications according to different schools. The pilgrim man or woman arrives in Mecca in a formal and psychological state of *ihram*, performs the ritual ablution, and pronounces the declaration known as *labbayka*, meaning 'Here I stand, Lord, at Thy service!' The pilgrim circumambulates the Ka'ba, walking seven times around, and, if possible, approaching and kissing the Black Stone. At the Station of Abraham, said to contain an imprint of Abraham's foot, he or she performs a prayer of two *rak'ats*. The pilgrim drinks water from the Zamzam spring, and then proceeds to walk seven times between the hills of Safa and Marwa, honouring Hagar's desperate search for water for herself and her son Ishmael. On the 9th day of the month of Dhu'l-Hijja, the pilgrim joins the crowd for the 'standing' prayers at the plain of 'Arafat, usually lasting from noon to sunset. The *labbayka* prayer is uttered frequently, each time reconfirming the pilgrim's commitment to God. The 10th of the month is a day of sacrifice, commemorating the exchange of a ram for Ishmael as Abraham's sacrifice to God. It is also the day to cast stones at three pillars representing the three times Satan appeared to the boy Ishmael warning him of Abraham's sacrificial intent, and the three times Ishmael stoned Satan out of obedience to his father and God.

Nasir Khusraw describes the minor pilgrimage in the *Safarnama* as follows:

For people who have come from faraway places to perform the minor pilgrimage, there are milestones and mosques set up half a parasang away from Mecca, where they bind their *ihram*. 'To bind the *ihram*' means to take off all sewn garments and to wrap an *izar*, or seamless garment, about the waist and another about the body. Then, in loud voice, you say, '*Labbayk, alla-humma, labbayk,*' and approach Mecca. When anyone already inside Mecca wants to perform the minor pilgrimage, he goes out to one of the markets, binds his *ihram*, says the *labbayk* and comes back into Mecca with an intention to perform the minor pilgrimage. Having come into the city, you enter the Haram Mosque, approach the Ka'ba, and circumambulate to the right, always keeping the Ka'ba to your left. Then you go to the corner containing the Black Stone, kiss it, and pass on. When the Stone is kissed once again in the same manner, one *tawf*, or circumambulation, has been completed. This continues for seven *tawf*s, three times quickly and four slowly. When the circumambulation is finished, you go to Maqam Ibrahim [Station of Abraham] opposite the Ka'ba and stand behind the Station. There you perform two *rak'ats* called the 'circumambulation prayer.' Afterwards you go to the Well of Zamzam, drink some water, or rub some on the face, and leave the Haram Mosque by the Safa' Gate. Just outside this gate are the steps up Mount Safa', and here you face the Ka'ba and say the prescribed prayer, which is well known. When the prayer has been said, you come down from Safa' and go from south to north through the bazaar to Marwa. Passing through the bazaar, you go past the gates to the Haram Mosque where the Prophet ran and commanded others to run also. The length is about fifty paces, and on either side are two minarets. When the people coming from Safa' reach the first two minarets, they break into a run until they pass the other two at the other end of the bazaar. Then they proceed slowly to Marwa. Upon reaching the end they go up Marwa and recite the prescribed prayer. Then they return through the bazaar and repeat the run until they have gone four times from Safa' to Marwa and three times from Marwa to Safa', making seven runs the length of the bazaar. Coming down from Marwa the last time, you find a bazaar with about twenty barbershops facing each other. You have your head shaven and, with the minor pilgrimage completed, come out of the Sanctuary (*S*, 68–9).

## THE PILGRIMAGES OF NASIR KHUSRAW

From his own account, Nasir made four pilgrimages to Mecca. The first he undertook from Jerusalem even before his arrival in Cairo. The remaining three were all in the service of the Fatimid caliph, with the last becoming the first leg of his return journey to Balkh. In the *Safarnama*, when he is writing about Jerusalem, he declines to describe the details of his trip to Mecca, explaining, 'I will describe it all under my last pilgrimage,' giving further proof that the book was compiled later and is not merely his day-to-day journal. In fact, he retains this position throughout, telling the reader of sights along the way for the first three journeys, mentioning Mecca somewhat, but saving the major description of the city and the actual pilgrimage rituals for the fourth.

For example, in his few sentences about the first pilgrimage, Nasir provides a number of points which hint at the physical experience of the journey. He set out on foot in the middle of Dhu'l-Qa'da 438/May 1047 with a group headed by a guide, also travelling on foot, named Abu Bakr Hamdani, 'a strong, pleasant-featured man.' The travellers arrived in Mecca in something less than three weeks and were back in Jerusalem by 5 Muharram/2 July, having stayed in Mecca itself for only two days. He gives two explanations as to why they hurried to leave. 'That year there were no caravans from anywhere, and foodstuffs were not to be found.' In addition, perhaps as a result of the lack of food and pilgrim traffic, 'the people were in danger of marauding Arabs,' especially during some of the exposed portions of the pilgrimage itself, such as the standing and praying on the plain of 'Arafat (*S*, 37).

The next year, when Nasir was securely ensconced in the higher levels of the Fatimid court in Cairo, a severe drought and famine again kept many away from Mecca, and 'people were fleeing the Hijaz in every direction.' Even the Fatimid caliph in Egypt, who was accustomed to outfitting an enormous official caravan with soldiers, horses, camels, slaves and supplies to protect pilgrims and to deliver the annually embroidered covering for the Ka'ba, warned the people away and issued the following edict:

The Prince of the Faithful proclaims that in this year, owing to drought and the resulting scarcity of goods, which has caused the deaths of many, it is unwise for pilgrims to undertake the journey to the Hijaz. This we say in Muslim commiseration (S, 59).

While thus discouraging a multitude from embarking on the pilgrimage, the Caliph-Imam nevertheless wished to fulfil his twice-yearly commitment to send the drapery for the Ka'ba. Nasir went along on this trip with the official retinue, attracted by the prospect of a new adventure, an ocean voyage. 'Because the covering was being sent via the Red Sea, I went along.' After a fifteen-day journey by boat, they landed on the Arabian peninsula at the port of al-Jar and then travelled four days overland to Medina, the city of the Prophet, where they stayed for two days. Nasir Khusraw describes the Prophet's Mosque, which is built around his tomb. The tomb itself is pentagonal, he notes, with a traditional grating surrounding it and a railing so that no one can go in. There is even a net across the top to prevent birds from getting in. When worshippers are facing front, toward the *qibla*, the tomb is to the left and the pulpit is to the right, 'so, when the preacher mentions the Prophet from the pulpit, he turns to his right and points to the tomb.' Such generous detail is given solely to help the reader visualise the setting. Heading south for Mecca, they come upon the narrow mountain pass named Juhfa about 110 miles from Mecca, one of the traditional sites for putting on the *ihram*. Nasir Khusraw learns that one year a great number of pilgrims had stopped there and were donning the pilgrim garments 'when suddenly a flashflood swept down and killed them all, which is why it is called Juhfa,' meaning 'sweeping away.'

From Juhfa, it took eight more days to reach Mecca where they witnessed the effects of the drought. Not only were scarcely any pilgrims arriving that year, but even the pious *mujawirs* (those who choose to stay and live in Mecca, close to the centre of faith) were leaving. Bread could only be obtained at exorbitant cost (one Nishapuri dinar for four maunds, Nasir notes). His group arrived on Sunday and left on Friday, hurriedly completing both the *hajj* rituals and the royal duty of delivering the gifts and Ka'ba coverings. When they returned home, even more evidence of the drought's devastation awaited them: over 35,000 refugees had streamed into Egypt from the Hijaz seeking the help of the Fatimid state. The caliph fed and clothed them and provided them some funds until the next year, 'when the rains came and food was once again plentiful enough in the Hijaz to support these people. The caliph gave them all clothing and gifts and sent them back home.'

Well, perhaps he sent them back too soon, because the next year, at pilgrimage time, the Fatimid palace again announced that due to famine in the Hijaz, it was unwise to go on the *hajj*. To calm the believers, the caliph invoked Qur'anic verses (3:97) which indicate that one is not required to perform the pilgrimage if serious conditions exist, such as poverty, illness or, as in this case, famine.[1] But the caliph still had to send his embroidered covering for the Ka'ba, along with gifts for the emirs of Mecca and Medina, including the stipend for each of 3,000 dinars a month, plus a horse and a robe of honour. Nasir again was selected to accompany the royal mission, this one conducted under the leadership of a judge from Syria, Qadi 'Abd Allah. After crossing the Red Sea, Nasir mentions that because it was pilgrimage time, prices were high, and 'a camel could not be hired for less than five dinars.'

When they arrived in Medina, Nasir Khusraw and his company learned first-hand of the dangers awaiting pilgrims on the road. In one case, he relates that a large caravan had come from the Maghrib (present-day Morocco, Algeria and Tunisia generally) to Medina. At the gates of the city some Arabs demanded protection money and a fight broke out. In the end, more than 2,000 Maghribis were killed and, of the others, 'not many ever returned home.' Besides the emotional impact of this event, Nasir Khusraw's record also suggests what a 'large' caravan meant, even allowing for rounding up; if 2,000 were killed, how many more had been travelling with them and did not enter into the fighting? His account also brings home the serious consequences of a person's decision to embark on this sacred ritual. Depending on how far the pilgrim had to travel, the entire journey could take years and at every stage, even on the way home, dangers of illness, robbery and murder could end the trip in disaster.

In a second tragedy, Nasir himself appears to have spoken with the victims. A group from Khurasan had travelled by land through Syria, Egypt, and then by boat to Medina. Behind in schedule, with only three days to reach Mecca to perform the pilgrimage on time, they offered forty dinars to anyone who could get them to 'Arafat in three days. Some locals cruelly took them up on their offer; after taking the money, they tied each pilgrim to a camel and drove them non-stop from Medina to 'Arafat. Nasir Khusraw recounts how he was standing with the crowd at 'Arafat, performing the afternoon prayer, when the miserable troop arrived, 'unable to stand up or speak.' On closer inspection, they saw that two men had died, still tied to the camels, while 'the other four were more dead than alive.' When he could finally get his countrymen to speak, the four reported that they had begged the Arabs to stop, to keep all the money, and simply 'to release them, as they had no more strength to continue.' Their pleas were ignored and the camels driven onward. Nasir concludes, 'In the end the four of them made the pilgrimage and returned via Syria.'

While Nasir renders no moral verdict on what he has seen, we may be able to detect an emotional reaction on his part, if not a judgement, in the next sentence which states that he returned to Egypt because 'I had my books there and had no intention of returning.' He writes this even though both he and the reader know, and are anticipating, his final visit to Mecca when, in fact, he stayed for six months as a *mujawir* himself (*S*, 60).

The return journey to Egypt after this, his third pilgrimage, provides a glimpse of the high position Nasir had attained in the Fatimid court. Besides having accompanied the official visits from Cairo, now he travelled from Mecca in the company of the emir of Medina, most likely Taj al-Ma'ali b. Abu'l-Futuh, whom Nasir mentions later is also the emir of Jidda (*S*, 67). The emir was travelling to Egypt to collect his yearly stipend from the Fatimid caliph, which he was given because he was a descendant of the Prophet's grandson Husayn, son of 'Ali. They took a boat together north to Qulzum. 'From there we continued in each other's company to Cairo.' Whether we can surmise from this anecdote that the twice-yearly stipend paid by Cairo to the emirs of Mecca and Medina was presented once at Hajj time with the gifts coming from Cairo, and the second time in Cairo occasioned by a visit from one of the emirs, is not clear. Or perhaps the emir, because he had already received the gifts in this instance, was paying a courtesy call on one of his most significant benefactors.

### THE LAST PILGRIMAGE

Nasir Khusraw timed his departure for home so that he could leave Cairo immediately after performing the prayers for one of the two canonical festivals of the Muslim calendar, the Feast of the Sacrifice, Eid al-adha. It is a momentous day, the day he truly sets out for home, and he records the date, place and circumstances of his departure. He moves quickly into the role of guide again, pointing out the special features of each area:

I performed the prayer of the Feast [of Sacrifice] in Cairo and departed by boat on Tuesday, the 14th of Dhu'l-Hijja 441 [9 May 1050], bound for Upper Egypt, which is to the south and is the province through which the Nile flows before reaching Cairo. It is part of the realm of Egypt, and most of Egypt's prosperity derives from there (S, 63).

The teacher in him remembers to mention that Upper Egypt is to the south, 'upper' because it is more mountainous. Even though he pleads that there are too many towns and villages along the Nile to describe, he does refer to some of them. Asyut has two notable features: it produces opium and some of the finest woollens, 'unequalled anywhere in the world.' In his usual punctilious manner, Nasir explains how opium is produced.

Opium is derived from a poppy with a black seed. When the seed grows and forms a pod, it is crushed and a molasses-like syrup comes out. This is collected and preserved, for it is opium. The poppy seed is small and like cumin (S, 63).

He explains to his Persian audience that the 'fine woollens imported into Persia and called "Egyptian" are all from Upper Egypt, since wool is not woven in Egypt proper.'

At a town called Akhmim, with 'a fortified wall, many date groves and orchards,' he and his companions (including his brother) stayed twenty days because they 'could not decide' whether to take the desert route or the river route. They finally decided on the river and proceeded to Aswan.

Aswan represents the Fatimids' southernmost post in this area; a little way to the south begins the province of Nubia, 'the population of which is all Christian.' We noted earlier Nasir's report that the king of Nubia 'continually sends gifts to the caliph of Egypt and makes treaties so that Egyptian soldiers will not enter his land and molest the populace.' But Aswan itself is heavily fortified against attack from the south, with a permanent garrison for defence. They stayed in Aswan for twenty-one days, seemingly quite comfortable in a luscious island in the middle of the Nile, opposite the city itself. The island was 'like a garden, with date groves, olives, and other trees and crops irrigated by waterwheels.' Besides enjoying the comfort of this grand garden, they were also waiting for the next caravan to arrive from its journey across the desert between the Red Sea and the Nile so that they could join it for the return trip back over. During these days, with the wait for the camels, Nasir Khusraw befriended a man named Abu 'Abd Allah Muhammad son of Falij, 'a pious and righteous man [who] knew something about logic.' This man also knew something about camels, because Nasir sought out his help in hiring a camel, which they succeeded in doing for the price of one-and-a-half dinars. Nasir records his gratitude for this kindness as well as the letter of reference this man wrote for him to present when he reached the other side of the desert.

Once finally underway, while crossing the desert Nasir's scientific interest in water supplies and wells becomes personal, and the camels' capabilities underscore his appreciation of God's creatures. A little distance outside Aswan, they came to a stopping-place where a well had been dug and the 'water was plentiful but not very good.' Good or not, the next five days of travel would have no water ('you cannot stop just anywhere'), so each person had to draw a jar of water for himself. It seems the five-day schedule stretched into seven, before they finally arrived at the second water station, which consisted of a stone mountain with two entrances, caves perhaps, with water flowing inside. The water is fresh, he writes, but the entrances are too small for the camels to drink from, so someone has to go inside and bring out water for the camels, who had had neither food nor drink for seven days. During the seven days in the desert, they had travelled day and night, except for a few hours, 'from the time the sun got hot in the day until the afternoon prayer.' He noticed that it 'was almost as though the camels themselves knew that if they poked along they would die of thirst; they did not need to be driven and, setting their own direction, went of their own accord, although there was no trace whatsoever of a road' (*S*, 65).

The journey to the shore of the Red Sea took fifteen days. 'Aydhab, the town on the shore with a population of 500, belonged to the Fatimid caliph and functioned as a customs station for ships. The camels shuttled across the desert frequently, between 'Aydhab and Aswan, transporting goods in both directions. It was while waiting in port to cross the Red Sea that Nasir came into contact with the people mentioned earlier as the Bajawis, who frequently suffer slave raids 'by Muslims and others.'

In the tedious days spent waiting for the right wind to sail, Nasir was asked to preach to the local population. 'I obliged and acted as a preacher until the winds changed and the boats could sail north and on to Jidda.'

The preaching would have earned him a little money, but strangely after those months, he reports, 'everything I had was spent.' Nasir's poverty on the trip home from Cairo (mentioned here and further on) is one of the most serious bafflements of his travelogue. If he was travelling in the service of the Fatimid caliph, why would he so soon have run out of funds? His solution each time is to rely on his own wit and talent, but it is puzzling why he should have had to. In order to confront his lack of funds, Nasir 'of necessity' presented the letter from Muhammad b. Falij and was surprised at the generous response. 'The man acted very politely and said, "Oh yes, I am holding a great deal of his money. You may just sign for any amount you require".' Nasir was surprised that Muhammad b. Falij was so kind, having had no previous dealings with him. 'Had I been a rogue and of a mind to do such a thing, I could have taken a great sum of money from him by means of that letter. Anyhow, I took one hundred maunds of flour, which was extremely valuable there.' He signed the paper and the man sent it back to Aswan. 'Before I left 'Aydhab, Muhammad sent a reply that not only should he give me whatever I need from his funds, but if the man dipped into his own pocket to help me, that amount also Muhammad would repay, for the Prince of the Faithful 'Ali, son of Abu Talib, had commanded, "The believer does not hold back or take advantage".' Genuinely touched by the trust and generosity showered on him, Nasir finds a moral lesson in it and explains:

I have included this little vignette so that my readers may know that people can rely on others, that generosity exists everywhere, and that there have been and still are noble men (S, 67).

When the boat finally sailed across to the Arabian peninsula it put in at the port of Jidda, a large city with a population of 5,000 and a 'strong wall' that touches the sea. Nasir went to see his friend, the emir of Jidda, who happened also to be the emir of Medina, Taj al-Ma'ali b. Abu'l-Futuh, most likely the same prince whom he had accompanied to Egypt on the way back from the previous pilgrimage. 'He was generous enough to exempt me from the customs duties that would have applied to me.' The emir also helped him by writing a letter to Mecca announcing that Nasir Khusraw 'was a scholar and that nothing was to be taken from me.' All along his journey, we see evidence of Nasir's privilege and prestige in the Fatimid ruling hierarchy.

### DESCRIPTIONS OF MECCA AND THE KA'BA

Whereas Jerusalem is a city on a hill in the middle of a plain and Cairo rises from a rocky promontory with Nile waters on all sides, the city of Mecca lies 'low in the midst of mountains such that from whatever direction you approach, the city cannot be seen until you are there.' Nasir Khusraw figures the population of Mecca to be not more than 2,000 citizens plus about 500 foreigners and *mujawirs* (pilgrims who reside near a holy place for an extended period). The extent of the city itself is modest, measuring 'only two arrow-shots square.' Its focal point, the Ka'ba, 'is situated in the middle of the Haram Mosque, which is in the middle of the city of Mecca.'

Describing this physical centre of the faith and pilgrimage, Nasir Khusraw writes that the Ka'ba is a rectangular structure positioned lengthwise on a north-south axis, with four corners, four walls, a door and a roof. He records that the door faces east. Three of the corners of the Ka'ba are known by the direction in which they point (the Iraqi, Yemeni and Syrian corners), while the fourth is the Black Stone corner. He says the Black Stone is set within another large stone in one corner of the Ka'ba 'at about the height of a man's chest.' The space between the Stone and the Ka'ba door is called the Multazim. The door of the Ka'ba is actually several feet above the ground, 'so that when standing on tiptoe you can reach the threshold.' When it is time to open the door, a wooden staircase 'wide enough for ten men abreast' is moved into place and people climb the stairs to the door. He records the detail that the door is made of teak, a double door about ten to twelve feet tall, containing inscriptions in gold and silver. Two large silver rings from Ghazna (another detail he knows will interest his readers in eastern Iran) are set high above the ground out of reach, for ornamentation; the door is opened by smaller silver rings at normal height.

The Ka'ba is covered in cloth decorated with bands and medallions of embroidery in gold thread. He states that the cloth covering is white,[2] with two bands of embroidery which divide the covering into three equal segments. It was these richly embroidered fabrics which Nasir Khusraw helped bring to Mecca several times from the Fatimid fabric and embroidery workshops.

Praying inside the Ka'ba itself is especially felicitous. Nasir remarks that from inside one generally faces the door, 'although any other direction is also licit.' This is because the Ka'ba is the sacred centre and all directions are, in a way, actually looking out.

Nasir writes that within the walls of the Haram Mosque are four buildings: the Ka'ba, the well of Zamzam, the pilgrims' drinking place, and the structure for storing oil (to be used for lamps). The Station of Abraham, 'a rock that has two imprints of Abraham's feet,' has been set in another rock and surrounded on all four sides by carved wood 'worked as finely as can be imagined.'

He remarks that, as a precaution, this fine wooden covering is chained to rocks on two sides 'so that no one can tamper with it.'

Nasir arrived in Mecca the day before the first of the month of Rajab, a month for minor pilgrimages, 'a great season, like the Ramadan feast and the pilgrimage time.' Many pilgrims had arrived from the nearby Hijaz and the Yemen to perform the minor pilgrimage. He observes that since 'they are nearby and the way is easy, they come three times a year' to Mecca. As part of the major celebrations of the month of Rajab, the door to the Ka'ba is opened at sunrise everyday, a very special ceremony because during other months, even Ramadan, the door is only opened a few days a week, if at all. Worshippers stream inside the Ka'ba to say their prayers.

An Arab clan called the Banu Shayba holds the key to the Ka'ba. They function as servants to the House and receive a stipend and robes of honour from the [caliph] of Egypt. Their chief keeps possession of the key, and when he comes to the mosque, five or six persons accompany him. As they approach the building, ten or so pilgrims bring the stairs we have previously mentioned and place them at the door. The old man mounts and stands at the threshold, and to open the door, a man on either side of him holds back the brocade covering as though holding a great robe with which he has been vested. He opens the lock and removes it from the rings. A great number of pilgrims will have assembled at the door, and when it is opened, they raise their hands and shout in prayer. Since the voices of the pilgrims can be heard throughout Mecca, all know that the Ka'ba door has been opened and, all at once, shout in prayer so that a great tumult fills the city. Then the old man goes inside, with the other two men holding back the covering, and prays two *rak'ats*. Both wings of the door are then opened and the chief, standing at the threshold, delivers a sermon in a loud voice and invokes blessings upon the Messenger of God and his family. Then the old man and his two assistants stand aside from the door, and the pilgrims begin to pour in. Everyone prays two *rak'ats* and then leaves. This continues until nearly noon (*S*, 79–80).

True to his character, Nasir Khusraw looks carefully around the Ka'ba while the crowd is praying and writes that he 'counted the number of people inside when the building was filled to capacity and reckoned 720.'

### THE MEANING OF THE PILGRIMAGE

Nasir's great journey began in response to his dramatic acceptance of the Ismaili Muslim faith. In his *Safarnama* he tells us how, after the dream which woke him up spiritually, in which a male figure pointed toward Mecca, Nasir set out, announcing his intent to perform the *hajj*. He tells of the physical nature of the *hajj*: the months of hard travel, the tedious waiting in oases to assemble the caravans, the dangers from robbers, drought and famine. He details the rituals: the four places for donning the *ihram* clothes and how often the doors to the Ka'ba itself are opened. The *Safarnama* thus provides a record and recommendation for how to actually carry out the external requirement of the *hajj*.

But mere public piety is almost sacrilegious, near anathema, for Nasir Khusraw, since for him no religious obligation is really fulfilled unless the believer also understands the meaning of the act performed. In the *Khwan al-ikhwan*, he writes that the religious duties of the *shari'a* 'have been specified for the sake of those things which lie veiled beneath them' (*KI*, 282). Along with other Ismaili theologians, he taught the necessity of both the *zahir* and the *batin*, that true faith entails observing both its exoteric and esoteric aspects. The required acts must be performed, but they are not valid without a concomitant understanding of the inner meaning of each gesture. Likewise, however subtle and advanced one's understanding of the meanings of the acts of religion, this does not excuse the believer from the requirement of performing them. The *zahir* and the *batin* constantly inform each other in a creative dialectic, each deepening the experience of the other.

Nasir's philosophical books and poetry provide many passages with esoteric explanations (*ta'wil*) of religious phenomena. The *Wajh-i din*, for instance, contains an entire chapter devoted to the inner meaning of the *hajj*, from which the following section is taken, in which he draws parallels between the outer, physical acts of the pilgrimage to the Ka'ba and the inner, spiritual journey of the Ismaili devotee to the recognition of the Imam (*WD*, 262–6). For Nasir, even the verb 'to make the pilgrimage' carries a deeper connotation than merely going to a particular physical place such as Mecca; it is to go toward something thoughtfully, not rashly. It is to act with meditative deliberation and conscious thought, eschewing all haste and hurry in one's deeds; to pursue goals with reason and not, like beasts of habit, with reckless passion.

The Ka'ba is not only the focus of the pilgrimage, with pilgrims travelling from all directions toward it. It is also the focus of Muslim ritual prayers said at any time, anywhere in the world. Each prayer is said with the whole body of the believer directed toward Mecca and the Ka'ba. Nasir Khusraw points out that those who pray within the vicinity of the Grand Mosque built around the Ka'ba can actually be facing any of the four cardinal directions when they pray, but those far away need to have a niche (*mihrab*) set in the wall of their mosque to indicate the proper direction of Mecca. From this he draws his parallel between prayer and pilgrimage. That is, in prayer one turns one's face toward the House of God, and in pilgrimage one takes a journey, constantly directed over long periods of time, toward the holy house.

Thus, while any Muslim's prayer is ultimately directed spiritually at God, the believer faces the Ka'ba physically. For the Ismaili worshipper, who also faces the Ka'ba, however, this orientation is made spiritually through the Imam. Nasir writes that the Imam, as the focus of devotion for the Ismaili believer, thereby corresponds symbolically to the holy mosque itself. The *da'i* corresponds to the niche in the wall, the direction to turn to, for just as the niche faces the holy mosque, the *da'i* faces the Imam. Those who listen to the *da'i* receive that which he receives from the Imam. When far away from the Ka'ba, the believer needs a *mihrab* to point the way, but this need disappears in the vicinity of the Ka'ba. Correspondingly, when an Ismaili believer reaches a spiritual level where he has access to the knowledge of the Imam, that is, 'where the Imam pours knowledge on him,' he is no longer required to follow the *hujjat*s and *da'i*s, the senior dignitaries of the Ismaili *da'wa*.

It has come down through tradition, writes Nasir Khusraw, that the Ka'ba on earth corresponds to the Eternal House (*bayt al-ma'mur*) in Heaven, and the pilgrims circumambulating the Ka'ba correspond to the angels circling around the heavenly House. He explains that the *ta'wil* or esoteric interpretation of this tradition is that Heaven corresponds to the level of the Imam, in the sense that beneath the Heavens lie all the bodies of creatures while beneath the Imam all the human souls are situated. And just as the material property of men lies hidden inside their houses, within the house of the Imam lies hidden the spiritual property of the Imam, which is the knowledge of truth. The physical act of travelling to reach the Ka'ba requires provisions and beasts of burden. The spiritual analogy for provisions is knowledge, and the modes of transportation are found in the personages of the *hujjat* and the *da'i*. The stations along the road to Mecca signify the stations of knowledge which the believer achieves through taking action and acquiring knowledge. Each time a pilgrim leaves one of the stations (signifying his house, his current situation), it corresponds to his rejection of a false faith in order to arrive at the way of truth. For Nasir, this destination is 'the Imam of the Time, who is the house of the knowledge of God.' Thus we see again that while the Ka'ba may serve as the physical goal of all Muslims, the Imam and his knowledge are in fact the spiritual goal of the Ismaili Muslim.

There are four stopping places (*miqat*) for changing into pilgrim clothes along the way to the Ka'ba, which correspond to the four *hujjat*s who never leave the side of the Imam and who take knowledge from the Imam and transmit it to the common people. For Nasir, no one may reach the stage of receiving words from the Imam except through one of these four *hujjat*s, just as whoever wants to reach the Ka'ba has to pass through one of the four *miqat*s.

Nasir Khusraw defines the act of 'putting on the *ihram*' as 'when one puts on unsewn garments and bares one's head and does not approach women.'[3] This corresponds to the stage when the believer reaches the Imam and must not speak to another, signifying that he has set aside his own beliefs before he arrives in the presence of the Imam. His bared head indicates that 'nothing covered remains,' that he is not concealing or holding anything back.

Discarding the everyday clothes also represents the relationship of body and soul. 'Shapes of the body are a sign of the beliefs of the soul.' There is a moment, between removing the regular clothes and putting on the consecrated ones, when beliefs are exposed and vulnerable. But since 'nakedness should be covered,' the new garments are donned. The putting on of the new clothes thus relates to the twin acts of faithfully performing the exoteric acts of faith and aspiring to understand their esoteric significance.

During the ablutions, the pilgrim pours water over himself, which means, according to Nasir, that he accepts the clear knowledge and washes his soul (*jan*) with it. Then he performs two *rak'ats* of prayers, signifying that he attests to the status (*hadd*) of both the Imam and his deputy, the *hujjat*.

The physical and mental preparations being completed, certain acts become forbidden to the pilgrim, who has now entered into a state of consecration. These acts include hunting or killing anything, sexual intercourse, cutting trees, cutting nails, scratching oneself or removing lice. According to Nasir Khusraw, the prohibition of these acts is analogous to the prohibitions imposed on a believer who reaches the presence of the Imam, such as making oaths and declarations, asking forgiveness (*kasr kardan*), seeking manumission (*bizari*), taking someone to court as his own *wali*, and defeating someone in an argument.[4]

Nasir Khusraw then presents the *ta'wil* of rituals relating to the Ka'ba. Entering into the mosque through the door of the Prophet signifies the believer's acknowledgement that he cannot reach the Imam except through obedience to the *lahiq* (another title for *hujjat*). The Black Stone is analogous to the Imam's position as the *asas* (foundation), and the pilgrim's approaching the Black Stone signifies his submission to the level (*hadd*) of the *asas*. Circumambulating the Ka'ba in seven rotations signifies the believer's acceptance of the level of the first seven Imams. When he circles the house he sees the whole of it with all four corners, which signifies the believer's seeing the four *hujjat*s through whom one comes to know the Imam.[5]

The pilgrim leaves the mosque itself and goes out to the hills of Safa' and Marwa. Going back and forth between them seven times signifies the passage of the believer between the *lahiq*s and his staying, through the mediation of the *lahiqs* at the level of the first seven Imams. Running between the hills signifies the believer's struggle to open himself into higher levels of understanding, and their completion marks the end of the ritual and a spiritual change in status. Marking this change, the pilgrim then covers his head, 'signifying the moment when the believer passes by what is over him, finds the Lord of the Time [i.e. the Imam] over him in his own level, who commands him to hide his level from the unworthy.'

Emerging from the purified state of *ihram* makes lawful for the pilgrim those actions forbidden in *ihram*. For Nasir Khusraw this means that when the believer accomplishes what is required of him, a commandment is placed on him to call others to the higher levels. The focus now shifts from internal to external purification, and the believer moves back into the profane world, with this added responsibility of teaching others. Then he puts his own clothes back on, in accordance with the command that he take notice of all the external (*zahir*) and internal (*batin*) conditions which will now confront him. That is to say, now that the inner transformation is secure, the believer is equipped to integrate the exoteric and the esoteric, the physical and the spiritual, aspects of faith into a composite and balanced way of life for him or herself.

The completion of the pilgrimage is marked by the pilgrim making an animal sacrifice, eating some of the meat and distributing the rest to the poor. For Nasir, this rite signifies more than a mere physical meal; it is a meal suffused with spiritual significance. The acts of sacrificing and eating represent the believer's struggle against those of false faith. Sharing the sacrificial meat represents a public effort to bring others to the truth so that they can partake of it also. The pilgrim shares the sacrificial meat with others so that his opponents will come to believe what he believes, and so that they too can partake of the rich spiritual offering he makes to them.

Nasir Khusraw ends his chapter on the esoteric significance of the pilgrimage here, saying that, by the generosity of God, he has explained, one by one, each of the meanings underlying the vocabulary and ritual requirements of the *hajj*.

In his poetry as well, and taking, of course, more license for emotional expression, Nasir emphasises the importance of balancing the *zahir* and the *batin*. In one poem he points an accusatory finger at hypocrites who perform religious duties but do not adjust their lives to live ethically. For him, such a person is religious only on a superficial, *zahir* level. In the following lines, he declares that dishonest business dealings will not be washed away by ablutions from the well of Zamzam. He warns a merchant that his acts of selling linen for the price of silk and skimping on the scales are not hidden from God. For Nasir, acts of devotion must be reflected ethically in the daily acts of living.

> O you who have washed your face and head in Zamzam water,
>> made the *hajj* like men, and come back without a care,
> For more than forty years you've struggled,
>> given little, but didn't take less for yourself.
> You've used every kind of trick,
>> sold cheap cloth for the price of silk.
> When will all your sins be washed clean now?
>> Don't let this corrupt fancy for the world possess you.
> There is no doubt at all that the pans of the scales
>> are never washed clean by Zamzam water.
> While you may hide what you do with them even from yourself,
>> there is no such ambiguity before the sight of God.
>> (*Divan*, 130: 1–4, 8–9)

Nasir devotes one of his most celebrated poems to an exposition of understanding the inner, spiritual significance of the pilgrimage. In the poem, a caravan has just returned from Mecca and the pilgrims are being welcomed and honoured for having completed their difficult journey. Nasir goes out to greet them and finds a good friend among the crowd of returning pilgrims. Through a series of questions, he exposes and reproaches his friend for performing his pilgrimage only superficially, content with the observation of bare formalities. We can only hope their friendship survived his relentless critique, about which even he confesses, 'perhaps I overstepped my bounds.'

The pilgrims had arrived, with full honours and respect,
    grateful that with the kindness of God's mercy
They had escaped the suffering and hardship of the Hijaz
    and been saved from Hell and a painful punishment.
They had arrived in Mecca from 'Arafat, and
    asserted clearly the pilgrim's 'Here I stand, Lord.'
Having performed the *hajj* and all the pilgrim's rites,
    they now returned home, safe and sound.
I went out to meet them for a while,
    but perhaps I overstepped my bounds.
Among the travellers in the caravan
    was a dear friend of mine, gracious and sincere.
I asked him, 'Tell me how you managed it,
    to make this frightening and difficult journey.
'For until you returned, my thoughts have ever been with you
    and I have had no companion but sorrow.
'I am delighted at your completion of the *hajj*;
    there is no one like you in the whole land!
'Please tell me how you venerated
    the venerable sanctuary itself:
'When you wanted to don the pilgrim clothes,
    what inner intentions did you declare at that moment?
'Did you take as forbidden to yourself
    all that does not suit us?'
He said, 'No.' I said to him, 'Did you say "Here I stand, Lord,"
    with full understanding and reverence?
'Did you hear the call of God and, then,
    like Moses, did you answer it?'
He said, 'No.' I said to him, 'When you were
    standing at 'Arafat and close to God,
'Did you become a knower of God and a denier of self?
    Did the breeze of knowledge reach you?'
He said, 'No.' I said to him, 'When you sacrificed a sheep
    for the good of prisoners and orphans,
'Did you feel yourself within it first,
    and then see it equal to the killing of your carnal soul?'
He said, 'No.' I said to him, 'When you walked
    in the Sacred Mosque, just like the *ahl-i kahf* and *raqim*,[6]

'Were you safe from the evil of your carnal soul,
    the sadness of separation, and the punishments of Hell?'
He said, 'No.' I said to him, 'When you were throwing stones
    at the accursed demon,
'Did you throw out of yourself
    all your blameworthy habits and actions?'
He said, 'No.' I said to him, 'When you went to pray
    at the Station of Abraham,
'Did you surrender your inner self to God,
    in truth, faith, and utter certitude?'
He said, 'No.' I said to him, 'When it came to the time
    for circumambulation, which you ran trotting like an ostrich,
'Did you think of the angels
    who circle round the Throne of God?'
He said, 'No.' I said to him, 'When you made the run
    between Safa' and Marwa,
'Did you see within your own purity the two worlds
    and your heart become free of both Hell and Heaven?'
He said, 'No.' I said to him, 'Now that you have returned,
    is your heart bleeding from separation from the Ka'ba?
'Did you prepare a grave there for your carnal soul,
    just as if now you turned into decomposed bones?'
He said, 'Everything you've said about all this,
    I haven't known the right from wrong.'
Then I said, 'In that case, my friend, you have made no *hajj*,
    you have not become a dweller in the station of self-effacement.
'You have merely gone to Mecca, seen it, and come back,
    and bought the suffering of the desert with silver.
'After this, if you really want to make the *hajj*,
    then go and do as I have taught you.'

                                 (*Divan*, 141)

### SETTING OUT FOR HOME

In the end, for Nasir Khusraw a pilgrimage to a physical place
in this world must bear a symbolic correspondence to the greater
journey of the soul in faith. Islam is known to its believers as the
*sirat al-mustaqim*, the straight path, the middle road between

extremes, such as between asceticism and worldliness. Our poet asks:

> How long will you turn from the path, left and right?
>   Why not travel straight with this caravan?
>
> (Divan, 7:23)

This image of a journey and the provisions necessary for its undertaking echo all through Nasir Khusraw's works. Indeed, he named one of his major theological works *Zad al-musafirin*, that is, *The Travellers' Provisions*, a work he praised elsewhere as one of his finest examples of prose:

> The *Zad al-musafir* is one of my treasures;
>   I write prose like that, and poetry like this.
>
> (Divan, 177:56)

Even the very days and years of one's life are a journey, a path to be traversed to return to a spiritual home. The things of this world are to be approached cautiously, chosen wisely and applied creatively in preparing the provisions for the spiritual journey:

> This world is your bazaar; search for all your needs.
>   Do not return from the bazaar empty-handed.
> For if you fall ill and cannot leave your bed,
>   you shall never find your way to the bazaar again.
>
> (Divan, 180:51–2)

Nasir Khusraw ended his six-month stay as a *mujawir* in Mecca immediately after completing the major pilgrimage in 443/1051. On 9 Dhu'l-Hijja, 'after the preacher had left 'Arafat,' Nasir followed the crowd to the shrine of Muzdalifa and spent the evening there. 'It is customary to spend the holiday eve in this spot and then to proceed to Mina early the next morning after the dawn prayer for making the sacrifice.' The tenth day he spent at Mina where stones are cast at the three large rocks symbolising Satan, an act which he describes as 'a supererogatory act connected with the pilgrimage.' Then everyone leaves, he says, on the 12th of the month, some returning to Mecca to stay there a while longer, others setting out for the journey home. And so, 'hiring a camel from an Arab for the thirteen-day journey to Lahsa, I bade farewell to God's House.'

# CHAPTER TEN

# The Journey Home

> We are travelling through that which can be passed
> until there comes that journey which cannot be
> by-passed.
>
> *Safarnama*, 104

It is not clear when it happened. Nasir mentions nothing of it while he is in Mecca, but within a few months he is so completely destitute that he cannot afford to hire a camel, even for one dinar. He and his brother had left Mecca in the beginning of 443/ May 1051. By July, 'nothing remained in my possession except two satchels of books.' How had he come to this point?

The two intervening months were filled with 'enduring much hardship and suffering great discomfort' as they travelled toward the city of Lahsa (also known as al-Ahsa). They had hired one of the camels of the caravan of an Arab who led the group as far as his hometown, Jaz', where they were delayed for fifteen days waiting for another *khafir* (safe conduct) to take them on the next leg of the journey. Along the way to Jaz', they stopped in the 'wretched little town' of Ta'if, with its 'pitiful little mosque.' They passed mountains and rubble, small fortresses and villages. But we see no hint yet of pennilessness. As if to pass the time of the tedium of waiting, Nasir inserts an explanation of the role of the *khafir*s. The Arab tribes protect their grazing territory seriously and no stranger is allowed to pass through except with designated *khafir*s. 'Anyone who does not have a *khafir* will be captured and plundered.' Finally, after two weeks the leader of the Arabs with whom they had travelled arrived and Nasir and his brother took him as their *khafir*. After they had been travelling for a while, a tense moment occurred when another 'group of Arabs, thinking they had found "prey" (as they call all strangers), came headed toward us.' As they approached, they recognised the *khafir* as their own leader and 'they passed by without saying anything.' Nasir's fear was visibly relieved; 'Had he not been with us, they most certainly would have destroyed us,' he reports.

Nasir had previously shown his amazement at the camels' ability to make their way across unmarked desert. In Arabia now, he praises the people:

As these people travel night and day, without the slightest trace of a road visible, they must go by instinct. What is amazing is that with no indication or warning, suddenly they come upon a well (*S*, 86).

At the next stop, they again had to wait for days before they found two men who would take them to the next tribe. They paid them each ten dinars. In this way, they were passed from tribe to tribe, 'the entire time in constant mortal danger.'

The way was extremely difficult, with little water or food. 'Among one tribe, some seventy-year-old men told me that in their whole lives they had drunk nothing but camels' milk, since in the desert there is nothing but bitter scrub eaten by the camels. They actually imagined the whole world was like this!' Nasir has great trouble with the local food; this cosmopolitan traveller, who has been so open to experiencing foreign cultures and customs, still cannot bring himself to enter into the world of the Arab bedouins.

Along the way, whenever my companions saw a lizard they killed and ate it. The Arabs, wherever they are, milk their camels for drink. I could neither eat the lizard nor drink camels' milk; therefore, wherever I saw a kind of bush that yielded small berries the size of a pea, I picked a few and subsisted on that (*S*, 84).

The worst was yet to come. He and his brother had to stay four months in the decrepit town of Falaj in the middle of the desert.

Once a flourishing area, Falaj had now been reduced to warring camps of 'filthy, ignorant bandits' in an area only about a mile wide. The people produced very little food for themselves, since 'in those four months, I never saw five maunds of wheat in one place,' and even that was severely rationed.

I stayed four months in this Falaj under the worst possible conditions: nothing of this world remained in my possession except two satchels of books, and they were a hungry, naked, and ignorant people. Everyone who came to pray brought his sword and shield with him as a matter of course. They had no reason to buy books (S, 85).

Had our traveller been poor all along his journey but never admitted it? Had he been robbed but never mentioned it? No answer arises from the clues he gives us; nevertheless, here he is, poverty-stricken, yet unable even to sell his beloved books because he is surrounded by brutish, illiterate people indisposed to buying books.

One day, to occupy himself, Nasir used the red and blue paint he had with him to write a line of poetry on the wall of the mosque in which they were living. To his calligraphy he added an artistic embellishment, painting a branch with leaves winding up through the writing. The people were so enthralled that 'everybody in the compound gathered around to look at what I had done.' They offered him 100 maunds of dates if he would paint the *mihrab* in the mosque. He knew exactly how precious this offer was, and he explains from his own experience:

Now a hundred maunds of dates was a fortune for them. Once while I was there, a company of Arab soldiers came and demanded five hundred maunds of dates. They refused to give it and fought, which resulted in the death of ten people from the compound. A thousand palms were cut down, but they did not give up even ten maunds of dates (S, 85).

So he painted the *mihrab* and was paid in dates, as promised, 'and that hundred maunds of dates was an answer to our prayers, since we had not been able to obtain any food.'

But as the weeks stretched into months, the lack of food, the mindless violence, the lack of intelligent conversation, and the interminable waiting, all took their toll. 'We had almost given up hope of ever being able to get out of that desert, the nearest trace of civilisation in any direction being two hundred parasangs away through fearful, devastating desert.'

But when the caravan comes, they cannot afford it. The 200 parasangs to Basra cost nearly half the price of purchasing a camel outright. That was exorbitant enough, but because he could not afford even one dinar, Nasir had to accept an even more exorbitant arrangement, putting himself in great debt. 'Since I had no cash with me, they took me on credit on condition that I pay thirty dinars in Basra. I was forced to agree to these terms, although I had never in my life so much as set foot in Basra!'

The Arabs packed my books and seated my brother on a camel, and thus, with me on foot, we set out, headed toward the ascent of the Pleiades (*S*, 86).

### THE PEOPLE OF LAHSA

On the way north, the travellers stopped in the remote town of Lahsa, a town so isolated among vast expanses of desert that even from the nearest city of Basra 'there has never been a ruler ... who has attempted an attack' on it. Their stop turned into an extended stay. Nasir notes that what he records 'is told from my own experience and not from false rumours, since I was there among them for nine consecutive months, and not at intervals.' In contrast to Falaj, he leaves the impression that he quite admires the people of Lahsa for their administration, even though they 'were as close as anyone could be to irreligiosity,' because these are people 'who, one year to the next, never perform ritual ablutions.' Their claim to be Muslims and follow the Prophet, coupled with their conviction that certain external practices were unnecessary, would have been a challenge to this Ismaili missionary on his way to establish himself as the *hujjat* of Khurasan.

Indeed, Lahsa had a notorious reputation. One of its rulers, Nasir writes, once led an attack on Mecca and killed a number of pilgrims circumambulating the Ka'ba. These attackers also picked up the Black Stone itself from its corner and carried it away to Lahsa. This historical event, carried out by the Qarmatis in Dhu'l-Hijja 317/January 930, struck deep into the Muslim psyche, and was referred to with horror in contemporary and subsequent accounts.[1] Although Nasir shared this horror, his disdain for this act derives from his contempt for ignorance in general. He becomes especially perturbed when ignorance causes people to miss the main point, the inner message. These thieves he ridicules for foolishly believing the stone to be a sort of a 'human magnet' that attracted people, 'not knowing that it was the nobility and magnificence of Muhammad' that drew them to the Ka'ba and Mecca, and not the stone itself. Nasir explains further that 'the Stone had lain there for long ages without anyone paying any particular attention to it.' He thus ignores the pre-Islamic role of the stone and the Ka'ba, preferring to believe, along with most believers of all faiths, that true religion sprang forth only with the formulation of his own particular faith. But in any event Nasir repudiates the violence, the taking of the stone, and the misplaced zeal of the attackers.

Given his fascination with engineering, it is the walls and water systems of Lahsa that will first summon forth Nasir's praise and admiration. Four strong, concentric walls enclose all the outlying villages and fields. Inside the walls of the town, there are enormous wells, each one the size of five millstones around. 'A really splendid town is situated inside these fortifications, with all the appurtenances of a large city, and there are more than 20,000 soldiers.' He records that there are also 30,000 African slaves from Zanzibar and Abyssinia working in the fields and gardens.

Governance is particularly unique in Lahsa, with the city ruled by a group of six kings with six viziers, and 'all affairs are handled in mutual consultation.' A single throne accommodates all six kings, and when they are seated on their throne the six viziers sit opposite them on another bench. 'They rule in complete accord and harmony.' The kings are called simply 'lord' and the viziers 'counsel.' 'The ruler answers most politely and humbly anyone who speaks to him, and wine is not indulged in.'

The city's consultative method of government is directly re-lated to its religious views. 'When you ask the townspeople what sect they belong to, they say they are Bu Sa'idis. They neither pray nor fast, but they do believe in Muhammad and his mis-sion.' Abu Sa'id (after whom the people name themselves) was a Qarmati ruler of Lahsa who claimed ultimate authority on religious matters and informed the people they did not have to pray or fast. He also declared that he would return after his death, but warning, 'When I come again among you, you will not recognise me. The sign will be that you strike my neck with my sword. If it be me, I will immediately come back to life.' Nasir observes insightfully, 'He made this stipulation so that no one else could claim to be him.' Abu Sa'id instructed that six of his sons[2] should rule together 'with justice and equity and without dispute among themselves.' In anticipation of his re-turn, 'a horse outfitted with collar and crown is kept always tied close by the tomb of Abu Sa'id, and a watch is continually main-tained day and night for such time as he should rise again and mount the horse.'

Nasir especially admires how Lahsa's official policies have been established to help individuals. He reports that not only do the rulers take no tax from the peasantry, they take care of anyone who falls into poverty or serious debt until the person is able to take care of himself again. Those who lend money are not allowed to claim more than the amount of the debt. If a stranger arrives and wishes to set himself up in business he 'is given enough money to buy the tools of his trade and establish himself,' at which point he repays what was given. And 'if anyone's property or implements suffer loss and the owner is unable to undertake necessary re-pairs, [the kings] appoint their own slaves to make the repairs and charge the owner nothing.' The rulers also operate a number of gristmills where the people can have their meal ground into flour for free, and the rulers pay for the maintenance of the build-ings and the wages of the millers.

Even the currency of Lahsa is designed for the benefit of those within the city walls. In an arrangement designed just for the city, customers make purchases with uniform pieces of lead which are wrapped together in 6,000 dirham-weight units each. 'When paying for something, they do not even count out the wrappers but take them as they are. No one takes this currency outside, however.'

Palm-dates are a major commodity and in such abundance 'that animals are fattened on them and at times more than one thousand maunds are sold for one dinar.' In the meat market, 'they sell all kinds of animals for meat, such as dog, cat, donkey, cow, sheep, and so on.' The merchants place the head and hide of the slaughtered animal next to its meat so that shoppers will know which is which. Besides this shopping detail, Nasir also adds a sentence about the dogs. 'They fatten up dogs, just like grazed sheep, until they are too heavy to walk, after which they are slaughtered and eaten.' This is perhaps the only citation, anywhere, of the custom of eating dog meat among Muslims. The city also drew wealth from a sizeable export trade in fine fabrics and scarves, as well as the pearl harvest from the sea near Bahrayn, seven parasangs to the east, from which the ruler of Lahsa took one half of the pearls collected.

While, according to Nasir, no ruler of the large city of Basra ever attempted an attack, Lahsa did not escape the covetous designs of nearby bedouin chieftains. Nasir reports a conversation he himself had with one of these rulers, a man from Qatif (where there is 'a large town and many date-palms') who had once laid siege to Lahsa for over a year. While he was able to capture one of the protecting walls and 'wrought much havoc,' according to Nasir, 'he did not obtain much of anything.' In their conversation, the chieftain asked Nasir's opinion about trying another attack, 'whether or not it was in the stars for him to take Lahsa, as they were irreligious.' The bedouin's argument for an attack seemed hardly convincing to Nasir, for he did not see much difference in religiosity between the bedouins and the people of Lahsa, both of whom were 'as close as anyone could be to irreligiosity.' For Nasir Khusraw, both the Qarmatis, who neither prayed nor fasted, and the bedouins, who practised these religious duties blindly, were equally irreligious. When Nasir ends with, 'I told him what was expedient [for me to say],' are we to conclude that he answered positively, shrugging his shoulders at the idea of an attack, there being no great difference between them in his own mind, or that he tried to steer the bedouin away from such an idea, perhaps for the very same reason?

After nine months in Lahsa, Nasir and his brother continued their journey to Basra where, they felt assured, they could make connections to pay their debt for the hired camel and guide. They arrived in this city on the confluence of the Tigris and Euphrates Rivers on 20 Sha'ban 443/27 December 1051.

## THE LESSON OF THE BATHS AT BASRA

Founded around 16/637 as an army camp in the Arab Muslims' war against the Sasanian Empire of Iran, Basra was by Nasir's time an important hub in the maritime and overland trade routes and a major centre of Shi'i piety and learning.

Basra is situated between the Tigris and Euphrates rivers, at the point where they join to make one river flowing to the Persian Gulf. The ground there lies very flat so that the saltwater tide, coming in from the Gulf, reaches far inland. Nasir notices that 'the Tigris and Euphrates indeed flow so calmly that in places it cannot be determined which direction the water is flowing.' Many canals have been cut into this fertile wetlands area of southern Iraq, leaving numerous islands for planting orchards and palm groves.

During his stay in Basra, Nasir heard that once, at the mouth of one of the many river channels threading throughout the area, a huge whirlpool had developed that made it impossible for boats to pass through. Of all the ideas put forward to resolve this problem, the solution was finally found by a wealthy lady who ordered 400 boats to be built and then filled with date pits. When this was done, the boats were sealed shut and sunk in the whirlpool, allowing free passage for ships. This story is consistent with Nasir's habit of recording the strange sights and ingenious inventions he learns of in his travels. But at the same time, the story is remarkable not only for being one of the few times Nasir mentions women, but even more so for the suggestion it gives about waste products. How were such enormous quantities of date pits normally stored – in buildings, silos, or the open air? Were they used for anything else such as fodder or fertiliser? Who was in charge of them? How long would it take to assemble 400 boatloads of date pits? Nasir's vignette does not answer these questions.

But for Nasir and his brother, more immediate concerns pressed in on them, like simply taking a bath.

When we arrived we were as naked and destitute as madmen, for it had been three months since we had unloosed our hair. I wanted to enter a bath in order to get warm, the weather being chilly and our clothing scant. My brother and I were clad only in old lungis with a piece of coarse fabric on our backs to keep out the cold. 'In this state who would let us into a bath?' I asked (S, 91).

In order to be allowed into the bath, Nasir needed money. The only possessions remaining were his books but, loathe to part with them, he managed to sell his bag instead, for 'a few rusty dirhams.' However, when they presented themselves at the bath, the attendant

looked at us as though we were madmen and said, 'Get away from here! People are coming out of the bath.' As he would not allow us in, we came away humiliated and in haste. Even the children who were playing at the bathhouse door thought we were madmen and, throwing stones and yelling, chased after us. We retired into a corner and reflected in amazement on the state of the world (S, 91).

The two were now really in despair, evicted like beggars even from a bathhouse, and they still had to find a way to repay the camel driver his thirty dinars. 'We had no recourse save the vizier of the king of Ahwaz [a city further to the north in Iran],' a man known as 'a worthy man, learned in poetry and *belles-lettres*, and very generous,' who was now living in Basra. Nasir has to find a way to contact the vizier, and this he does through another Persian, 'also a man of learning.' His Persian connections work extremely well, for the vizier, 'as soon as he heard, sent a man with a horse for me to come to him just as I was.' But Nasir, 'too ashamed' of his poverty and ragged clothes, sought a delay in order to be able to show his own substantial level of learning and literary accomplishment. So he wrote a note of regret, saying he would come at a later date.

I had two reasons for doing this: one was my poverty, and the other was, as I said to myself, that he now imagines that I have some claim to being learned, but when he sees my note he will figure out just what my worth is so that when I go before him I need not be ashamed (*S*, 91, 93).

Nasir's plan works. The vizier immediately sends thirty dinars for him to have a suit of clothing made. He buys two fine outfits (probably one for his brother) and on the third day presents himself at the vizier's assembly. Nasir has only respect and praise for the vizier, 'a worthy, polite, and scholarly man of pleasant appearance, humble, religious, and well spoken.' Of the vizier's four sons, Nasir was especially taken by the eldest, 'not only a poet and administrator,' but an eloquent, polite and reasonable youth, 'wise and devout beyond his years.'

The two brothers stayed in these felicitous surroundings for several weeks. The vizier paid the debt to the camel driver ('May God thus deliver all His servants from the torment of debt!') and subsequently provided the travellers with even more generous gifts.

During his time in Basra, Nasir visited all the thirteen shrines dedicated to Imam 'Ali in the city. He notes that one of the shrines, named the Lady Mazin, was the house of Layla, a woman whom 'Ali had married while he stayed in Basra 'at the time A'isha was waging war against him.'[3] Layla was the daughter of Mas'ud Nahshali, and 'Ali stayed with her for seventy-two days. He also records that at the cathedral mosque of the Bab al-Tib Shrine, there is a 'wooden post thirty cubits long and five spans, four fingers thick, although it is somewhat thicker at one end,' placed there by 'Ali himself. Nasir Khusraw's visit to these and other shrines of Shi'i reverence may have been the spiritual high points of his stay in Basra but, true to his style, he gives no further information of their religious or historical significance.

Once their 'worldly condition had taken a turn for the better and we each had on decent clothing,' Nasir and his brother finally made a trip back to the bath in Basra. This time they were greeted as the gentlemen they appeared to be. Everyone stood up respectfully and even the scrubber and attendant hurried over to take care of them. Again, when they came out from the bath, everyone stood up and remained standing until they had put on all their clothes and departed. While they were dressing, Nasir overheard their conversation in Arabic, which the speakers thought Nasir would not understand. When the attendant helping them said to his friend, 'These are those same young men whom we refused admission one day,' Nasir responded in Arabic, 'You are perfectly correct. We are the very ones who had old sacks tied to our backs.' Nasir reports that the man was ashamed and quite apologetic about his conduct.

While the whole scene certainly gave Nasir and his brother great pleasure, and the contrast between the two visits to the bath could hardly be more extreme, Nasir draws a moral lesson from these events in his life. 'Now these two events transpired within twenty days, and I have included the story so that men may know not to lament adversity brought on by fate and not to despair of the Creator's mercy, for He is merciful indeed.' He himself must have been surprised at how quickly his fortunes changed. It is an important lesson – not to despair – one which Nasir would invoke many times later in his life. Here he shares it with the reader and with posterity from his own real experience that things can change from bad to good.

### SAILING ALONG THE COAST

Nasir and his brother left Basra by boat. Instead of travelling directly to Isfahan by land, they went down river and followed the coast of Iran in the province of Fars. In Abadan everyone disembarked; some bought carpets and others something to eat. That boat then shuttled back to where it had started from, and the group continued on another boat the next morning.

As the dawn rose, Nasir writes, something like a small bird could be seen far out in the sea. 'The closer we approached the larger it appeared.' Upon inquiring, Nasir was told it was called a *khashshab*.

It consisted of four enormous wooden posts made of teak and was

shaped something like a war machine, squarish, wide at the base and
narrow at the top. It was about forty ells above the surface of the
water and had tile and stone on top held together by wood so as to
form a kind of ceiling. On top of that were four arched openings
where a sentinel could be stationed. Some said this *khashshab* had
been constructed by a rich merchant, others that a king had had it
made (*S*, 96).

As the boat sailed on, this *khashshab* faded into the distance
and another one 'of the same shape' came into view. These giant
wooden structures not too far from shore served two functions,
Nasir records. The first was that of a lighthouse, to mark the shal-
lows so that boats would not run aground. At night, their lamps
encased in glass 'were lit for people to see from afar and take
precaution, since there was no possibility of rescue.' The second
function was also precautionary, to allow sailors to avoid pirates
who might be hiding close to the coast, and upon seeing them 'to
steer the ship away.'

They put in to the port city of Mahruban but could not sail
further south to visit the towns of Tavva and Kazarun because of
infighting among the local rulers. The port of Mahruban served
as a customs station and transportation hub between the inland
routes and the sea routes. Nasir was intrigued to find inscribed
on the pulpit of the mosque the name of a prince of Khurasan
from the century before his own time. He asked and found out
that Ya'qub b. Layth had indeed conquered this far south.

But they were unable to find safe passage out or to tour safely
further down the coast, and Nasir became 'weary of staying in
that town.' He must therefore have leaped at the news that somewhat inland lived a great and learned man, Shaykh Sadid
Muhammad son of 'Abd al-Malik. Nasir took the opportunity once
again to appeal as one learned man to another, and wrote to the
scholar, describing his sorry situation and asking him directly to
'get me out of there and into a safe place.'

Once again, Nasir's pleas were answered. 'Three days later thirty
armed foot soldiers approached me and told me they had been
sent by the shaykh to take me to Arrajan.' Nasir must have been
very pleased to be so 'hospitably' escorted to Arrajan, where

streams ran through the basements of every home making them very comfortable even in summer, and where gardens and orchards provided abundant food. Nasir met with other religious scholars in this town where 'the people there are of most every sect,' and he must certainly have enjoyed the discussions on dialectical theology and mathematics that he had with the leader of the Mu'tazilis there, Abu Sa'id of Basra, who he described as 'an eloquent man with some claim to knowledge of geometry and mathematics.'

From Arrajan, they continued northward, inland to Isfahan, through the mountains. Now back in completely Persian territory, Nasir continues to point out items of interest to his Persian-speaking audience in Khurasan. One was a narrow mountain pass called 'Cut by the Sword' (*shamshir-burid*), said to have been carved out by Bahram Gur with his sword. Nasir does not have to explain this historical figure to his audience nor recount his glories.[4] He simply continues on to Lurdajan and then to Khan Lanjan, two towns along the way to Isfahan. As his caravan passes under the gate to Khan Lanjan, Nasir notices the name of Tughril Beg inscribed over the gate. This is the same Tughril Beg, the Saljuq Turk who had conquered Nasir's homeland of Khurasan, evidently victorious even this far south and west. Nasir keeps his feelings about the Saljuq quiet, even allowing that 'the people of Khan Lanjan were remarkably safe and secure, everyone occupied with his own business.'

### INTERLUDE IN ISFAHAN

'Of all the Persian-speaking cities, I never saw a finer, more commodious, or more flourishing city than Isfahan.' It was fortunate, then, that 'the caravan was not going to leave for some time' and Nasir was able to stay in Isfahan for twenty days. This city which, 500 years later under the Safavids, would become Iran's capital, already showed signs of its importance.

Blessed with a 'delightful' climate and an accessible supply of underground water ('wherever one sinks a well ten ells into the ground, refreshing cold water comes out'), Isfahan was an important link in the caravan routes travelling between the Persian Gulf

and the interiors of Iran and Central Asia. 'There were many bazaars; one that I saw was only for money changers and contained
two hundred stalls.' The embroidery district itself had fifty 'fine'
caravanserais, each of which housed large numbers of retail merchants and shopkeepers. Nasir notes that the caravanserais, which
provided lodging for all the camels and other animals as well as
room for the goods of the caravans, were exceptionally clean and
extensive. As specific evidence he adds, 'The caravan we entered
with had 1,300 *kharvar*s of goods, yet there was no difficulty in
finding space since there seemed to be no lack of room or fodder.'

The city was secure from without and within. Its walls were high
and strong, complete with gates, embrasures, and battlements all
around. Within were channels for fresh running water. The walls
were so effective they were blamed for compromising the air within
the city and thereby causing stored grain to spoil. Someone nostalgically recalled for the traveller that, before the walls were
erected, wheat, barley and other grains could be stored for twenty
years without spoiling. In administration, the Saljuq conqueror
Tughril Beg had appointed as governor 'a young Nishapuri' who
had formerly served the Ghaznavids in Khurasan. Nasir admired
this governor's personal and professional style. 'A good administrator with a fine hand, composed, well met, a patron of learning,
well spoken, and generous,' this man had followed Tughril's orders not to tax the people for three years, and thus provided the
peace which allowed peasants who had fled the invasion to return
home and resume their lives. Based on his generous description
of the governor and their common Khurasani background, as well
as Nasir's access to people of power and learning, we can assume
that his account stems from personal meetings. The anecdote, it
should be noted, gives an example of how the court administrators
kept their posts even as the nominal conquerors changed places.

### THE SOUL'S JOURNEY

As we have seen, mere physical travels and pilgrimages had little
value for Nasir Khusraw if these were not accompanied by an
equally rigorous spiritual journey. The pilgrim must undergo an
inner transformation and not just experience a change of scenery.

But from what inner source does a person make the decision to embark on such a journey, with all its internal and external dangers? And what aspect of the human personality oversees the drive to continue on and to seek change?

Nasir Khusraw holds that within each human being is an individual soul (*nafs-i juz'i*) which directs the person's life.[5] For Nasir, it is this soul – not the intellect – which decides to seek knowledge, which directs both the person's intellect and senses, and which chooses between good and evil. It is this soul which will be saved or damned on Judgement Day. Since this individual soul is comprised of the same substance (*jawhar*)[6] as the Universal Soul (*nafs-i kulli*) it therefore functions in the same manner, that is, desiring perfection, moving toward it, assembling the tools necessary to achieve perfection, creating products that did not exist before, occupying the middle ground and moving between the intelligible and material worlds.

Having followed Nasir's journey to Jerusalem (where we analysed his philosophy of God) and to Cairo (where we discussed his philosophy of the Intellect), we now see him nearing home, which presents an appropriate juncture to discuss his philosophy of the Soul, thereby following his own presentation of the unfolding of the spiritual and physical realms.

Nasir Khusraw's doctrine of the Soul can be found in several of his prose philosophical texts as well as his poetry. In his *Shish fasl*, for example, he describes how the Universal Soul fits into the coming to be (*padid avardan*)[7] of the realm of being. He begins with God (*bari*), whose Word, the primordial 'Be!' (*kun!*), was the cause (*'illat*) of the Universal Intellect (*'aql*). As we have seen, the Universal Intellect knows perfectly, without the discursive act of thinking, and without motion. From the Intellect then proceeds the Universal Soul (*nafs-i kulli*).

The Universal Soul immediately realises that it is separated from God by the Intellect. The Soul is imperfect because it is separated from its real source. While, on the other hand, the Soul is perfect *in potentiality* because it is capable of the intimacy that the Intellect enjoys with God, it is imperfect *in actuality* because of its separation from God. However, the Soul desires to remedy this imperfection, and longs to reunite itself with God. As a result of this desire for perfection, the Soul moves to return to its source, a move that introduces the first motion into the cosmos. Nasir states clearly that the Soul's motion (*junbish*) was 'actually started by its attempting to attain its own perfection' (*SF*, 51) – a significant concept in its implications for human souls, given the connection between the spiritual and physical realms.

The Soul's initial motion begins the formation of the heavenly spheres and the revolution of the entire cosmos. Along with motion, time is also introduced since time is the measure of motion. From the movement of the spheres, the four elements are produced, from which develop minerals, plants, animals, and then human beings. Humanity is thus the pinnacle of all creation, which was stimulated originally by the Soul's desire for perfection. The optimism inherent in such a doctrine will be what sustains Nasir Khusraw, as we shall see, at moments when he feels despondent and sunk in despair.

In the *Khwan al-ikhwan*, Nasir explains the connection between the individual and the universal. He declares, 'individual souls are possessed of the universal' (*KI*, 103). That is, because each thing comes into being through the action of the Universal Soul, each thing contains some of the very same substance of the Universal Soul. This World Soul, then, runs as a thread through the whole fabric of creation. Sharing the same universal substance (*jawhar*), individual souls mirror the Universal in that everything, every creature, desires its own perfection and struggles to attain it. Plants struggle to grow and ripen to their fullest in order to reproduce and thereby continue themselves. Animals eat and grow and reproduce; in addition, they are 'animated' and move around. Human beings can perform all the actions of plants and animals but, in addition, can decide to use their intellects to make ethical choices in behaviour and to make things that have not existed before (such as silk which, Nasir points out, is produced by combining two species, the mulberry tree and the silkworm, to create a totally new product). The human intellect is thus one tool that the individual soul can call upon to perfect its world and life.

This philosophy that the soul is the driving essence of action is echoed by Nasir in several places in his poetry, as these verses show:

Drape your soul with intellect, like rich brocade,
Lest any learned man call you foolish.

*(Divan,* 83:6)

Your soul is king of your body,
Your mind the scribe, your intellect the vizier.

*(Divan,* 91:15)

But also in his poetry, he frequently reminds the reader of the transitory nature of this world, which is no more than a temporary stopping place on a more important journey:

This world is like a house along the way,
    where people pass through quickly, rank on rank.
Brother and father and mother have all passed through.
    How long then will you linger on this journey?

*(Divan,* 15:19–20)

Indeed, the true goal of every pilgrimage is to return home; the journey is incomplete if the traveller remains suspended in a state of flux. After making the commitment, enduring the hardships, and experiencing inner growth, the newly transformed person must eventually go home:

The world is like a two-doored house –
    one for the beginning and one the end.
You were brought imperfect to this place
    that one day you would leave here, perfected.

*(Divan,* 32:13, 21)

### GUIDING THE TRAVELLER HOME

It would take Nasir Khusraw and his brother another four months to reach Balkh, their caravan travelling through perilous roads plagued by bandits and shifting sands. Nasir has remarked several times about the dangers, as well as the security measures that had been established to make the journey possible. We have already seen how impressed he was by the lighthouses along the shores of the Persian Gulf and, back in Egypt, how the camels had known how to find their own way from well to well in the desert between the Nile and the Red Sea. In all the cities he visited, he took careful note of the durability of the walls and the quality of the water supplies, essential for military protection and physical sustenance.

On the final leg of his journey, we find him still sobered by the possible dangers that lie ahead. From Isfahan, they pass through desert and mountains to reach the town of Na'in, then on out to the desert district (*biyaban*). Because of the crucial need for water along the desert road, small towers had been built every six miles or so to collect rainwater in tanks. These towers provided not only water, but guideposts and shade, 'so that people will not lose their way and also so that travellers may stop and rest for a while out of the heat and cold.' But for about eighteen miles the terrain itself held its own unique terrors:

We saw great areas of shifting sands along the way. If anyone were to stray from the markers and wander into these shifting sands, there is no way he could come out again and he would surely perish. We continued past there, when brackish earth came into view, all pocked and pitted; this lasted for six parasangs. If anyone went off the path, he would sink in (*S*, 99–100).

It took ten days to reach the large village of Tabas, where 'water is scarce and agriculture minimal.' Tabas, however, is remarkable for what Nasir calls the security of the people. This 'security and justice' is exacted by the rule of its conqueror, Prince Gilaki, 'who had taken it by sword':

The people were so secure that at night they did not lock their doors and even left their animals in the streets, despite the fact that there was no city wall. No woman dared speak to a stranger, for if she did they would both be killed. On account of this prince's protection and justice there was neither thief nor murderer (*S*, 100).

Nasir's praise of the prince may be partly due to the fact that he and his brother (and maybe others of his group) stayed as the prince's guests for seventeen days. When they left, 'he bestowed presents and apologised for any shortcomings' and sent a horseman along with them for the next 253 miles or so (72

parasangs). As they travelled, the horseman told them of a tragedy he had witnessed in the same region, a story that fits Nasir's
interests exactly. Once they had been travelling when a band of
thieves attacked. To escape, several people threw themselves down
a canal well where they apparently perished. After the danger of
the attack was past, the people came to see how to retrieve the
bodies from the well. One of those who had jumped into the well

had a kindly father who came and hired someone to go down into
the well and bring out the body of his son. They collected all the
rope they had while lots of others gathered around to watch. Seven
hundred ells of rope went down before that fellow reached the
bottom. He tied the rope around the son's dead body and they hauled
him out (*S*, 101).

On 23 Rabi' II/22 August they reached Qa'in, a city having
not only strong fortifications but also a trench all around the main
city. Nasir sent Prince Gilaki's man back at this point, but could
not continue on immediately because of 'disturbances in Zuzan
occasioned by 'Ubayd of Nishapur and the rebellion of the head
of Zuzan.' The traveller gives no other explanation, seeming to
assume the reader will know of the uprising or perhaps deeming
it politic to refrain from judgement.

In his month in Qa'in, Nasir met with Abu Mansur Muhammad
son of Dust, 'who knew something of medicine, astronomy, and
logic.' He records this conversation on philosophy in which the
man quizzes Nasir on the universe and infinity:

'Outside the celestial spheres and stars, what is there?' he asked me.
    'Things that are inside the spheres have names,' I said, 'but not
anything outside them.'
    'What say you then?' he asked, 'Is there substance outside the
spheres or not?'
    'The universe must of necessity be finite,' I said. 'And its limit is
the last sphere. Indeed, it is called "limit" precisely because there is
nothing on the other side. When this limit has been realised, it
becomes necessary that what is outside the spheres not be like what
is inside them.'

'Therefore,' he continued, 'that substance, which reason must hold to be existent, is finite and ends at that limit. If it then be finite, up to what point does it exist? If it is infinite and without end, how then can it ever pass out of existence?' He went on in this manner and finally said, 'I have suffered much perplexity over all this.'

'Who hasn't?' I replied (*S*, 102).

The preacher must have been tired.

At the end of September, Nasir and his brother reached Sarakhs, which Nasir reckoned to be 390 parasangs from Basra, approximately 1,270 miles. They then passed through the caravanserais of Ja'fari, 'Amravi and Ni'mati, which are 'close together on the road.' On 12 Jumada II 444/19 October 1052, they reached Marv Rud, near the site of the fateful dream that first provoked his conversion and set him out on his journey. They were now coming close to home. It would be only a matter of days before their return to Balkh.

Khurasan at this time was under the control of Tughril Beg's brother, Chaghri Beg. Halting at one caravanserai, Nasir learned that another of his own brothers was travelling nearby in the company of Chaghri Beg's vizier. This other brother, Khwaja Abu'l-Fath 'Abd al-Jalil, was evidently one of those bureaucrats and courtiers who had successfully made the transition from Ghaznavid to Saljuq rule, a path Nasir had declined emphatically. Nasir's excitement to be getting nearer to home runs just beneath his words, 'Now it had been seven years since I had left Khurasan.'

When they reached the next stopping place, they saw a bustle of activity, as supplies were loaded onto animals and shipped out. Nasir's brother found out that the goods belonged to the vizier and immediately asked those standing around if they knew of a certain Abu'l-Fath 'Abd al-Jalil. They replied that one of his men was with them.

And immediately, a man came to us and asked where we were coming from.

'From the pilgrimage,' we answered.

'My master, Abu'l-Fath 'Abd al-Jalil, had two brothers,' he said, 'who went on the pilgrimage many years ago, and he still longs to see them, but no one he has questioned has had any news of them.'

Instead of revealing their identities, Nasir and his brother draw out this moment and accentuate its emotional impact by playing a practical joke:

'We have a letter from Nasir,' my brother said. 'When your master comes, we will give it to him.' A moment later, however, the caravan began to move, and we started to join it.

At this, the servant tries to secure the letter that he knows would make his master very happy:

'My master is coming just now,' said the fellow, 'and if he misses you, he will be disappointed. Why don't you give me the letter so I can give it to him and make him happy?'

Nasir's brother then relieves the tension:

'Would you rather have Nasir's letter,' asked my brother, 'or Nasir himself – for here he is!'

'The man was so overjoyed he did not know what to do,' Nasir writes. The message of their imminent arrival in Balkh was rushed on to their brother who, on hearing the news, returned from the entourage of the vizier 'and waited for us at the Jumukian Bridge' (*S*, 103).

Nasir Khusraw ends the record of his seven-year journey with these words:

On Tuesday, the 26th of Jumada II, 444 [23 October 1052], after having had little or no hope and having at times fallen into perilous circumstances and having even despaired of our lives, we were all together again and joyful to see each other. We thanked God for that, and on that same day we arrived in Balkh, wherefore I composed these lines of poetry:

> Though the toil and travail of the world be long
>     an end will doubtless come to good and bad.

The spheres travel for us day and night:
> whatever has once gone, another comes on its heels.
We are travelling through that which can be passed
> until there comes that journey which cannot be by-passed.

The distance we traversed from Balkh to Egypt and thence to Mecca and then via Basra to Fars and finally back to Balkh, not counting excursions for visiting shrines and so on was 2,220 parasangs. I have recorded my adventures as I saw them. If some of what I heard narrated by others does not conform to the truth, I beg my readers to forgive me and not to reproach me. If God grants me success in making a journey to the East, what I may see will be appended hereto, if God the One wills.

Praise be to God, the Lord of the Universe, and prayers be upon Muhammad and his House and Companions all! (S, 103–4)

# CHAPTER ELEVEN

# The World Turns Dark

His heart swells fuller with sorrow
than a pomegranate bursting with seed.

*Divan,* 208:4

Exactly what happens next is sketchy at best. While we have seen in the *Safarnama* that Nasir Khusraw was called upon several times to preach and teach in various places on his journey home to Khurasan, nowhere in that work does he refer to the life he was about to embark on as the *hujjat* of Khurasan, the head of the Ismaili missionary effort throughout eastern Iran, which included parts of today's Central Asia and Afghanistan. The only forward-looking comment he makes is the hope that someday, God willing, he might make a trip 'to the East' and record that journey also. Such a journey probably never came to be. The few details we have of the remaining portion of his life can be deduced only from his later poems, a few remarks he penned in his books on philosophy, and from the biographical references others have left of him.

As far as the kind of life he would live, we know that the active, expansive life best suited his character. That is, doctrinally and personally, he did not consider it either ethical or sufficient to acquire knowledge and then hold that knowledge within himself. This emphasis on personal responsibility for the expression of his faith led him to actively preach and call others to the truth. He saw two sources for this special vocation. One call came from God:

The Master Craftsman who made the universe entire,
    why does he call me and what does he want from lowly me?
Since of all the creatures it is me he calls,
    without a doubt he has a duty for me, his weak slave.

              (*Divan*, 46: 34–5)

The other call came from the Ismaili Imam of his time, the Caliph al-Mustansir:

He has made me shepherd over the flock,
    which I shall not abandon for another.
If you are not too drunk, my thirsty one,
    I will guide you on a path to the edge of a mighty sea.
And if you accept this advice I give,
    you shall be lifted from dark well to heaven's highest sphere.[1]

              (*Divan*, 130:32–4)

For Nasir Khusraw, the imperative to share knowledge with
those without such knowledge has its model in the intelligible
world. That is, the cosmic hierarchical interplay of Universal Intellect, Universal Soul and the physical world is reflected here on
earth in the pyramidal structure of the Ismaili *da'wa*, with the
Prophet and the Imam above and the lower ranks of preachers
and proclaimers below them. Within the Fatimid *da'wa*, teachings were transmitted in a descending order from higher to lower
ranks. In such a structure, each believer who receives knowledge
from someone above, either the Imam himself or an intermediary teacher, must then convey this knowledge and the benefits
received to others. From understanding flows responsibility for
action, and higher levels of understanding demand greater action. This continual give-and-take thus occurs at the highest
intelligible level (Universal Intellect, Universal Soul, and so forth),
at the religious or social level (prophet, imam, *hujjat*, *da'i*, and so
forth), and at the personal or individual level (teacher, student,
and so forth).

The life of an Ismaili *da'i* was often dangerous. The Sunnis,
with their Abbasid caliph based in Baghdad, had no doubt that
they needed to stop both the religious and political expansion of

Ismailism. They saw Ismaili preachers as political threats and often put them to death.[2] At the same time, the Shi'is of the Ithna'ashari or Twelver school did not always support Ismailism. There was a great deal in common theologically between these two branches of Shi'ism, but they differed fundamentally on the succession to the Imam Ja'far al-Sadiq (d. 148/765). The early Ismailis were also more organised and active in seeking to dislodge Sunni hegemony and establish a Shi'i political state. All Shi'is viewed the Sunni Abbasid caliphate in Baghdad as illegitimate. But while the Ismailis had achieved several visible successes toward their avowed political goal (such as Egypt in 297/909 and Yemen in 430/1038) and were interested in achieving more, the Twelvers would take a few more centuries; it was not until 907/1501 that Twelver Shi'ism became officially instituted in Iran as the state religion.

In spite of this opposition, many did convert to Ismailism because of Nasir Khusraw's preaching. Even today, over broad expanses of Tajikistan, northern Afghanistan and Pakistan, large numbers of people proudly declare that their ancestors, or their entire region, was converted by Nasir Khusraw. However, the full extent of the territory covered by his preaching is difficult to confirm. We have seen in his *Safarnama* how quickly he could traverse enormous territory and how successfully he dealt with the vicissitudes and perils of travel. He even gives us an indication that he carried out his Ismaili mission not only throughout the lands of greater Khurasan but also in the provinces closer to the Caspian Sea, specifically in Mazandaran:

> Though my roots are originally Khurasani,
>     due to my experience, excellence, and rank,
> The friendship of the Prophet's family and relations
>     have made me a Yumgi and Mazandarani.
>
> (*Divan*, 26:35–6)

### THE CALL OF THE PREACHER

The doctrines Nasir Khusraw preached were those of Ismaili Shi'i Islam: Islam, in that God chose Muhammad as His ultimate and final Prophet and sent His message to humanity through the heart and voice of Muhammad in the form of the Qur'an; Shi'i as distinct from Sunni, in that the Shi'is believe that the spiritual and political leadership of the Muslim community after the Prophet Muhammad passed to his cousin, Imam 'Ali – who was married to the Prophet's daughter Fatima – and then continued through his sons and descendants; Ismaili, as distinct from Twelver Shi'ism, in that Ismailis believe the eternal imamate is present and visible in the physical world in the person of a living Imam of the Time, belonging to a particular 'Alid line, rather than in a line of twelve imams ending in the person of the Twelfth Imam of the Ithna'asharis who went into 'occultation' in 260/874 and whose messianic return is still awaited.

Both Ismaili and Twelver Shi'is insist on the absolute necessity of an authoritative spiritual guide to interpret God's message. This guide and interpreter is the imam. While Twelver Shi'is hold that a class of learned clergy can act on behalf of their absent Twelfth Imam until he returns to usher in a new era, Ismailis believe that God would not leave the world without a living imam as God's 'proof' on earth and guide to the ultimate truths of religion.

Nasir's teachings also focused on the theological imperative of understanding the oneness (*tawhid*) of God. Not that a human being can understand God directly or comprehend His reality in any real or 'comprehensive' manner, for human beings cannot possibly get their minds around the immensity and uniqueness of God, but rather to understand the principle of divine unity and what it means. After attempting to understand *tawhid*, Nasir instructs, the believer must understand God's command or order (*amr*) for the world, with all its consequences for the creation of the intelligible and physical worlds. The believer must come to understand the relationship between the physical world and the spiritual world, the message of God brought by the Prophet Muhammad, and the inner meaning of this message conveyed by the Imam of the Time.

The believer must also express these beliefs in life. Whether in private acts, personal prayer, or public displays of faith such as the pilgrimage, Nasir maintains, the believer must look deep within his or her soul to fathom the esoteric meanings of such acts. He preaches both the necessity of performing acts of devotion and the inner changes that must follow on from the soul-searching performance of these acts. Unthinking obedience to dogma and superficial expressions of the outer rites of faith are invalid for him.

Nasir was well aware that his preaching activities on behalf of the Ismailis would put him at risk in the eyes of the political and theological authorities, especially the Sunni scholars. Nonetheless, he remained dedicated to his mission, buoyed by the deep conviction that his message provided sustenance for the spiritually hungry, its truth a shield against evil. One poem reflects this assurance in his calling:

> I am a shepherd for the Moses of our time, to a flock
>> which feeds on knowledge through the night of this world.
> No shepherd can go without crook or bowl;
>> my bowl is a book, my crook my tongue.
> When you come to me, you will eat the bread of divine law,
>> softened by the milk of my eloquence.
> O you who have thought my face ugly,
>> I am not at all what they think I am,
> I am a mirror. If you are ugly, I am ugly.
>> If you are beautiful, then my face and form are beautiful to you.
> Learn wisdom. Take me as your teacher.
>> Become a glittering sword and I shall be your whetstone.
> The hand of God of the world, the Imam of the Time,
>> has sown the seed of humanity in my speech.
> Come under my tree, if it be your desire
>> that I place you upon the branch of humanity.
> Like flowing water I am, freshening with my speech
>> the fields planted with wisdom in the garden of true religion.
> If the dust of demons should settle on them,
>> I shall wash the dust away with pearl-like words of wisdom.
> The devil can never disgrace me[3]
>> because my spear, with sharpened point, is fixed on him.
> My arrowhead is my speech, my arrow the pen,
>> my fingers a sufficient bow.

If my enemy is in the east, then from the west.[4]
I shall easily send my flying arrows into him.
                    (*Divan*, 97: 32–44)

## FLIGHT AND EXILE

Nasir Khusraw was correct in his perception that his enemies would persecute him on account of his preachings. As discussed above, one of the major topics of theological debate in his day was how to interpret the Qur'anic anthropomorphic descriptions of God's attributes, such as the image of God sitting upon His throne, which implies that He has an anatomical limb that can sit on a throne. For Nasir Khusraw, of course, such images fall within the external realm of the *zahir* and require the application of *ta'wil* to understand their esoteric significance, the *batin*. He protests that those who do not adhere to the superficial interpretation given to the masses are repudiated by those sitting in high positions of religious authority:

You say that some so-called jurisprudent,
    'His eminence, the imam of glorious Balkh,'
Has declared that the people shall see God
    seated on His throne on Judgement Day,
And whoever does not follow in this belief
    is an unbeliever, a heretic, and godless.
                    (*Divan*, 24:39–41)

In many places in his poetry he argues back at his detractors, often calling them Nasibis, a term for the enemies of 'Ali. In one poem that foregoes any traditional sweet prelude to springtime or the beauties of nature, he launches directly into a forceful complaint about the Nasibis, sarcastically contrasting these enemies of 'Ali's family with the Kafirs, the same term for heretic that had been used against Nasir Khusraw:

Is there any surprise that a Nasibi
Is not sated with heresy?
There is no surprise to find heresy in a Nasibi

Since you wouldn't be surprised to see a donkey act like an ass.
Nasibi, you ass, how long will you move on toward Hellfire,
Following after Samiri's invention.[5]
If you stand in Samiri's army, what good does it do you
To wear the Prophet's armour on your body?
Your Prophet's armour is Islam,
Your life secure within this helmet and armour.
But you have no use for this armour and helmet
Except for eating and sleeping here and now.
How do you expect to take the Prophet's helmet
Down to Hell with you, you miserable ass?
You call yourself Muslim in name, for sure,
But can't you see how you're lost in a well?

(Divan, 26:3–10)

Nasir speaks frequently in his poems of the intense opposition he encountered for his views and many of his verses reflect his struggle to make some sense of it:

What madness has taken over everyone,
    that they are so frightened, even of my name?
No one's reputation was ever ruined because of me
    and I have never stolen even a crust of bread.
No youth did I ever beat into senility.
    So why do young and old now turn on me in enmity?
No sermon did I ever seek to preach in Kashgar or Baghdad.
    So why do khan and caliph now malign me so?
If I'm so repugnant, of carrion and blood,[6]
    note how all my enemies have turned into ravenous dogs.

(Divan, 97: 5–9)

At some point – we do not know the year – the calumny and slander of his opponents became a serious threat to his life. The *Majma' al-fusaha* reports that the clerics and nobility called him infidel and heretic (*zandaqa*).[7] We have reports that he first came under serious criticism in Nishapur, from whence he fled further east to Balkh, where he again aroused condemnation. The *Tarikh-i Nishabur* (*History of Nishapur*)[8] relates that during his second visit to Nishapur, he encountered an already hostile situation since, based probably on the teaching and preaching he had conducted previously, 'the clerics and other scholars did not have a good opinion of him.' So, for greater security, he took up residence in the home of the chief justice and leading cleric (*imam-i buzurg*) of the city, Abu Sahl Sa'luki. But it seems that even with the protection of so eminent a man, Nasir Khusraw's stay was still in danger. One day, Sa'luki came to warn him. 'You are an exceedingly accomplished and great man, testing out many issues, and your message has become louder and more apparent. I see that the exoteric clerics of Khurasan are coming after you. It would be wise for you to leave this region.'9 Nasir Khusraw decided to leave Nishapur under cover, and headed for Balkh.

He settled for a while in Balkh and 'preached allegiance to the Caliph al-Mustansir and adherence to Ismaili precepts.'10 His preaching lasted until a fanatical mob set out to kill him and wantonly beat him up. In the end, Nasir Khusraw was forced to flee from Balkh.

Besides the emotional statements he placed in his poetry referring to this event, he also inserted this key sentence in the *Zad al-musafirin* in a passage otherwise dedicated to explaining the need to accept the precepts of the true faith (*din-i haqq*):

I bring forth proofs on what I preach so that the ignoramuses of this world who have called me 'heretic' (*bad din*) and fought and won out over me, and who have run me out of house and country, shall be despised by those of wisdom who reflect carefully on this book of mine (*ZM*, 402).

He found refuge further east under the protection of the Ismaili prince 'Ali b. al-Asad, and was able to live out the remainder of his years in the district of Yumgan in the province of Badakhshan. But Nasir Khusraw has left a highly sensitive record of his sorrow and anger at this forced exile. His profound outrage at this unjust turn of events, in which evil overtakes good, where injustice prevails, and where his own pious actions are misunderstood, comes across in many sombre moments in his poetry:

Everyone has turned away, repulsed and disgusted at my words,
  even my neighbours, my relations, my countrymen.

No one reads my writings, no one speaks my name;
  the ignorant out of ignorance, the scholars trembling at
  trouble.

(Divan, 44:15–16)

From here on, the Nasir Khusraw we know from the *Safarnama* – open, adventurous, inquisitive and humorous – often turns bitter, resentful and angry in his *Divan*. He fills his pen with eloquence and academic training, and then flings stinging poetry at the forces of oppression and hypocrisy he sees arrayed around him: fanatical clergy, fawning poets, the cruel Saljuqs, the inconstancy of nature. There are times when he regrets the loss of his youth and the onset of old age. Sometimes his mood turns to sorrow, sometimes to rage, but either way his artistic talent turns these emotions into exquisite poetic images, as in this dramatic opening line to one *qasida*:

The scorpion of exile has stung my heart so,
  that you would say heaven invented suffering
  just for me.

(Divan, 6:1)

Another ode begins with these memorable lines, full of the nostalgia, sorrow and bitterness of exile:

Pass by, sweet breeze of Khurasan,
To one imprisoned deep in the valley of Yumgan,
Who sits huddled in comfortless tight straits,
Robbed of all wealth, all goods, all hope.
Cruel fate has rudely stolen away by force
All peace from his heart, all rest from his body.
His heart swells fuller with sorrow than a pomegranate
  bursting with seed,
His body shrinks, more consumed than a shrivelled winter reed.
That beautiful face and that handsome figure
Are now fallen into weakness, ugliness and ruin.

That face, once bright as spring's anemones,
Crackles now like autumn leaves from exile's miseries.
Even family turn away from him like strangers.
None can help him now, save the mercy of God.

(Divan, 208:1–7)

### AGAINST FALSE FAITH

Stripped of all possessions, all connections, his life in danger, Nasir Khusraw fled east into the high mountains near the Hindu Kush and found refuge in Yumgan, in the court of a local Ismaili prince. In this remote place, safe from danger but far from any centres of worldly activity, Nasir Khusraw lived out the remaining fifteen or twenty years of his life, 'sending a book a year' out into the world and writing philosophical poetry laced with anger at his fate and contempt for his enemies. He objects that he has been unjustly accused of irreligion (*bad din, bad madhhab, rafidi*) by people whom he regards unqualified to make such a judgement. They only know Islam superficially, he says. What good are eloquent, well-crafted arguments against these demons, dogs, calves and idiots, as he calls them. In the following verses, continuing immediately from the lines above, his disdain for his accusers keeps his complaint at the level of sustained anger rather than allowing it to sink into self-pity:

Though sinless, I have become the ancient enemy
Of the Turk, the Arab, the Iraqi, and Khurasani.
Always searching for a fault and finding none but this:
'You are "unorthodox" and an enemy of
The Prophet's companions.'
What can I say to this army of demons?
God did not give me the charms of Solomon.[11]
They dare not approach me but from afar,
Howling and yowling like dogs in the barn.
As the *hujjat*, a host of such enemies would not bother me.
But God, Thou knowest best.
But, it is not wise *not* to defend oneself from demons.
What is an educated, articulate man supposed to say

To such demons from the desert?
For futile it is to write proofs for an idiot;
You don't recite the Qur'an to a calf.
The smart man does not waste words on idiots.
Who would put expensive Kermani rye in cheap barley bread?
They call me irreligious yet know naught of Islam but the name!

In the next lines, the poet turns to directly address the clerics who oppose him:

O you who wear on your head the cap of false knowledge,
Your soul is hidden under coats of ignorance.
Tell me, to whom should one pay allegiance after Muhammad,
And what is the proof for your claims?

(*Divan*, 208:18–19)

Then he directly accuses them of hypocrisy:

By day you fast and moan and finger your rosary,
By night you're enjoying music and wine.
You've memorised the texts of deception quite smoothly,
So now you're grand *mufti* of Balkh, Nishapur and Herat.
When you speak, a luscious date palm you are, full of fruit,
But your actions reveal you full of thorns like acacia.

(*Divan*, 208:32;34;37)

Besides criticising the clerics for their attacks on him and for hypocritically not practising what they preach, Nasir also holds in contempt those religious leaders who plant simplistic visions of paradise in the minds of common people, magnifying a literal view of the pleasures of heaven, rather than its spiritual pleasures. Of course people will flock to them, he sneers, with all their promises of feasts and physical pleasures in the afterlife. He warns other Ismaili *da'i*s to be careful in their teachings, lest the other preachers promising earthly delights in paradise turn against them and they suffer the same fate as Nasir himself:

From pulpit-tops they preach to the common folk,
    dazzling them about paradise and the food to be had there.[12]

Go on, spread the word about 'Ali, if you can be sure they won't
    lock you up too, like me, in the mountains of Yumgan.

They crow and cry in hope of food;
    asses always bray when you speak of barley.

And if you do not preach that heaven is a place of eating and sex,
    they'll send arrows of ridiculous rage flying from their eyes
    at you.

                  (*Divan*, 68:21–4)

Not only the Muslim clerics of the kind mentioned here, but also
Zoroastrian priests and other scholars of these ancient scriptures[13]
receive his rebuke:

You who have read the Zand and the Pazand,
    how much longer will you go on reading this Zand?
Scriptures on your lips, but mischief in your hearts;
    is this what Zoroaster wrote in his Zand?
By your words, you are full of knowledge and wisdom;
    by your actions, though, fiercely hypocritical.
Increase the nobility of your actions,
    and quiet down a little with your words.
What sort of advice would you give me?
    You should gird your loins tight with your own advice.
For when you do not do as you say,
    everything you say comes out as lies and fraud.

                  (*Divan*, 11:1–6)

As mentioned before, Nasir Khusraw, along with the other
Ismaili preachers, offers a religion which holds intellectual inves-
tigation of the faith to be one of the supreme virtues of the
believer. The human intellect is seen as the primary tool in the
soul's activity to cleanse itself and gain a more lucid understanding. The Ismaili intelligentsia under the Fatimids actively
engaged each other as well as non-Ismaili thinkers in debates
on theological and philosophical issues, such as how human

beings can be said to truly have free will if God is the continual creator of all acts. A flavour of such intellectual debates is captured in these lines:

> Why were we given an intellect if, even with this intellect,
>     we sometimes sin and sometimes worship God?
> Why did God command us to do good and avoid evil,
>     if we are not alive and free to choose?
> Why is the vicious wolf not condemned before God
>     for his acts, while we are held responsible for ours?
> Why, with its meaningless crowing and cawing,
>     is the crane not held in contempt, but we are?
> Why are you and I weighed down with prayer and fasting,
>     while deer and other creatures we hunt are not?
>                                          (*Divan*, 33:23–7)

Drawing on this comparison of the difference between God's requirements for human beings and animals, the poet poses the fundamental problem of divine justice: if God is the agent for all acts, then it is not just of God to punish human beings for their acts; but if, on the other hand, God is not in control of every act in the universe and some human acts are judged to be sinful, then we can conclude that human beings are not subservient to God:

> If He does not will us to sin, and we do,
>     then we are not slaves of God, but masters.[14]

> If all sin derives from His will,
>     then we are not sinners, but good and doers of good.
>                                          (*Divan*, 33:33–4)

Nasir then challenges the religious scholars opposed to him, giving some sense of the vigorous intellectual environment he was used to:

> If you do not wish to be engaged in these questions,
>     don't, and get away from us, for we do.
> If you challenge us about these problems,
>     we shall resist firmly against your attack.

With shining minds we construct towers of debate
   as high as the heavens, and lavish them with gold.
                                        (*Divan*, 33:36–8)

Firm in his faith, Nasir Khusraw knows he is right. In the next few lines, he confirms his faith in Islam and devotion to 'Ali, and showers his disdain upon his opponents even if he is outnumbered:

Warriors we are, in the army of the Qur'an and the *Shari'a*;
   for we are the Shi'a of 'Ali, the persistent.
Sick people think sugar isn't sweet.
   No wonder you think we are unbelievers.
One of me and a thousand of you; though you swarm like
   snakes and ants and we are not many,
An army cannot be five hundred mounts on one man;
   better we not even count you an army.
                                        (*Divan*, 33:39–42)

### LAMENT FOR KHURASAN

It is not only for himself that Nasir Khusraw complains. While he certainly sees himself as a victim, this pain of his personal misfortune sits within the context of what he sees as the even larger loss of his homeland. Not only is Khurasan in the hands of a corrupt clerics, but it is also now ruled by vagabond and untutored (*bi-khwan u bi-man*) invaders who have wreaked ruin on his cultured world. He sees his own loss of country and home as proof that Khurasan is now ruled by barbarians:

They threw me out of house and home, those lowest of the
   low, those ignorant and careless of their prayers.[15]
Khurasan has become the haven of the low;
   Could one house hold both the noble and the low?
No one can understand me, except for one
   whom the lowest eject from his home.
                                        (*Divan*, 65:12–14)

This Persian poet has lost the world he loved, one based on literature, ancient culture and intellectual achievement. He opens the same poem with an outpouring of nostalgia, wondering:

Who asks, from this miserable, sad exile,
'O Khurasan, how goes it without me?'

Are you still as I saw you in springtime?
Send news, if still you are the same.

Are your trees still draped in multi-hued streamers,
Your willows still bound up with turbans of red?

In April, do eastern breezes still cover the face of the desert
With veils yellow from China and red from Byzantium?

In late winter months, do breezes still scatter the coins and
The jewels of all colours on the heads of the brides in the orchards?

Do they still make the crown for narcissus
Out of gold from the treasure chest and pearls of fine lustre?

If you are still so, and this is how it goes,
May your nights be sweet and your days happy and full.

(*Divan*, 65:1–7)

From this tender reminiscence of his homeland, Nasir shifts to a contrast with his own debilitated state, using metaphors to describe his loss of hair, sallow skin and weakening body:

But for me, things have been quite different for some time now,
Even if you, without me, have not changed.

Little by little, the hand of time has washed
The silken turban from my head.

Fickle time has sallowed my rosy complexion
With too many washings in yellow water.

By the tyranny of time, my body, once straight as the letter *alif*
Is now changed into the round letter *nun*, the letter *nun*!

(*Divan*, 65:8–11)

Nasir Khusraw's poems on Khurasan demonstrate a strong sense of Persian identity combined with an acute awareness of injustice and oppression which he condemns.[16] He feels it could only be God's anger that would allow the nomadic homeless Saljuqs to take root like some noxious weed in his beloved homeland. From his complaint at being forced from his home, Nasir now moves directly into criticising the people of Khurasan for bringing God's wrath down on themselves in the form of these nomadic invaders:

> In this way, the heavens have rained God's anger
> Down on Khurasan, upon these base-born folk,
>
> That this mob of homeless rabble
> Now sit as kings and queens there.
>
> On that ground where God's wrath rains
> The seed of calamity will grow from rotting soil.
>
> An evil seed will grow upon the land
> Whose people spring from Haman and Qarun.
>
> This evil plant is the Turkish tribes of Ghuzz and Qifchak,
> Who have grown up along the banks of the River Jayhun.
>
> This is God's surprise attack by night on them,
> Fitting indeed is God's surprise attack by night.
>
> (*Divan*, 65:15–20)

Elsewhere, Nasir extrapolates beyond Khurasan into the whole of the Iranian world itself:

> The demon himself has thrown religion out of Iran,
>     that's why Iran is now so ruined.
>
> (*Divan*, 48:14)

In the same vein of blaming his fellow Khurasanians for not attending to religion properly and thus bringing divine punishment on themselves, he also frequently evokes scenes from the *Shahnama*, the Iranian national epic, and popular mythology to remind them of the earlier conquest of Iran by the Arabs:

You have heard how, even with his elephantine strength,
    Rustam was the slave of Kavus.
Seek honour through religion, for the wise man
    gains respect from the people through religion.
Through religion did he glory till Resurrection Day,
    he by whom the Arabs gloried over Iran.

                    (*Divan*, 30: 29–31)

In all, Nasir Khusraw considers the conquest of Khurasan by
the untutored Saljuqs from the steppes of Central Asia as a vivid
symbol of how the world can turn topsy-turvy, with slaves raised to
rulers and knowledge reduced to ignorance.

Demonland it has become, Khurasan.
    Hail pelts down from clouds of ignorance.
                    (*Divan*, 197:28)

### AGAINST FALSE POETS

Nasir particularly holds in contempt the poets who oil themselves
into comfortable positions by composing panegyrics to the powerful that drip with flattery, hyperbole and exaggerated praise.
He cannot restrain his disgust at their willingness to sell their art
and their souls for such worldly and, therefore, transient masters.
A true *hakim*, he writes (employing the term for sage often used
for himself), does not act this way:

A *hakim* is one who does not concern himself with kings,
Not like those fools who recite poems for kings in hope of gain.
                    (*Divan*, 19:20)

In another poem, he actually goads the poets directly:

O poem-hawkers of Khurasan, harken to
    these deep words of mine, if indeed you be poets.
                    (*Divan*, 213:14)

Drawing on his own experience in Ghaznavid and Saljuq courts, Nasir thus distances himself from the behaviour of such courtly poets. In the following selection, he specifically derides the panegyrists of the Ghaznavid conqueror, Mahmud, the descendant of Turkish slaves whose armies swept across eastern Iran, Afghanistan and parts of India in the early years of the 5th/11th century, massacring a multitude of people along the way, including many Ismaili communities, only to have the Saljuqs trample his empire a few decades later:

How were you so deceived by the empire of the Turk? Recall
    the might and majesty of Mahmud of Zabulistan.
Where is it now, that terror with which he, by his own hand,
    caused the Farighunians to lose Juzjanan;
When he destroyed India under the hooves of horses of Turks,
    and Khutlan was crushed under the feet of his elephants?
Never before did the world record the likes of him;
    even his arrow could pierce an anvil.
When he took Sistan from the Khalafs and Rayy from the Razis,
    he raised the hand of his palace far past the zenith of Saturn.
Dazzled and deceived, he went throughout the world,
    indeed many has the world deceived like him.
You deceived ones stood before him shouting,
    'Long live the Sultan! A thousand years more!'
By the mighty glory of his rule, whatever ventured near,
    even the powerful turned to wax within his jaws.
Yesterday, Zabulistan was the *qibla* of the free,
    as today the Ka'ba is for those who believe.
But where is it now, that glory, might, magnificence that
    saw the constellation of the Crab spread out beneath itself?
His claws fell out, his teeth decayed,
    when death sharpened up its claws and teeth on him.

                              (*Divan*, 52:9–19)

### REFLECTIONS ON OLD AGE

Besides his sorrow and bitterness over his exile, his contempt for hypocritical clerics and poets, and his regret that barbarians rule over cultured Khurasan, Nasir Khusraw also rails against the effects of old age. The encroachment of age and the deterioration of his physical condition are bitter proof for him of the capricious and unreliable nature of all physical existence. He opens many poems with a lament against the relentless passage of time. In the following lines, he leads with a complaint about the contrast between his former, young, robust self and his current, decrepit, bent body:

> That strength of youth, that heavenly face –
> O mindless body of mine, why did you ever leave them behind?
> When your body was beautiful you acted pretty ugly,
> Now that you're ugly, you should beautify your actions.
> Time has made your torso feeble:
> Yesterday a peacock, today a porcupine.
>
> (*Divan*, 174: 1–3)

Even the material world cannot be trusted. In one common image of the time, Nasir portrays the world as a beautiful but deceitful woman who ensnares young men with her charms and then mocks them for their infatuation:

> So many years and months and days and nights have passed by over me,
>    so many wonders did they make, strange, like a magician.
> So many days and nights passed over me that
>    my hair now shines like day and my face like night.
> My boy, the world is a beautiful woman who deceives fools frequently,
>    she makes herself bewitching as when she takes the bachelor's hand.
> You laugh and cackle merrily over her, yet do not see
>    she laughs day and night at you secretly under her lips.
>
> (*Divan*, 44:1–4)

On other occasions, the poet depicts the world as a cruel witch-like matriarch who is reborn each time she gives birth to her offspring. While she stays ever young and beautiful, her children grow old and weak.

> This old globe takes freshness from all the new children;
>     we have turned old, but she is young, a beautiful sorcerer!
> Did you ever see a mother whose children grow old
>     while their old mother becomes younger all the time?
> Usually whoever turns young, his mother turns old, but
>     just the opposite happens here, by inverse logic.
> How can you be deceived by this one's garish, false clothing
>     when you take note of the terrible deeds of this smelly old hag?
>                                                   (*Divan*, 164:1–4)

Applying the same analogy of the physical world as mother, Nasir warns against becoming too involved with her:

> The world is a stinking, old mother. Do not be seduced by her,
>     if in rank you are worthy to receive a houri in paradise.
> Do not marry your mother, for your mother is forbidden to you,
>     if you are one of the people of religion.
>                                                   (*Divan*, 8:5–6)

Besides this frightful figure of a mother who remains youthful even as her children grow old and die, another iconic image of a deceitful world is the sorceress, and Nasir makes full use of the image of one who gives pleasure for a price but cares nothing for the soul. By analogy, the world's pleasures are a deceptive trick which keeps believers away from the path of tending to their souls. The heavens revolve, not caring that with each turn they make people older. Nasir gives a strong warning to resist the lures of this world.

> O oppressing sphere, O sister of Ahriman,[17]
>     why don't you admit what has happened between you and me?
> You've turned me soft and yellow like an apricot,
>     with the clear intention of devouring me.
> This yellowing and wearing out has happened to the shirt of
>     the soul; for the body is the covering of the soul and mind.

On loan I had it from you, this old, worn-out shirt,
  until such time as I shall cast it down before you.
Why should I fear a battle with one like you, O Ahriman,
  when my sword is devotion and my armour the mind?
Since I have ceased desiring all your blessings and glory,
  you must cease desiring my worship and obedience.
The world is a sorceress; I do not buy her trickery.
  Whoever is deceived by a woman, is a woman.
You never heard of the guile that woman inflicted on Bizhan?[18]
  That, in the end, what happened to the head of Bizhan?
Just as Bizhan remains trapped in a dark well, O son,
  it will happen to you if you are devoted to the world.
O fools, following down the path of Bizhan,
  how can you say that the same will not happen to you?
If you cultivate conversation with this evil, wicked woman,
  you will not be worth one single grain.
Don't buy her talk, don't let your life slip away,
  because only an idiot would barter an axe for a needle.
Cut off the appetite of your soul, or with the marriage price
  you'll be giving away Qarun's treasure or Qaran's army.[19]
I have had enough of this woman, since
  sixty or more winters and springs have I spent with her.
Her nature is this, my man, she sells naught to the wise
  but artifice, lies, and guile.
Stupid and filthy and miserable is the world, and vile,
  the whole thing built of nothing but rubbish and filth.

(*Divan*, 17:1–16)

# CHAPTER TWELVE

# Glory Regained

He said, 'Do not be sad, for the jewel
has been found in thy mine.'

*Divan*, 242:75

Despite the often disheartening spirit of pessimism which colours
Nasir Khusraw's *Divan*, his verse and rhyme in the final analysis
convey no message of existential gloom or grief, the joy of his
spiritual certitude dispelling the depression we have seen him
express. In his poems we can watch how he moves from mood to
mood and thereby lifts himself from grief and sorrow, progress-
ing, for example, from an observation of nature to a reflection on
the passage of time, to anger at being misunderstood, or regret
for lost opportunities. But there comes a moment in each poem
when he stops complaining and answers himself. At this point he
shifts tone, moving from sorrow to anger in some poems or, in
others, from sorrow to calm assurance. In all circumstances, whatever his state of mind, he remains absolutely sure of himself,
confident of his faith, and committed in his actions. He does not
doubt himself. Any questions he poses in his poetry are purely
rhetorical. His eye remains firmly fixed on his ultimate purpose.
He is confident that the universe revolves according to divine
purpose and that just as the mighty wheel of heaven full of planets and stars must follow certain rules, then so too must human
beings.

> In the sky, there is no escape from the black eclipse,
>   not for the shining sun, nor for the glowing moon.
>
> (Divan, 52:25)

Since the heavens themselves revolve by divine order and even
the mighty sun is a servant to Heaven's dictates, comfort can be
found in discerning the grand design and following it. Part of the
design can be found in the very structure of the universe and the
components of a single human being. But beyond these structures lies the purpose within the design. Nasir draws hope from
his certitude that he has observed the structures, understood their
underlying purposes, and lived his life according to these purposes as well as possible. By comprehending the structures and
their purposes, Nasir gains his faith in God, in the Prophet Muhammad and in his descendants, the Ismaili imams, and with this
faith finds a way of living wisely in the world.

### THE ORDER OF THINGS

The first structure to understand about the world is the duality of
*zahir* and *batin*, that there is an apparent world which we see and
feel, and a hidden world which we can only apprehend with our
minds and hearts. Beginning with what is close at hand, we can
physically see and feel our own bodies and at the same time have
an inner awareness of ourselves and our thinking, but we cannot
employ our physical senses to touch our thoughts or see our feelings. From this microcosmic level, the duality applies also to the
macrocosmos; there exists a spiritual world beyond this physical
universe. Just as our physical bodies abide in this material world
of *zahir*, Nasir teaches that the non-physical part of our beings –
whether called soul or mind or heart – resides in the spiritual
universe of the *batin*, to which in fact it yearns to return, to regain
its proper home. Thus, the ultimate journey is the journey of the
soul which starts here and now, in this world. And for Nasir
Khusraw this is not mere philosophy but a personal statement of
faith:

Though day and night I dwell upon the earth,
My journey is unfolding up on the seventh sphere.
One day, you shall see me on wings of devotion,
Flown from this lofty dome, like a bird on the wing.
(*Divan*, 6:14,32)

This is a creed which he advises others to adopt as well:

Your true abode is the bright and everlasting world,
    not for you the lowest world.
Light the candle of reason within in your heart
    and go quickly with shining heart on to the shining world.
(*Divan*, 78:14–15)

Although the spiritual world is preeminent and superior, it is
only half of the whole. The *batin* coexists with the *zahir*; neither of
them can be done away with. Accordingly, Nasir nowhere espouses
monastic withdrawal from the world itself. Of course, when he is
sad or angry, he says it is better to sit alone than with fools, but he
has no desire for a cloistered life or one spent in constant contemplation. For even though he stridently warns against being
seduced by the attractions of the world and against following sen-
sual pleasure for its own sake, he also calls for active engagement
with the world, since it holds clues to the next world as well as
tools to make the journey possible. Thus, the physical is to be
used in the service of the spiritual. The clues to guide this search
and journey can be found in this physical world:

Why do you not think God the All-Knowing would have supplied
All the needs for the pure soul in this earthen casket,
    when He breathed life into it?
How long will the tall and disagreeable, difficult blue wheel
Chase around after this little black ball?
The secret of God is under this blue veil, my son.
Who can rip asunder the veil of the secret of God?
If you ask 'Why did God hide His secrets from us?'
What shall I say but 'This is fitting, by His order.'
(*Divan*, 25:30–3)

Another structure to understand in this ordered universe is the mutability and the inevitability of change. While no one wishes the good to pass away, it is comforting to know that even the worst evil will pass away too. This is precisely the lesson one finds in Nasir's poem lamenting the loss of Khurasan to the Turks, after having pointed out that the mighty Mahmud of Ghazna – who 'crushed India beneath the hooves of the Turks' horses' and for whom his fellow poets wished a thousand more years – is gone, swept away by a new wave of nomadic conquerors. After the crescendo declaration, 'His claws fell out and his teeth decayed when Death sharpened up its teeth and claws,' the poet falls quiet, observing that things naturally change:

> The heavens often have turned tears to smiles,
> And also just as easily, turned smiles into tears.
> How can you hope to find consistency here under the
> revolving wheel,
> When the wheel itself never stays in one single state?
> Step back from it, for a crazy galloping rider it is,
> And no one ever embraces a crazy galloping rider.
> Be on your guard when something difficult turns easy,
> For the heavens soon make the easy thing hard.
> When Heaven's revelations turn angry, they throw out just as they
> Take in: Caesar from his palace, the khan from house and home.
> (*Divan*, 52: 20–4)

Thus, since change is the natural order of things, we should find consolation rather than sorrow in the passage of time, even as the years progress and our bodies grow old and gradually decay toward death. On earth, we can be confident in the regular divinely ordained progression of the seasons. Therefore, when life is at its worst, we can find hope, for spring will surely follow even the deepest winter of despair.

### SEEKING THE JEWEL WITHIN

In addition to looking at the world with an attitude of trust in the inherent order found in its contents and processes, Nasir Khusraw

also looks within himself and all humanity with optimism, confident that the inner core is ultimately good. What really matters,
what really counts for him is the spiritual side of human beings,
not their worldly station in life and certainly not, given his own
predicament, their worldly location. One may be king or outcast,
but only the goodness of the soul counts, and its creative expression in worldly deeds. Nasir repeatedly confirms the inner
goodness of someone trapped in terrible surroundings, likening
this person to a jewel in a muddy mine or a pearl in an ugly shell:

> The world is a deep ocean, its water is time;
> Your body is like a shell, your soul the pearl.
> If you wish to have the value of a pearl,
> Raise up the pearl of your soul by learning.
>
> (*Divan*, 145:47–8)

He sees himself as the prime example of the imprisoned jewel,
and thereby turns his exile in Yumgan into a badge of honour.

> You ask me, 'If you are so intelligent and of high birth,
> Why are you sitting here in Yumgan, alone and lowly?'
> Under God's protection I am here in Yumgan.
> Look closely, and consider me not a prisoner.
> No one says that silver or diamonds or rubies
> Are prisoners in the rocks or lowly.
> Even though Yumgan itself is lowly and worthless,
> Here I am greatly valued and honoured.
> Although the serpent is lowly and reviled,
> The snakestone in its head is precious and praised.
> No one deems the perfect pearl less dear
> For having come from a worthless shell.
>
> (*Divan*, 9: 4–9)

Nasir can admit that he has landed in an undesirable situation –
an isolated backwater with little intellectual stimulation, within a
larger world now governed by those he views as barbarians – and
he places the blame for this wholly outside himself. He uses this
grim external reality to point out what is hidden and how deeply

it differs from the external. Jewels are found within stone and dirt, such that it requires great effort to find and extract them, but the jewel is not debased by its base surroundings. In fact, in the verse immediately following the selection above, he remarks that we find it possible to enjoy flowers in their own beauty and fragrance and completely ignore the fact that they spring from mud and manure. In judging the value of something, the inner essence must on no account be confused with external conditions.

Besides using the jewel motif to characterise his own forlorn condition in a hostile place, Nasir also uses the same motif to refer to the soul in the body. For him, the physical body is a complex container for the soul. For while it offers the means to gain knowledge, it also offers the means to enjoy physical pleasure, an excess of which can block the path to knowledge. For Nasir, the body is merely a shell to encase the soul, something to protect and nurture the pearl within. Of the two, that which is contained is superior to the container.

In addition, when surrounded by an ugly situation, the poet counsels not only awareness of one's unique goodness, but also appreciation of the solitude that often accompanies excellence.

> When being with others does not work out, to be alone is better,
> A hundred times better than being with idiots.
> The sun's solitude brings no shame; indeed it is better
> Than the Pleiades, which is made of seven stars.
>
> (*Divan*, 2:17–18)

Thus, while he nowhere advocates a cloistered or monastic life as an ideal, in these verses Nasir suggests that solitude is to be preferred when the only alternative is to mingle with stupid people. Just as the ruby's solitude signals its worth, so too does the sun's glory lie partly in that it has no peer. Indeed, the singular sun is treasured more than several suns shining together in constellation.

In the same way that a jewel in the mine needs to be found and polished with great expertise and effort, and a pearl requires a diver, the fullest effort is required of each individual to become his or her most noble self. God provides tools, such as the five senses, the intellect, the things of the world, and teachers, but it is

each individual's responsibility to take and use these instruments
to his or her best advantage. Since, according to Nasir's philosophy, within each soul's nature lies the innate desire for excellence
and the longing for perfection, one is actually rebelling against
the universe and God's purpose if one remains content at a lower
level of existence. For Nasir, human heights of happiness are to
be found in intellectual and spiritual pursuits and by the constant
increase of one's knowledge.

> Peace of mind from the torment of ignorance
>> comes from knowledge;
> Only with knowledge can the basil of peace blossom forth in
>> one's soul.
>
>> *(Divan,* 25:26)

### SUSTENANCE IN TRUE FAITH

Besides drawing hope from the natural order of things and the
human soul's pursuit of excellence, Nasir also sustains himself
through his sadness by certitude that his faith is true. He rests
assured that, after much searching, he has found God's true message in the Ismaili interpretation of Islam, sure that, through his
allegiance to the family of the Prophet Muhammad and the Ismaili imams, he has found the true path to knowledge and
salvation. And he affirms this commitment fearlessly, even though
it resulted in the miseries and torments of a life in exile. In fact,
he even comes to see that in the remote valley of Yumgan he may
be freer than ever, far from the corruption and hypocrisy of king
and clergy which he so despised.

> Do you know what became of me when I fled the devils?
> All of a sudden I became acquainted with angels.
> When the light of the Imam of the Age shone on my soul,
> I, once darkest night, now became the shining sun.
> The Greatest Name is the Imam of the Time, and from this,
> I have ascended to Heaven, like Venus risen from the earth.
> If I said, 'From Muhammad, 'Ali is the leader (*wasi*) of the people,'
> why does this make me worthy of incrimination?

And if I said, 'All praise and glory to the family of the Prophet,'
Why do you think this earns me cruelty and scorn?
They find fault with the very source of my pride:
My pride is that I became one of the Shi'a of the cloak.
They drove me out of house and home because of religion,
Till I became like the Prophet of Truth with his migration.
Famous but hidden was the star Suha in the sky,
Now on earth, have I become a veritable Suha.
Thanks be to that God by whose grace I have come to Yumgan
And reign over the soul and treasure of the Shi'is,
So that when the Prince of the Faithful of the world
    welcomed me.
I became worthy of the welcome of believers.

(Divan, 62:24–6; 31–7)

Nasir Khusraw's faith rests in the certainty that there is more to
understand than is readily apparent in the outward forms of nature and religion, and that this hidden knowledge was given to
the Prophet Muhammad and Imam 'Ali. The secrets of the universe and the meanings of the scriptures were all entrusted to
'Ali, the lion (*haydar*) of God.[1]

Consider this: what is man, that God calls him to Himself?
What does He want from man that He sends,
    from time to time, one prophet after another?
Why did this boundless motion fall into this great corpus of
    the universe?
In this veil, no one finds his way except one who actually seeks
    the way from a guide.
Who knows the secret way of God? The Prophet,
    and the Prophet entrusted this secret to Haydar.

(Divan, 145: 49–51; 58–9)

As part of his faith, Nasir Khusraw also proclaims his allegiance
to the descendant of 'Ali who leads the Ismaili believers, the Fatimid Caliph-Imam al-Mustansir, who governs from Cairo. The
poet dreams of the day al-Mustansir would wrest Baghdad from

the Abbasids and rule over the whole Muslim world.[2] For Nasir, al-Mustansir is

> That lord to whom Caesar would give a hundred thanks
> To be appointed gatekeeper at Cairo's Zahhab Gate.
> As heaven lords o'er all the earth, he has honour, and from his
>     glory
> Even a pebble from his courtyard outshines a Badakhshani ruby.
> Children of kings and lords aplenty are present at his court,
> Hailing from the Khans, the Razis and the Samanids.
> Who can shower such goodness on the people
> But one who has no equal in the world?
> When you descend on Baghdad, the Abbasid devil himself
> Will make an offering to you of his very own child.
> To me, your devoted slave, the very stones of Yumgan
> Are far more precious than any grand Omani pearl.
> Since you gave me the blessings of the eternal world,
> What is worth thinking of in this tasteless, transitory world?
>
> (*Divan* 208:43–7; 54–6)

### WORKING IN THE WORLD

Nasir Khusraw's fourth source of hope lies squarely in his own hands in the work and conduct of his life. While the three sources of hope we have already considered can be seen as intellectual concepts – the divine order inherent in the physical and spiritual worlds, the intrinsic goodness of the human soul, and his religious commitments – the fourth, what one actually does with the gifts given and how well one carries out one's purposes, has a more empirical basis and can only be judged by the person's acts. In the midst of his exile, Nasir looks at the activities of his life and consoles himself with his considerable achievements:

> The hovel of Yumgan has become famed and glorified because
>     of me,
> Just as the Arab desert became glorified by the excellence of
>     the Prophet.
> No harm comes to the grape since it is pure and good and sweet,

Even though all its vines come out of manured dirt.
Though I am hidden in Yumgan, my knowledge is well known,
Just as the actions of the soul of growth are visible in berries
    and roots.
What is the comforter to my heart and soul? Prayer and the Qur'an.
What is the foundation of my intellect? Poems and sermons.
I do three things, my brother, each the work of the acquired
Intellect: I speak well, I exercise knowledge, and I worship God.

(Divan, 44: 28–32)

He takes special pride in his accomplishments as a teacher and preacher:

But to the wise ones of Khurasan,
I am recognised as the *hujjat* of Mustansir.
Through my words, the wisdom of religion became
Like drops of rain, making the desert bloom.
No one ever saw in the words of Hermes
The likes of what they find in the words of Nasir.
Even though I am concealed in Yumgan,
This has served to make me even greater.

(Divan, 26:37–40)

Nasir Khusraw has lived a life fully engaged in the circumstances of the present world, always exploring and questioning. In all aspects of his life, from his early education, his teaching, preaching, writing poetry and travelling, he sets out to challenge himself and others to search for the truth and to reject the easy way out. Besides his success in preaching, he also takes solace in his ability as a poet and scholar:

Life has been this way for me, that through poetry
I thread together rows of gold and pearls and coral.

(Divan, 52:54)

Nasir sees each human life as a progression from ignorance to knowledge, an intellectual and spiritual journey which can be ever side-tracked by earthly pleasure or despair. He sees that not only have the provisions for the journey been supplied by God and wait to be gathered, but also that each person possesses an inner core of excellence, the soul, which drives the individual forward to seek sustenance and growth. Even infants exhibit this drive, or else they die:

> Even though God makes the mother, the breast and the milk,
> the baby still has to suckle the milk by himself.
>
> (*Divan*, 25:22)

Once in Yumgan, Nasir was awake all night until morning. In a poem remembering his thoughts as the hours went by, he describes day and night as the two sons of Noah, one light and one dark. He revels in the sight of the star-filled sky, a thousand pearls strewn throughout black curls with streaks of red and gold so bright that, 'No one ever saw a bride so beautiful.' The immensity of the evening and the beauty of the dawning light lead him to think of God and the many languages He uses to communicate. But, the poet notes, one needs to have the 'ear of the heart' completely open to hear the internal speech which communicates without physical voice. We shall let this distinguished poet and man of letters speak for himself and have the last word.

> Last night, from eventide till break of dawn,
> The cup of contemplation sat nestled in my hand.

> From the east advanced the army of the Abyssinian king,
> When the Byzantine king descended into the west.

> Like the two sons of Noah they are, O wonder!
> Day just like Sam and dark night like Ham.

> Night did strew thousands of pearls throughout her curls,
> Scarlet and golden, some in designs and some without.

> No one ever saw in all the world a bride such as this –
> With tresses illumined and countenance dark.

> None but evil-doers were awake at that hour;
> Alas for me, no one else beheld such a fabulous scene.

The face of all these lights of the world
Looked to me like a thousand sleepless eyes,

As if each one were a prophet sent down to us by God,
And the lights of each one were the prophecies.

These are the languages of God, O son!
And all creatures are like the words of these languages.

No one hears their conversation but one
Whose mind opens completely the ear of the heart.

How could you hear speaking without voice,
When you've never seen walking without feet or legs?

Even if a sinner never with tongue declares, 'I am a sinner,'
Surely his actions always do:

The hand of the fool bespeaks 'wine,'
The one seated by the sodomite bespeaks 'boy.'

Words like dates, but deeds like thorns –
This is not faith, O friend, but pure hypocrisy.

I, who never acquiesce to any ugly deed,
How could I have anything but Yumgan as my home?

If I have been busy with religion, of course
I'm now deemed a heretic, one lost in error on the way.

Take my hand, O God of all the worlds!
From this miserable place, this darkest well.

A just adjudicator You are among all your creatures,
Free from the need of 'Where?' and 'Which?'

Whoever speaks falsely of me, cast over his head
A bridle of fire on Judgement Day.

Still I stayed on, marvelling at all I saw,
From dusk of evening until the morning dawn,

When bright dawn in its wisdom drew
The golden glinting sabre from its cobalt sheath,

The face of the earth became like the inner being of the wise,

And that trap besmeared with tar was lifted from the world.

'This is how it shall be,' I said, 'the day the Fatimid
Draws the sword of truth from out its scabbard.'

The religion of his ancestor he shall renew afresh,
That Imam, son of the Imam, son of the Imam.

Fruit of the branch of the justice of God is Abu Tamim,[3]
Perfect in calmness, knowledge, authority and justice.

Except by way of the ladder of his knowledge,
No other way exists for you to ascend this roof of light.

The intellect does not accept mere talk, except with his
    explanation,
Just as the raw should only be eaten after the fire.

In his teachings of the true religion, he passes along
To the people the message of his father and ancestors.

His soul is the pure substance of divinity,
And the world just an accident of that substance.

Lift your head out of the trap of this dome and see
The perpetual spinning of the heavens.

See how Time, just like a crocodile,
Has opened wide its mouth to devour us all,

And how this endless army has fallen on itself,
Just like dogs on bones.

Like beasts, the eye of their heart sees and seeks
Nothing but food and fine raiment

Ignorance and brashness are now rampant and permitted,
While knowledge and liberty have been rendered forbidden.

The world has turned the fur-coat inside out;
Free men now bow meekly to slaves.

If it pleases you to follow the way of that group,
Then shamelessly set your face like alabaster.

Set all modesty and thought aside at the door of insolence,

Then strut yourself along, impudent and arrogant.

When you unsheathed shame from your body,
O son, you gained silks and horses and all their trappings.

When will Heaven submit to your command,
Since you've made yourself its perpetual slave?

And if Heaven never even returned your 'salam,'
Do you think it will just come up and say 'salam' to you?

But if, like me, you've given up all hope in them,
Then sit like me and sunder all connections to these sordid types.

Better to sleep in a furnace with noble intellect
Than in silky tents with base-born fools.

With wisdom, put into practice the counsel of Hujjat
So that your days and your name shine brightly on.

                                        (*Divan*, 173)

# Notes

**Chapter One: A Soul Higher Than Fortune**

1. See Chapter Three for further discussion. Also, Nasir Khusraw's *Risala dar bayan-i nadamat-i ruz-i qiyamat* is considered to have been written first in Arabic. See Ismail K. Poonawala, *Biobibliography of Isma'ili Literature*, (Malibu, C.A., 1977), p. 123.

2. Part of the confusion on the issue of Nasir's date of birth derives from two different dates given in two poems. The poem with the earlier date ('I was born in 357 [967 CE] in the month of Dhu'l-Qa'da') was identified in the Taqavi edition of the *Divan* as not belonging to Nasir Khusraw. Mohaghegh's edition places it in the Appendix (*Mulhaq*, 1, line 56). The poem with the later date ('Three hundred ninety four years after the Hijra [1004 CE] my mother placed me in this abode.') appears in Mohaghegh's edition of *Divan*, 247:27. If we followed the first date, he would have been at least 120-years-old at his death. However, Nasir provides other benchmarks of his life. One of the strongest appears in his *Safarnama* (p. 2), where he asks himself the pivotal question, 'When are you going to wake from your sleep of forty years?' He tells us this was in the late autumn months of 437/1045. His commitment to God was anchored a few weeks later on 19 December 1045, a day so important to him that he recorded it in both his contemporary Islamic calendar and the pre-Islamic Persian calendar: 'On Thursday the 6th of Jumada II of the year 437, which was by Persian reckoning the middle of the month of Day, the last month before the year 414 of the Yazdigirdi era, I cleansed myself from head to foot, went to the mosque, and prayed to God for help both in accomplishing what I had to do and in abstaining from

what He had forbidden.'

If we accept Nasir Khusraw to be around forty rather than eighty at the time of his conversion and the start of his journey, then this argues for a date of birth closer to 394 than 357. This date is further corroborated in another verse, where he writes, 'Forty-two years had the celestial dome passed over me when my speaking soul began searching for wisdom.'

Among the biographers, Riza Quli Khan Hidayat records this later date of 394/1004. In his extensive introduction to the 1925 edition of the *Divan*, Taqizada criticises those who accept the date of 357 for 'falling into an error of rhythm.' He explains that the two dates have the same number of metrical feet and the same rhythm and could be confused for that reason; but the earlier date makes no chronological sense. Following this, there is no excuse for two other dates in the 350s, 358 and 359. Thus, the accepted date for Nasir Khusraw's birth is 394 in the Islamic calendar and 1004 in the Common Era.

3. Nasir Khusraw, *Safarnama*, trans., Wheeler Thackston, Jr., *Naser-e Khosraw's Book of Travels (Safarnama)*, (Albany, N.Y., 1986), p. 1. This and all subsequent references to the *Safarnama*, from Thackston's English translation, are given in the text.

4. Nasir Khusraw, *Jami' al-hikmatayn: Le livre réunissant les deux sagesses ou harmonie de la philosophie grecque et de la theosophie ismaélienne*, ed. H. Corbin and M. Mu'in (Tehran and Paris, 1953), pp. 307–8. The original work by Nasir Khusraw, *Ghara'ib al-hisab*, is now lost.

5. I began the task of distinguishing the relative characteristics and functions of the intellect and the soul according to Nasir Khusraw in A. Hunsberger, 'Nasir Khusraw's Doctrine of the Soul: From the Universal Intellect to the Physical World in Isma'ili Philosophy,' Ph.D. thesis, Columbia University, 1992.

6. *Divan*, 103:26.

7. A lithographed edition of the *Safarnama* was published in Tehran in 1314/1896, along with his *Divan* of poetry. Of translations, we have no record of an Arabic version of the *Safarnama* until this century when Yahya al-Khashshab published his translation in 1945 and the second edition in 1970. A Russian translation came out in 1933, reflecting a strong interest in Nasir Khusraw's works in certain areas of the former Soviet Union, notably Tajikistan. The Urdu version appeared not long after in 1937 and the Turkish in 1950. These translations in languages spoken in countries geographically adjacent to Iran actually came after the 1881 edition and French

translation by Charles Schefer (hereafter cited as Schefer). While a few passages on Syria and Palestine were translated into English a few years later (in 1883) by Guy Le Strange, a full century had to pass before the next complete English translation appeared, by Wheeler Thackston, Jr. Scholarly editions of the Persian text itself were produced first by Schefer with his translation mentioned above, then in Delhi (1882) and Bombay (1892); these were followed by editions by the Iranian scholars Zayn al-'Abidin al-Sharif al-Safavi (1895), M. Ghanizada (1922), Muhammad Dabir Siyaqi (1957), Dabir Siyaqi (1976, 2nd edn) and Nader Vazinpur (1972).

8. Nasir Khusraw's *Divan* was first compiled in a lithographed version in Tabriz in 1280/1863, with a second lithographed edition appearing in 1314/1896 in Tehran. In Calcutta a few poems were published for teaching purposes at the University of Calcutta in 1926, and there is a report of another copy, undated, in India. (See the Foreword to Mohaghegh's edition of the *Divan* for additional information.) In the 20th century, the *Divan* appeared in two scholarly editions, both based on several original manuscripts. The first was prepared in 1925–28 through the creative collaboration of Hajj Sayyid Nasr Allah Taqavi, 'Ali Akbar Dihkhuda, Sayyid Hasan Taqizada and Mujtaba Minuvi, using the 1314/1896 edition as the basic text but incorporating other copies in circulation, plus verses attributed to Nasir Khusraw in literary anthologies. Taqizada wrote an in-depth introduction covering the poet's biography and an analysis of his thought, while Minuvi contributed a piece on the sources used for the edition. The second edition was published in 1974 by Mujtaba Minuvi and Mehdi Mohaghegh in Tehran, under the auspices of the Tehran branch of the Institute of Islamic Studies, McGill University, Montreal. For this major undertaking, the editors increased the number of manuscripts under review and used much older sources than had been the case for the 1925–28 edition, including the oldest complete version of the *Divan* found to date, located in the Chelebi Abdullah Library in Turkey and dated 736/1335. The editors note the existence of a microfilm copy (no. 290) of this manuscript in the Central Library of Tehran University. Other manuscripts consulted include one in the India Office Library in London, copied between 712 and 714 AH during the reign of Sultan Khudabanda Uljaitu, and another prepared for Sultan Muhammad Fatih who ruled during 855–886 AH, as well as individual odes in a few other manuscripts. Both these editions provide introductions with further detail.

9. P. L. Wilson and G. R. Aavani, trans., *Nasir-i Khusraw: Forty Poems from the Divan* (Tehran, 1977).

10. Annemarie Schimmel, *Make a Shield from Wisdom* (London, 1993).

11. Malik al-Shu'ara Bahar, *Sabk shinasi* (Tehran, 1355/1976), vol. 3, pp. 188–9.

12. The *Sa'adatnama* has had two other editions by E. Fagnan (1880, 1882) and M. Ghanizada who published it as a supplement to his edition of the *Safarnama* in Berlin, 1922. G. M. Wickens' translation, 'The "Sa'adat-nameh" Attributed to Nasir Khusraw,' *Islamic Culture*, 2 (1955), pp. 117–32, improves on Fagnan's French prose version and corrects some of F. Teufel's commentary in the German edition. Wickens also brushes aside the Russian scholar Berthels' view of the work as 'a sort of outspoken revolutionary tract on land-reform.'

13. See Ismail K. Poonawala's *Biobibliography of Isma'ili Literature*, pp. 123–5. The missing works which Nasir Khusraw himself refers to in his other books are: *Muftah; Musbah* (these first two being, perhaps, one work); *Dalil al-mutahayyirin; Bustan al-'uqul; Ikhtiar al-imam wa ikhtiar al-iman; Lisan al-'alam; 'Aja'ib al-sun'a; Ghara'ib al-hisab wa 'aja'ib al-hussab; Dala'il; Kitab andar radd-i madhhab-i Muhammad Zakariyya al-Razi*. In addition, Poonawala lists five works with no reference: *Kanz al-haqa'iq; al-Iksir al-a'zam fi'l-hikma; Mustufa dar fiqh; Dastur-i a'zam dar fiqh; Qanun-i a'zam*.

14. The *Gushayish* was edited by Sa'id Nafisi in 1950 and reprinted in 1961 for the Ismaili Society, Bombay, and translated into Italian in 1959 by Pio Filippani-Ronconi. Nafisi's edition was made from a single manuscript dating from the 8th/14th century from the collection of Sayyid Nasr Allah Taqavi. A new edition and English translation based on this and another manuscript from the collection of the late Mujtaba Minuvi was produced by Faquir M. Hunzai under the title of *Knowledge and Liberation* (London, 1998). I have used the Hunzai Persian edition with my own translations for the present work.

15. The Corbin and Mu'in edition of the *Jami' al-hikmatayn*, the only one to date, was based on a copy held in the Central Library of Tehran University of a manuscript in the Aya Sofia Library in Istanbul. Along with the text itself the editors have included an excellent introduction in French which presents the historical and theoretical background for the work. Isabelle de Gastines published a French translation of the complete work: *Nasir-e Khosraw: Le Livre réunissant*

*les deux sagesses (Kitab-e jami' al-hikmatayn)*, (Paris, 1990).

16. The questions raised by Jurjani's poem inspired another commentary, the *Sharh-i qasida-i Abu'l-Haytham Jurjani*, by one of Jurjani's students, Muhammad b. Surkh al-Nishapuri. Both Nasir Khusraw's and al-Nishapuri's commentaries have been studied in *Commentaire de la qasida ismaélienne d'Abu'l-Haitham Jorjani*, ed. H. Corbin and M. Mu'in (Tehran and Paris, 1955).

17. The *Khwan al-ikhwan* has been edited twice, first by the Egyptian scholar Yahya al-Khashshab in Cairo, 1940, and then by A. Qavim in Tehran, 1338/1959. Al-Khashshab based his edition on an original manuscript in the Aya Sofia collection. It has been suggested (Poonawala, *Biobibliography*, p. 435) that it is likely that Qavim derived his edition from al-Khashshab rather than referring to an original manuscript.

18. See *Khwan al-ikhwan*, ed. al-Khashshab, pp. ix–x, 28, 85.

19. See Paul E. Walker, *The Wellsprings of Wisdom: A Study of Abu Ya'qub al-Sijistani's Kitab al-Yanabi'* (Salt Lake City, Utah, 1994).

20. *Shish fasl*, edited and translated by W. Ivanow from two manuscripts from Qanjut, was published as *Six Chapters or Shish Fasl, also called Rawshana'i-nama* (Leiden, 1949).

21. Mahmud Ghanizada and Muhammad Qazvini used a manuscript from Leningrad (now St. Petersburg again) to prepare their edition of the *Wajh-i din* in 1343/1924 at the Kaviani Press in Berlin. This edition was reproduced in Tehran in 1348/1970 under the auspices of the Kitabkhana-i Tahuri. But the first critical edition was produced in 1398/1977 in Tehran by Ghulam Reza Aavani for the Imperial Academy of Philosophy. Several manuscripts of the *Wajh-i din* are listed in a number of libraries in St. Petersburg, Tashkent, Dushanbe and Tehran. One chapter has been translated into Russian and analysed by A. Semenov (Tashkent, 1926).

22. The *Zad al-musafirin* is the earliest to date of all Nasir Khusraw's works, since he himself tells us (p. 280 of the printed edition) that he composed it in 453/1061. It has been edited once so far, in 1341/1923 by Muhammad Badhl al-Rahman, and published in Berlin by the Kaviani Press. This edition was based on two manuscripts, one from Paris and the second from Cambridge. Other manuscripts have been recorded in the Bodleian Library (with a microfilm in the Central Library of Tehran University), in the Mashhad Library, in Danishsara-yi Ali's collection of 'Abd al-'Azim Khan Gurgani, in the Majlis Library, Tehran; and the Central Library of Tehran University

holds a microfilm of Tabataba'i's manuscript of the same. In Russian, Semenov reviewed it in *Iran* I (1927), pp. 224–31, and G. Ashurov wrote two studies (both published in Dushanbe, 1965) on Nasir Khusraw's philosophy based on the *Zad al-musafirin*.

**Chapter Two: Heretic, Magician or King?**

1. Wladimir Ivanow published this work, *Problems in Nasir-i Khusraw's Biography* (Bombay, 1956) as the revised edition of his previous account *Nasir-i Khusraw and Ismailism* (Bombay, 1948). E. G. Browne's two earlier accounts, the article 'Nasir Khusraw: Poet, Traveller and Propagandist,' in *Journal of the Royal Asiatic Society*, (1905), pp. 313–52, and the chapter on the poet in his *A Literary History of Persia* (Cambridge, 1924), vol. 2, pp. 218–46, also occupy themselves considerably with questions of biography, rather than analysis of ideas.

2. The *Risalat al-nadama fi yawm al-qiyama* appeared in Dhikri's compendium of poets, *Khulasat al-ash'ar wa zubdat al-afkar*. Taqi al-Din Muhammad Kashi (known as Dhikri) was born in Kashan around 946/1539. There is some discrepancy in the completion dates of the *Khulasat*. Rypka reports that Dhikri finished his writing in 993/1585 (Jan Rypka, *History of Iranian Literature*, Dordrecht, 1968, p. 453). N. Bland's two dates mentioned in his manuscript (1038 and 1039/1629), probably refer to the completion of the manuscript itself ('On the Earliest Persian Biography of Poets,' in *Journal of the Royal Asiatic Society*, (1847), p. 20). Dhikri writes that he had the autobiography in its original Arabic but had now translated it into Persian for the collection. Other versions of this pseudo-autobiography are found in *Atashkada (Fire Temple)*, the compendium of poets by Hajji Lutf 'Ali Beg Adhar, as well as in the introduction to the Tabriz edition of Nasir's *Divan* published in 1280/1864.

3. For example, Riza Quli Khan Hidayat, *Majma' al-fusaha*, vol. 1 (Tehran, 1878), p. 608; Z. Safa, *Tarikh-i adabiyyat dar Iran*, (5th ed., Tehran, 1352/1993), vol. 2, p. 443.

4. This doubt is registered most recently by Wheeler M. Thackston, *A Millennium of Classical Persian Poetry* (Bethesda, Maryland, 1994) p. 21, where he writes, 'While credited with being the first to use poetry as a vehicle for philosophical and theological thought, he has been criticised on the same count for having versified philosophy devoid of poetry.'

5. Abu'l-Ma'ali Muhammad b. 'Ubayd Allah, *Bayan al-adyan*, ed.

A. Iqbal and S. M. Dabir Siyaqi (Tehran, 1376/1997), pp. 55–6.

6. The *Dalil al-mutahayyirin* is no longer extant.

7. In the *Wajh-i Din*, Nasir refers to himself as the *sahib* of the *jazira*.

8. I have translated the words *bad din, bad madhhab, mulhid* (all cited by Nasir Khusraw as accusations against him) variously as heresy/heretic, lack of faith, unorthodoxy or irreligion, and eschewed the use of the word 'atheism,' of which he was never charged even by his enemies. He was accused of having the wrong religion, *not* of denying God's existence. But, unfortunately, the word 'atheism' in reference to Nasir Khusraw has entered Western scholarship; see, for example, Browne, *A Literary History*, vol. 2, pp. 242–3.

9. Farid al-Din 'Attar (ascribed), *Lisan al-ghayb* (Tehran, 1965), p. 188, reading Yumgan for Mulkan. All six lines appear in Ja'far Shi'ar, *Tahlil-i Safarnama-i Nasir Khusraw* (Tehran, 1371/1992), p. 31. Browne, *A Literary History*, vol. 2, p. 509.

10. The *Nizam al-tawarikh* was written in 674/1275 by Nasir al-Din Abu Sa'id 'Abd Allah al-Baydawi (d. 685/1286 or 692/1292), (Hyderabad and Deccan, 1930).

11. Al-Baydawi errs in giving Isfahan (in central Iran) as Nasir Khusraw's city of birth. In several of his prose works, Nasir writes his name out fully, showing that he is Nasir, son of Khusraw from Qubadiyan in the district of Marv (which is considerably farther east in today's Afghanistan). While it is true he could have moved there, his deep loyalty and affection for Khurasan is revealed frequently in his poetry while Isfahan receives no mention.

12. On the debate about the date of Nasir Khusraw's death, see Taqizada's Introduction to the *Divan* (Tehran, 1925–28), pp. *mim-dal*; Ivanow, *Problems*, pp. 15–16, 47.

13. The descendants of the Prophet Muhammad are accorded special respect in Islam, especially in Shi'ism, and given the title *sayyid* or *sharif*, the first more common in Iran and its environs, and the second usually occurring outside Iran, for example in North Africa. Men who are *sayyid* can be distinguished by the colour of their turban, now most commonly black or green, but this has changed through time and location. Women (*sayyida*) do not usually show off their status in any visible way, but do pass it on equally to their children. Al-Baydawi reports that Nasir Khusraw was called a *sharif*, and Riza Quli Khan Hidayat refers to him as a *sayyid*. The most detailed research on whether or not Nasir Khusraw was a *sayyid* has been

carried out by Mehdi Mohaghegh, the co-editor of the second critical edition of the *Divan*. As an ardent Shi'i and Ismaili, Nasir often declares his allegiance to the Prophet and his family, specifically naming his daughter Fatima, her husband 'Ali, or their two children Hasan and Husayn. But he never gives himself the title *sayyid* or *sharif*. Based on some of Nasir's own verses and other evidence, Mohaghegh concludes that Nasir was not a *sayyid*. The fact that Nasir received this title often should then be understood more as a sign of honour and respect by his followers, which was transmitted to historians, rather than of physical genealogy.

14. See al-Khashshab, pp. 5–7.

15. This would not have been difficult, since al-Kharaqani's illiteracy was one of his points of pride. See Annemarie Schimmel, *Mystical Dimensions of Islam* (Chapel Hill, N.C., 1975), p. 222.

16. The second hemistich of this line, translated here as it is in al-Baydawi and Dawlatshah, *Tadhkirat* p. 14, differs from the one in both editions of the *Divan*: 'Beyond the seven heavens, revolving up above are two essences,/Their light illuminating the whole of both worlds and mankind too.'

17. Schimmel, *Mystical Dimensions*, pp. 89–90.

18. The *Athar al-bilad wa akhbar al-'ibad* (Beirut, 1960) was composed in 674/1276 by Zakariyya b. Muhammad al-Qazvini (d. 1282 CE). Compare Schefer, pp. iv–v, and al-Khashshab, p. 7.

19. Rashid al-Din Fadl Allah, *Jami' al-tawarikh*, ed. M. T. Danishpazhuh and M. Mudarrisi Zanjani (Tehran, 1338/1959), p. 77.

20. Mulla Nur al-Din 'Abd al-Rahman Jami was born in the town of Jam in Khurasan in 1414 CE and died in Herat in 1492. The *Baharistan*, composed in 1487, contains eight chapters, the sixth of which reviews about thirty-five poets. Browne, *A Literary History*, vol. 3, p. 515.

21. Schefer, pp. vi–vii, plus note 2. Al-Khashshab, p. 10, says Jami seems not to have had any of Nasir Khusraw's books before him when he wrote this, which is entirely possible; it seems he just borrowed information from several of the chronicles already cited.

22. W. Ivanow and several of his colleagues were unable to locate any such citation of Nasir Khusraw's poems in the *Tamhidat* of 'Ayn al-Qudhat al-Hamadani (d. 533/1138). Ivanow, *Problems*, pp. 7–8; al-Khashshab, pp. 4, 47.

23. Amir Dawlatshah, son of 'Ala' al-Dawla Bakhtishah Ghazi of

Samarqand (d. 900/1490 or 1495). Though widely acknowledged to be full of inaccuracies and exaggerations, his *Tadhkirat al-shu'ara*, ed. E. G. Browne (Leiden and London, 1901), still forms the basis of much opinion about Persian poets, including Nasir Khusraw. Browne, *A Literary History*, vol. 3, pp. 436–7; Schefer, pp. v–vi; al-Khashshab, pp. 10–11.

24. Portions from nos. 112 and 189 of the *Divan* (Mohaghegh edition).

25. See n. 2 above.

26. Ghiyath al-Din b. Humam al-Din, known as Khwandamir (born in Herat 879/1474, died in Gujarat 941/1533), wrote *Habib al-siyar fi akhbar afrad al-bashar* in 1523. Browne, *A Literary History*, vol. 4, p. 445; al-Khashshab, pp. 16–17.

27. Amir Khusraw of Delhi, a prolific poet and talented musician, was born in India in 1253 CE, where his father had fled from the region of Balkh to escape the Mongols. Browne, *A Literary History*, vol. 3, pp. 108–10.

28. Muhammad Muhsin Fani, born before 1618 in Patna, completed his *Dabistan-i madhahib* by 1657. See al-Khashshab, p. 19.

29. Lutf 'Ali Beg Adhar, *Atashkada-i adhar* (Bombay 1277/1860), pp. 202–8.

30. *Majma' al-fusaha*, lithographed in Tehran 1878, 2 vols. The entry on Nasir Khusraw is in vol. 1, pp. 607–33.

31. According to al-Khashshab, pp. 19–20, with no other bibliographical information.

32. Kungiri-yi Nasir Khusraw, *Yadnama-i Nasir Khusraw* (Mashhad, 2535/1976).

33. Browne, *A Literary History*, vol. 2, pp. 242–4. Here is Browne's translation of the verses. Far from supporting a charge of atheism, this first selection reflects the religious debate of determinism and free will:

O God, although through fear I hardly dare
To hint it, all this trouble springs from Thee!
Hadst Thou no sand or gravel in Thy shoes?
What made Thee suffer Satan willingly?
'Twere well if Thou hadst made the lips and teeth
Of Tartar beauties not so fair to see.
With cries of 'On!' Thou bid'st the hound pursue;
With cries of 'On!' Thou bid'st the quarry flee!

The second, instead of being taken as proof of Nasir's heresy, could be seen as warning of the transitory nature of the world:

> Dead drunk, not like a common sot, one day
> Nasir Khusraw went to take the air.
> Hard by a dung-heap he espied a grave
> And straightway cried, 'O ye who stand and stare,
> Behold the world! Behold its luxuries!
> Its dainties here – the fools who ate them there!'

Browne's third selection includes a two-couplet response by Nasir al-din Tusi who, two centuries after Nasir Khusraw, also wrote Ismaili philosophical works. See Taqizada's comments (Introduction to *Divan*, 1929, p. *mim*) that these cannot be Nasir Khusraw's lines because of their weak poetic style and ridiculous content; see also al-Khashshab, pp. 47–50.) The content addresses the doctrinal issue of the resurrection of the body and how literally that should be taken, a valid question for medieval religious scholars:

> Some luckless wretch wolves in the plain devour;
> His bones are picked by vulture and by crow.
> This casts his remnants on the hills above;
> That voids its portion in the wells below.
> Shall this man's body rise to life again?
> Defile the beards of fools who fancy so!

Nasir al-din Tusi replies:

> Shall this man's body rise to life again
> When thus resolved to elements? I trow
> God can remake as easily as make:
> Defile the beard of Nasir Khusraw!

34. Quoted in A. J. Arberry, *Classical Persian Literature* (London, 1958), p. 348.

### Chapter Three: The Wonders of this World

1. The brother's name, Khwaja Abu'l-Fath 'Abd al-Jalil, is recorded in the *Safarnama*, p. 103.

2. Mehdi Mohaghegh, *Tahlil-i ash'ar-i Nasir Khusraw* (Tehran 1965), pp. 3–4.

3. The remainder of the ode is translated and discussed in Chapter Eight.

4. Qarun was a rich and avaricious minister of Pharaoh who taunted Moses as being only a magician. After proudly displaying his wealth, Qarun was swallowed up by the earth, along with his palace. Known as Korah in the Old Testament (Numbers 16), Qarun is mentioned three times in the Qur'an (28:76–82; 29:39/38; 40:25/24).

5. Qipchaq (also Qifchak), a Turkish people and tribe.

## Chapter Four: The Turning Point

1. Compare Ivanow, *Nasir Khusraw and Ismailism*, p. 14.

2. Ivanow, *Problems in Nasir-i Khusraw's Biography*, pp. 21–40.

3. *Divan*, 242:52 (my translation). Alternate reading: 'Since today both these things have been gathered together beside me ...'

4. See Heinz Halm, *The Fatimids and Their Traditions of Learning* (London, 1997), pp. 31–2, 41–7.

5. An accomplished poet and theologian, al-Mu'ayyad was born in Shiraz in late 4th/10th century. Like Nasir Khusraw, he undertook a perilous journey to Cairo in 438/1046 and gained rapid promotion in the Ismaili *da'wa*. In 450/1058 he was appointed the chief *da'i* and head of the Dar al-'Ilm, a major Fatimid institution of learning, where he lived and lectured until his death in 470/1078.

6. On Azar, see Chapter Seven, note 5.

7. The House of Ma'mur literally means 'the eternal house in heaven.' See Chapter Nine.

8. *Wajh-i din*, p. 69.

## Chapter Five: Knowledge and Action

1. The passages of *Wajh-i din* (*WD*) cited in this chapter are from the 1977 edition by Aavani.

2. The references to *Zad al-musafirin* (*ZM*) are from the 1341/1923 edition by M. Badhl al-Rahman.

3. In fact, the connection between these two is so great that there is disagreement in various manuscripts of *Zad al-musafirin* as to whether *wahm* comes first or *hiss*, suggesting the difficulties of later copyists in coming to an understanding of the distinction.

4. We have reviewed above Nasir Khusraw's description (from *ZM*, 18–25) of five external and internal senses. In his *Khwan al-ikhwan*, Nasir Khusraw also describes the spiritual faculties of mankind.

5. *Divan*, ed. N. Taqavi et al. (Tehran 1304–7/1925–28), p. 499. A shorter version of the poem in four couplets is contained in the Minuvi and Mohaghegh edition of the *Divan* (Tehran, 1353/1974), p. 523. The full Persian text also appears in W. Thackston, ed., *A Millennium of Classical Persian Poetry* (Bethesda, MD, 1994), p. 22, and has been variously translated into English by A. Schimmel in *Make a Shield from Wisdom*, pp. 92–3, and F. Hunzai, *Shimmering Light: An Anthology of Ismaili Poetry* (London, 1996), p. 68. See also my 'Nasir Khusraw: Fatimid Intellectual,' in F. Daftary, ed., *Intellectual Traditions in Islam* (London, 2000), pp. 112–29.

### Chapter Six: The Journey Begins

1. Later poems and philosophical works in which Nasir Khusraw's answers to questions begin with 'O son' are rendered in such a formulaic and impersonal style that they bear no hint that a particular person is being addressed; the expression can refer to any younger man the speaker is advising. This would be the case especially in Nasir's role later as the *da'i* of Khurasan. Similarly, the counsel 'O brother' does not necessarily indicate a sibling relationship, even though one brother accompanied him on his journey and may well have stayed with him in exile. It is, of course, a very common appellation of men in the same religious faith.

2. Based on one parasang equal to 3.25 miles.

3. See, for example, Ian R. Netton, *Seek Knowledge: Thought and Travel in the House of Islam* (Richmond, 1996).

4. For references on this correspondence, see F. Daftary, *The Isma'ilis: Their History and Doctrines* (Cambridge, 1990), n. 133, p. 214.

5. Nasir does not explain the reason for this hostility of the local people, but it was probably because the Shi'is regard Abu Hurayra as an enemy of their first Imam 'Ali.

### Chapter Seven: Jerusalem, the Holy

1. At that time, the entire eastern shore of the Mediterranean Sea, extending hundreds of miles inland, was known as Syria (Sham).

2. *Shish fasl*, pp. 33–4; and also *Wajh-i din*, p. 21 ('to God pertains

neither limit nor attribute').

3. *Gushayish wa rahayish*, ed. Hunzai, p. 4.

4. For Nasir Khusraw, plants possess a rudimentary vegetative soul, the *nafs-i namiya*.

5. Azar, the father of the Prophet Abraham, stands as one of the clearest examples of unadulterated idol-worshippers. It was against his father's tradition that Abraham initiated the worship of the one God.

6. Al-Ash'ari's account of the Mu'tazila, quoted in W. M. Watt, *The Formative Period of Islamic Thought* (Edinburgh, 1973), p. 247 and n. 137.

7. For more information, see C. E. Bosworth, 'Karramiyya,' in *EI2*, vol. 4, pp. 667–9.

8. The phrase Nasir quotes, '*Ahdath-na*" ('He related to us') is the standard opening for the transmission of the Prophetic Traditions (*hadith*).

9. For a discussion of the incident, see Halm, *The Fatimids*, p. 37.

## Chapter Eight: The Splendour of Fatimid Cairo

1. See *Divan* 58:24, where, following the Prophet's command that all should seek knowledge even unto China (Chin) and a symbolic place called Ma-chin, Nasir Khusraw shows that he equated the Chin of Muhammad to the Imam: 'Commanded Muhammad, "Seek even to China for knowledge of religion." I went, I did, to the China of Muhammad.'

2. Based on the Qur'an 95:1–3: 'By the fig and the olive/and the Mount Sinai/and this land secure!' Each of these terms is loaded with a specific *batin* meaning for Nasir Khusraw. See *Wajh-i din*, pp. 97–100, where figs stand for Universal Intellect, olives for Universal Soul, Mount Sinai for the *natiq* (the prophet-messenger), and city of refuge for the *asas* (imam).

3. Luqman, a legendary figure from pre-Islamic Arabia famed for his wisdom, also appears in the Qur'an (31:12–19) as the recipient of wisdom from God who dispenses sage advice to his son on how to worship one God steadfastly and humbly. Luqman's image developed over centuries into an almost Aesop-like character.

4. For a brief overview, see Thelma K. Thomas, *Textiles from Medieval Egypt* (Pittsburgh, P.A., 1990) and for a more extensive examination, Maurice Lombard, *Les Textiles dans le monde musulman*

*du VIIe au XIIe siècle* (Paris, 1978), especially pp. 151–74, on the Egyptian Delta.

    5. Lombard, *Les Textiles*, pp. 219–22, which includes a long quote from Ibn Khaldun's *Muqaddimat*, as well as one from Ibn Mammati, quoted from Serjeant, *Ars Islamica*, vols 13–14, p. 104.

    6. There is also the suggestion that in 464–467/1071–1074 Mahmud of Ghazna sent a yellow brocade cloth to cover the Ka'ba. Lombard, *Les Textiles*, p. 172, n. 8.

    7. *Buqalamun* today generally refers to just one bird, the turkey, a specific extension of its reference to shimmering iridescence, like that of feathers.

    8. Due to the mineral content of the Pamir Mountains, the local rivers often appear red in springtime, when the powerful melting snows rush down the mountainsides, churning up silt. A recent traveller also remarked on the contrast of white snow and 'streams of scarlet' and the 'crimson gash of riverbeds.' Colin Thubron, *The Lost Heart of Asia*, (New York, 1994), pp. 266–9, 274.

    9. Nasir refers here to the Qur'anic story of Joseph (Yusuf) and Zulaykha in Sura 12. Zulaykha's love for Joseph became one of the central motifs of mystical love in Sufi poetry.

    10. Conqueror of Egypt and 'wily' politician (EI) at the time of the Prophet and the early caliphs, 'Amr b. al-'As (d. 42/663) is reviled by Shi'is for siding with Mu'awiya against 'Ali, both in the battle of Siffin and in the arbitration which paved the way for Mu'awiya's accession.

    11. From a Persian proverb meaning that, since the judge will hear only one side of the case, he will rule in its favour.

    12. For more on al-Qadi al-Nu'man, see Daftary, *The Isma'ilis*, pp. 249–53.

    13. While Ismaili law could be taught in public to all citizens, the esoteric doctrine (*hikma*) was conveyed to Ismailis in private sessions known as the *majalis al-hikma*. See Heinz Halm, 'The Isma'ili Oath of Allegiance ('*ahd*) and the Sessions of Wisdom *(majalis al-hikma)* in Fatimid Times,' in F. Daftary, ed., *Mediaeval Isma'ili History and Thought* (Cambridge, 1996), pp. 91–115.

    14. Al-Maqrizi, *al-Khitat*, vol. 1, pp. 458 ff, quoted in Halm, *The Fatimids*, pp. 73–4.

    15. Compare the *Safarnama*, where Nasir's conversion account mentions no person responsible for his conversion.

    16. Abu Hatim al-Razi, *Kitab al-islah*, ed. H. Minuchihr and M.

Mohaghegh (Tehran, 1998).

17. Hamid al-Din al-Kirmani, *Kitab al-riyad*, ed. 'Arif Tamir (Beirut, 1960).

18. Henry Corbin has carried out a comparison of Nasir Khusraw's *Khwan al-ikhwan* and al-Sijistani's *Kitab al-yanabi'*, in his *Trilogie ismaélienne* (Tehran and Paris, 1961). The *Kitab al-yanabi'* is now also available in English translation in Walker, *The Wellsprings of Wisdom*, pp. 37–111. For a summary of al-Sijistani's thought, see P. E. Walker, *Abu Ya'qub al-Sijistani: Intellectual Missionary* (London, 1996).

19. Hamid al-Din al-Kirmani, *Rahat al-'aql*, ed. M. Kamil Husayn and M. Mustafa Hilmi (Cairo, 1953); see also D. de Smet, *La Quiétude de l'intellect: Néoplatonisme et gnose ismaélienne dans l'oeuvre de Hamid ad-Din al-Kirmani (Xe/XIe s.)* (Louvain, 1995), and P. E. Walker, *Hamid al-Din al-Kirmani: Ismaili Thought in the Age of al-Hakim* (London, 1999).

20. See also W. Ivanow, *Nasir Khusraw and Ismailism* (Bombay, 1948) p. 53; and Hunsberger, 'Nasir Khusraw's Doctrine of the Soul,' pp. 91–100, for further analysis of the differences in Nasir Khusraw's views.

21. Plotinus, *The Enneads*, trans., A. H. Armstrong (Cambridge, Mass., 1966–88), vol. 3, 2.2.

22. For a careful review of eyewitness accounts and histories over several centuries showing the importance of these state rituals for Fatimid political and religious life, see Paula Sanders, *Ritual, Politics, and the City in Fatimid Cairo* (Albany, N.Y., 1994).

23. Drawing on a *hadith* of the Prophet Muhammad directed toward 'Ali, 'You are to me as Aaron was to Moses,' Nasir Khusraw here speaks of 'our Aaron' meaning 'Ali.

24. Drawing from another *hadith*, 'Imprison knowledge through writing.'

25. The poet is here playing with the contrasting sounds and meanings of '*baqar*' (cow) and Muhammad al-Baqir, the early Shi'i Imam famed for his knowledge and wisdom.

26. The line which reads, '*bi-khwan har du divan-i man ta bi-bini yiki gashta ba 'Unsuri Buhturi ra*' has been the basis for some speculation that Nasir Khusraw had two *Divans*, in Arabic and Persian, or that there was a second, separate *Divan*. However, until such time as we see some Arabic verses from him (not eliminating the possibility), I prefer to read the line as expressing the poet's prowess in the poetic skills of both languages. The line actually states that Buhturi has become one with 'Unsuri, referring to the highly successful 3rd/9th

century poet, Buhturi who wrote in Arabic, and 'Unsuri (5th/11th century), the court poet of Mahmud of Ghazna, who wrote in Persian.

## Chapter Nine: Mecca, City of Pilgrimage

1. Qur'an 3:97, 2:196; see also *Safarnama*, p. 60, n. 23.
2. See Chaper Eight, p. 148.
3. Reading '*na-dukhta*' for '*dukhta*.' See line 13, same page.
4. This series of prohibitions listed by Nasir Khusraw on the believer's conduct before the Imam require a full study of Fatimid Ismaili law.
5. On the higher rank of these four *hujjats*, see Daftary, *The Isma'ilis*, p. 229.
6. *Ahl-i kahf* (people of the cave) refers to the story of the 'Seven Sleepers' in the Qur'an (18:9–26) about a number of youths who concealed themselves in a cave to escape religious persecution. *Raqim* is the tablet of lead on which was inscribed the names and accounts of these youths.

## Chapter Ten: The Journey Home

1. The Qarmatis were originally a dissident group of Ismailis who broke away from the mainstream Fatimid *da'wa* around 286/899. The Fatimids denounced the taking of the Black Stone and, after establishing their rule in Egypt, engaged in numerous military campaigns in Syria against the Qarmatis of Bahrayn; see W. Madelung, 'The Fatimids and the Qarmatis of Bahrayn,' in Daftary, ed., *Mediaeval Isma'ili History and Thought*, pp. 21–73.
2. This is Thackston's translation; Bernard Lewis in his *The Origins of Isma'ilism* (Cambridge, 1940) used the word 'disciples.'
3. Nasir is very specific about her name as well as the duration of the marriage, 'Ali stayed with her for seventy-two days,' providing a very clear example of acceptable marriage practices among the early Muslims.
4. Bahram Gur, one of the most popular kings in Iranian history (reigned 420–438 CE), famed for his prowess in hunting and the promotion of music, as well as military and administrative achievements. More spectacularly, his romances are celebrated in many legends and epics, such as Firdawsi's *Shahnama* and Nizami's *Haft paykar* (*Seven Beauties*).

5. This topic has been examined in depth in Hunsberger, 'Nasir Khusraw's Doctrine of the Soul.'

6. *Shish fasl*, English trans., p. 32; Persian p. 5.

7. *Shish fasl*, English trans., pp. 30–70; Persian, pp. 4–31. Nasir's cosmogony follows closely al-Sijistani's *Kitab al-yanabi'*. Compare his *Khwan al-ikhwan*, section 48, with the latter's Section 15 (18th Source), in Corbin's ed. and trans., in *Trilogie*, pp. 67–8.

### Chapter Eleven: The World Turns Dark

1. For Nasir Khusraw, the image of the well generally, as here, refers to a dark, confining prison. In other poems, Nasir employs the Qur'anic story of Joseph thrown into a well (Qur'an, 12:1–20) to exemplify beauty and truth lost in darkness.

2. Muhammad al-Nasafi (d. 332/943) and Abu Ya'qub al-Sijistani (d. ca. 361/971) are among prominent Ismaili *da'is* executed by their opponents.

3. Meaning literally, 'pour water on my head,' an idiom beautifully echoing the pouring and flowing images from the preceding lines.

4. The term 'east' refers to Nasir's enemies in Khurasan, and 'west' to the Fatimid Caliph-Imam in Cairo, Nasir Khusraw's intellectual and spiritual mentor.

5. The Qur'an (20:85–97) recounts how 'the Samiri' made a calf statue out of melted jewellery for the children of Israel while Moses was away on the Mount for forty days and forty nights. When the Samiri brought the calf statue before the people, 'it seemed to low' (20:88). Upon his return, Moses banished the Samiri for misleading the people into idolatry and destroyed the statue.

6. Nasir Khusraw has here named two ritually impure (*haram*) substances (*murdar* and *khun*) which are forbidden to Muslims.

7. Riza Quli Khan Hidayat, *Majma' al-fusaha*, vol. 1, p. 607.

8. *Tarikh-i Nishabur*, ed. Sayyid 'Ali Mu'ayyid Thabiti (Tehran, 2525/1966), pp. 352–3.

9. This quotation is a paraphrase from *Tarikh-i Nishabur*, p. 352, which borrows from an earlier work, *Siyaq al-tawarikh* and Dawlatshah's *Tadhkira*, p. 15.

10. *Habib al-siyar*, pp. 456–7.

11. Solomon is famed, among other things, for having the ability to communicate with animals and other creatures.

12. The Persian poet Hafiz wrote a famous *ghazal* on the same subject, in the same metre and with the same final rhyme-word, apparently imitating Nasir Khusraw.

13. Zoroastrianism had been the religion of Iran for over a thousand years when the Arabs conquered it in 16/637 and introduced the new religion of Islam.

14. Nasir Khusraw has a discussion on humans as 'slaves' of God in *Gushayish wa rahayish*, 24th question.

15. An allusion to the Qur'anic verse 107:4–5.

16. Besides the verses cited, see also *Divan*, no. 37 for more on the decline of Khurasan.

17. Ahriman, the god of evil in Zoroastrianism.

18. Bizhan, an Iranian hero, is famed for his romance with Manizhah, the daughter of the enemy king, Afrasiab. Manizhah contrived to have Bizhan drugged and brought into her palace. When her father discovered them, he had Bizhan thrown into a well and a stone placed on top. Manizhah slipped food to him through a crack and eventually the two lovers were rescued by Bizhan's uncle, Rustam.

19. Nasir Khusraw here plays with the similarity in two names: Qarun (see Chapter Three, note 4) and Qaran, an Iranian champion at the time of Rustam.

## Chapter Twelve: Glory Regained

1. 'Ali's courage on the battlefield earned him the praise of the Prophet who called him *Asad Allah*, 'the lion of God.'

2. In Nasir Khusraw's lifetime, this political victory did actually occur, albeit briefly, in 451/1059, when the Turkish commander, Abu'l-Harith Arslan al-Basasiri, captured the Abbasid palace and sent the caliphal insignia to al-Mustansir. However, a change of Fatimid viziers halted the financial support of the campaign and al-Basasiri was defeated and killed by the Saljuq sultan, Tughril. See Daftary, *The Isma'ilis*, pp. 205–6.

3. Abu Tamim is a reference to the eighth Caliph-Imam al-Mustansir bi'llah (r. 427/1036–487/1094).

# Bibliography

## I. Works of Nasir Khusraw

*Divan*, eds Nasr Allah Taqavi et al. Tehran, 1304–1307/1925–1928;
eds, M. Minuvi and M. Mohaghegh. Tehran, 1353/1974. Partial
English trans., P. L. Wilson and G. R. Aavani, *Forty Poems from the
Divan*. Tehran, 1977. Partial English trans., Annemarie Schimmel,
*Make a Shield from Wisdom*. London, 1993.

*Gushayish wa rahayish*, ed. S. Nafisi. Leiden, 1950; revised ed., Tehran,
1340/1961. Italian trans., Pio Filippani-Ronconi, *Il libro dello
scioglimento e della liberazione*. Naples, 1959. New ed. and English
trans., F. M. Hunzai, *Knowledge and Liberation*. London, 1998.

*Jami' al-hikmatayn*, eds, H. Corbin and M. Mu'in, Tehran and Paris,
1953. French trans., Isabelle de Gastines, *Le Livre réunissant les
deux sagesses*. Paris, 1990.

*Khwan al-ikhwan*, ed. Y. al-Khashshab, Cairo, 1940; ed. A. Qavim. Tehran, 1338/1959.

*Safarnama*, ed. M. Ghanizada. Berlin, 1341/1922; ed. S. M. Dabir
Siyaqi, 5th ed., Tehran, 1356/1977. French trans., Charles
Schefer, *Sefer Nameh, relation du voyage de Nassiri Khosrau*. Paris, 1881.
Arabic trans., Y. al-Khashshab, *Safarnama, rahla Nasir Khusraw*, 2nd
ed., Beirut, 1970. Partial English trans., Guy Le Strange, *Diary of a
Journey through Syria and Palestine by Nasir-i Khusrau, in 1047 A.D.*
London, 1893. English trans., W. M. Thackston, Jr., *Naser-e
Khosraw's Book of Travels (Safarnama)*. Albany, N. Y., 1986.

*Shish fasl*, ed. and trans., W. Ivanow as *Six Chapters, or Shish fasl, also
called Rawshana'i-nama*. Leiden, 1949.

*Wajh-i din*, eds, M. Ghanizada and M. Qazvini. Berlin, 1343/1924;

ed. G. Reza Aavani. Tehran, 1977.

*Zad al-musafirin*, ed. M. Badhl al-Rahman. Berlin, 1341/1923.

## II. Works about Nasir Khusraw

Adib Pishavari, S. A. *Sharh-i mushkillat-i divan-i Nasir Khusraw*, ed. J. Surushyar. Isfahan, 1363/1984.

Bertel's, Andrei E. *Nasir Khusraw wa Isma'iliyan*, trans., Y. Ariyanpur from Russian into Persian. Tehran, 1346/1967.

Berthels, E. 'Nasir Khusraw,' in *The Encyclopaedia of Islam*, (1st ed.) vol. 6, pp. 869–70.

Browne, Edward G. 'Nasir-i Khusraw: Poet, Traveller, and Propagandist,' *Journal of the Royal Asiatic Society* (1905), pp. 313–52.

Corbin, Henry. 'Nasir-i Khusrau and Iranian Isma'ilism,' in *The Cambridge History of Iran*: Volume 4, *The Period from the Arab Invasion to the Saljuqs*, ed. R. N. Frye. Cambridge, 1975. pp. 520–42 and 689–90.

Fagnan, E. 'Notes sur Naçir ibn Khosrou,' *Journal Asiatique*, series 7, 13 (1879), pp. 164–8.

—— 'Le Livre de la Félicité par Nasir e Hosraw, texte persan et traduction française de Sa'adat Nameh,' *Zeitschrift der Deutschen Morganländischen Gesellschaft*, 34 (1880), pp. 643–74.

Hunsberger, Alice. 'Nasir Khusraw's Doctrine of the Soul: From the Universal Intellect to the Physical World in Isma'ili Philosophy,' Ph.D. thesis, Columbia University, New York, 1992.

—— 'Nasir Khusraw: Fatimid Intellectual,' in F. Daftary, ed., *Intellectual Traditions in Islam*. London, 2000. pp. 112–29.

Ivanow, Wladimir. *Nasir-i Khusraw and Ismailism*. Bombay, 1948.

—— *Problems in Nasir-i Khusraw's Biography*. Bombay, 1956.

al-Khashshab, Yahya. *Nasir è Hosrow: Son voyage, sa pensée religieuse, sa philosophie et sa poésie*. Cairo, 1940.

Kungiri-yi Nasir Khusraw. *Yadnama-i Nasir Khusraw*. Mashhad, 2535/1976.

Meisami, Julie Scott. 'Symbolic Structure in a Poem by Nasir-i Khusraw,' *Iran*, 31, (1993) pp. 103–17.

Meskoob, Shahrokh. 'The Origin and Meaning of *'Aql* (Reason) in the View of Nasir Khusraw,' *Iran Nameh*, 6 (1989), pp. 239–57, and 7 (1989), pp. 405–29.

Mohaghegh, Mehdi. *Tahlil-i ash'ar-i Nasir Khusraw*. Tehran, 1965.

—— 'Nasir Khusraw and His Spiritual *Nisbah*,' in M. Minuvi and I.

Afshar, eds, *Yadnama-i Irani-yi Minorsky*. Tehran, 1969. pp. 143–8.

Nanji, Azim. 'Nasir-i Khusraw,' in *EI2*, vol. 7, pp. 1006–7.

Semenov, Aleksandr A. 'A Review of Book of Travellers' Provisions (*Kitab Zadu'l-musafirin*) by Nasir Khusraw,' *Iran*, 1 (1927), pp. 224–31.

Teufel, F. 'Zu Nâsir Chusrau's 'Rushanâinâma' und zu 'Le Livre de la Félicité,' *Zeitschrift der Deutschen Morgenländischen Gesellschaft*, 36 (1882), pp. 96–114.

Wickens, G. M. 'The 'Sa'adat-nameh' Attributed to Nasir Khusraw,' *Islamic Quarterly*, 2 (1955), pp. 117–32.

Ziyah-i Nur, Fazlullah. 'Andishaha-i falsafi-yi Nasir Khusraw,' *Revue de la Faculté des Lettres et Sciences Humaines*. University of Isfahan, New Series, 1 (1983), pp. 262–80.

## III. Other Sources and Studies

Abu'l-Ma'ali, Muhammad b. 'Ubayd Allah. *Bayan al-adyan*, ed. A. Iqbal and S. M. Dabir Siyaqi. Tehran, 1376/1997. French trans., H. Massé, in *Revue d'histoire des religions*, 94 (1926), pp. 17–75.

Abu Hatim al-Razi. *A'lam al-nubuwwa*, ed. S. al-Sawi and G. R. Aavani. Tehran, 1977. Extracts in P. Kraus, 'Raziana II,' *Orientalia*, New Series, 5 (1936), pp. 35–56 and 357–78, reprinted in P. Kraus, *Alchemie, Ketzerei, Apokryphen im frühen Islam*, ed. R. Brague. Hildesheim, 1994, pp. 256–98.

—— *Kitab al-islah*, ed. H. Minuchihr and M. Mohaghegh. Tehran, 1998.

Adhar, Lutf 'Ali Beg. *Atashkada-i adhar*. Bombay, 1277/1860, Tehran, 1957.

Arberry, Arthur J. *Classical Persian Literature*. London, 1958.

'Attar, Farid al-Din (attributed). *Lisan al-ghayb*. Tehran, 1965.

'Awfi, Muhammad. *Lubab al-albab*, ed. E. G. Browne. London and Leiden, 1903–1906.

al-Baydawi, Nasir al-Din Abu Sa'id. *Nizam al-tawarikh (A General History of Iran)*. Hyderabad and Deccan, 1930.

Bland, Nathaniel. 'Account of the Ateshkedah, A Biographical Work on the Persian Poets, by Hajji Lutf 'Ali Beg, of Ispahan,' *Journal of the Royal Asiatic Society*, 7 (1843), pp. 345–92.

Browne, Edward G. *A Literary History of Persia*. 4 vols. Cambridge, 1924.

Bulliet, Richard W. *Islam: The View from the Edge*. New York, 1994.

Canard, Marius. 'Fatimids,' in *EI2*, vol. 2, pp. 850–62.

Casanova, Paul. 'La Doctrine secrète des Fatimides d'Egypte,' *Bulletin de l'Institut Français d'Archéologie Orientale du Caire*, 18 (1921), pp. 121–65.

Corbin, Henry, ed. and trans., *Trilogie ismaélienne*. Tehran and Paris, 1961.

—— 'L'Initiation ismaélienne ou l'ésotérisme et le Verbe,' *Eranos Jahrbuch*, 39 (1970), pp. 41–142, reprinted in H. Corbin, *L'Homme et son ange*. Paris, 1983. pp. 81–205.

—— 'The Isma'ili Response to the Polemic of Ghazali,' in Nasr, ed., *Isma'ili Contributions to Islamic Culture*, pp. 67–98.

—— 'Les conférences ismaéliennes de Mo'ayyad fid-Din Shirazi,' *Journal Asiatique* (1978/79), pp. 265–72.

—— *Cyclical Time and Ismaili Gnosis*, trans., Ralph Manheim and J. W. Morris. London, 1983.

—— *Temple and Contemplation*, trans., Philip Sherrard. London, 1986.

Daftary, Farhad. *The Isma'ilis: Their History and Doctrines*. Cambridge, 1990.

—— *The Assassin Legends: Myths of the Isma'ilis*. London, 1994.

—— ed. *Mediaeval Isma'ili History and Thought*. Cambridge, 1996.

Dawlatshah b. 'Ala al-Dawla. *Tadhkirat al-shu'ara*, ed. E. G. Browne. Leiden and London, 1901.

*The Encyclopaedia of Islam*, ed. H. A. R. Gibb et al. New ed., Leiden and London, 1960–.

Fani, Muhammad Muhsin. *Dabistan-i madhahib*, trans., Shea and Troyer as *The Dabistan or School of Manners*. London, 1843.

Feki, Habib. *Les idées religieuses et philosophiques de l'Ismaélisme Fatimide (organisation et doctrine)*. Tunis, 1978.

Fischel, W. J. 'The Jews of Central Asia (Khorasan) in Medieval Hebrew and Arabic Literature,' *Historia Judaica*, 7 (1945), pp. 29–50.

Friedlander, I. 'The Heterodoxies of the Shi'ites in the Presentation of Ibn Hazm,' *Journal of the American Oriental Society*, 28 (1907), pp. 1–80, and 29 (1908) pp. 1–183.

Goodman, L. E. *Avicenna*. London and New York, 1992.

Halm, Heinz. 'Die Sieben und die Zwölf: Die Isma'ilitische Kosmogonie und das Mazdak – Fragment des Šahrastani,' *Zeitschrift der Deutschen Morgenländischen Gesellschaft*, 18 (1974), pp. 170–7.

—— *Kosmologie und Heilslehre der frühen Isma'iliya: Eine Studie zur islamischen Gnosis*. Wiesbaden, 1978.

—— *The Empire of the Mahdi: The Rise of the Fatimids*, trans., Michael Bonner. Leiden, 1996.

—— 'The Isma'ili Oath of Allegiance (*'ahd*) and the Sessions of Wisdom (*majalis al-hikma*) in Fatimid Times,' in Daftary, ed., *Mediaeval Isma'ili History and Thought*, pp. 91–115.

—— *The Fatimids and their Traditions of Learning*. London, 1997.

Hamdani, Husain F. 'Evolution of the Organisational Structure of the Fatimi Da'wah,' *Arabian Studies*, 3 (1976), pp. 85–114.

Hidayat, Riza Quli Khan. *Majma' al-fusaha*. 2 vols. Tehran, 1878.

Ivanow, Wladimir. 'The Organization of the Fatimid Propaganda,' *Journal of the Bombay Branch of the Royal Asiatic Society*, New Series, 15 (1939), pp. 1–35.

—— *Ismaili Tradition Concerning the Rise of the Fatimids*. London, 1942.

—— *Brief Survey of the Evolution of Ismailism*. Leiden, 1952.

—— *Studies in Early Persian Ismailism*. 2nd edn, Bombay, 1955

—— *Ismaili Literature: A Bibliographical Survey*. Tehran, 1963.

Jami. *Nafahat al-uns*, ed. A. Tawhidpur. Tehran, 1957.

Khwandamir, Ghiyath al-Din. *Tarikh-i habib al-siyar*. Tehran, 1955.

al-Kirmani, Hamid al-Din. *Kitab al-riyad*, ed. 'Arif Tamir. Beirut, 1960.

—— *Rahat al-'aql*, ed. M. Kamil Husayn and M. Mustafa Hilmi. Cairo, 1953.

Kraus, Paul. ' "*Majalis*" de al-Mu'ayyad fid din as-Shirazi,' *Rivista degli Studi Orientali*, 14 (1933/34), pp. 93–129.

—— 'The "Controversies" of Fakhr al-Din Razi,' *Islamic Culture*, 12 (1938), pp. 131–53.

Laoust, H. *Les schismes dans l'Islam*. Paris, 1965.

Lewis, Bernard. *The Origins of Isma'ilism: A Study of the Historical Background of the Fatimid Caliphate*. Cambridge, 1940.

—— *The Assassins: A Radical Sect in Islam*. London, 1967.

Lombard, Maurice. *Les Textiles dans le monde musulman du VIIe au XIIe siècle*. Paris, 1978.

Madelung, Wilferd. 'Fatimiden und Bahrainqarmaten,' *Der Islam*, 34 (1959), pp. 34–88, English trans., 'The Fatimids and the Qarmatis of Bahrayn,' in Daftary, ed., *Mediaeval Isma'ili History and Thought*. pp. 21–73.

—— 'Das Imamat in der frühen ismailitischen Lehre,' *Der Islam*, 37 (1961), pp. 43–135.

—— 'Aspects of Isma'ili Theology: The Prophetic Chain and the God Beyond Being,' in Nasr, ed. *Isma'ili Contributions to Islamic Culture*, pp. 51–65, reprinted in W. Madelung, *Religious Schools and Sects in Medieval Islam*. London, 1985, article XVII.

—— *Religious Trends in Early Islamic Iran.* Albany, N.Y., 1988.

—— 'Abu Yaʻqub al-Sijistani and Metempsychosis,' in *Iranica Varia: Papers in Honor of Professor Ehsan Yarshater.* Leiden, 1990, pp. 131–43.

Majerczak, R. 'Les Ismaʻiliens de Choughnan,' *Revue du Monde Musulman,* 24 (1912), pp. 202–18.

Makarem, Sami N. *The Doctrine of the Ismaʻilis.* Beirut, 1972.

—— 'Ismaʻili and Druze Cosmology in Relation to Plotinus and Aristotle,' in M. E. Marmura, ed. *Islamic Theology and Philosophy: Studies in Honor of George F. Hourani.* New York, 1984. pp. 81–91.

Marquet, Yves. *La Philosophie des Ihwan al-Safa.* Paris, 1973.

—— 'Quelques remarques à propos de "Kosmologie und Heilslehre der frühen Ismaʻiliyya" de Heinz Halm,' *Studia Islamica,* 55 (1982), pp. 115–35.

Martin, R. C. ed. *Islam and the History of Religions: Essays in Methodology.* Berkeley, C.A., 1983.

Massé, Henri. *Aspects du pèlerinage à la Mekke dans la poésie persane.* Brussels, 1936.

McGovern, W. M. *The Early Empires of Central Asia.* Chapel Hill, N.C., 1939.

Mirza, Nasseh A. 'The Ismaʻilis and their Belief in Universal Divine Order,' *Glasgow University Oriental Society Transactions,* 20 (1963/64), pp. 10–22.

Nanji, Azim. 'Towards a Hermeneutic of Qurʼanic and other Narratives in Ismaʻili Thought,' in Richard C. Martin, ed., *Approaches to Islam in Religious Studies,* Tucson, A.Z., 1985, pp. 164–73.

Nasr, S. Hossein, ed. *Ismaʻili Contributions to Islamic Culture.* Tehran, 1977.

Netton, Ian Richard. *Seek Knowledge: Thought and Travel in the House of Islam.* Richmond, UK, 1996.

al-Nishapuri, Muhammad b. Surkh. *Commentaire de la qasida ismaélienne d'Abu'l-Haitham Jorjani,* ed. H. Corbin and M. Muʻin. Tehran and Paris, 1955.

al-Nuʻman b. Muhammad, al-Qadi Abu Hanifa. *Daʻaʼim al-Islam,* ed. Asaf. A. A. Fyzee. Cairo, 1951–1961. Partial English trans., A. A. A. Fyzee, *The Book of Faith.* Bombay, 1974.

Petrushevski, Ilya Pavlovich. *Islam dar Iran,* Persian trans., Karim Kashawarz. Tehran, 1354/1975.

Pines, Shlomo. 'La longue recension de la Théologie d'Aristote dans ses rapports avec la doctrine ismaélienne,' *Revue des Etudes*

*Islamiques*, 22, (1954), pp. 7–20.

Plotinus. *The Enneads*, trans., A. H. Armstrong. Cambridge, Mass., 1966–1988.

Poonawala, Ismail K. *Biobibliography of Isma'ili Literature*. Malibu, C.A., 1977.

al-Qazvini, Zakariyya b. Muhammad. *Athar al-bilad wa akhbar al-'ibad*, Beirut, 1960.

Rashid al-Din Fadl Allah. *Jami' al-tawarikh: qismat-i Isma'iliyan*, ed. M. T. Danishpazhuh and M. Mudarrisi Zanjani. Tehran, 1338/1959.

Rabinowitz, L. I. 'Notes on the Jews of Central Asia (Khorasan),' *Historia Judaica*, 8 (1948), pp. 61–6, (rejoinder by Fischel, pp. 66–8).

Rosenthal, Franz, 'On the Knowledge of Plato's Philosophy in the Islamic World,' *Islamic Culture*, 14 (1940), pp. 387–422; 15 (1941), pp. 396–398; reprinted in his *Greek Philosophy in the Arab World: A Collection of Essays*. Hampshire, UK, 1990.

Rypka, Jan. *History of Iranian Literature*, ed. Karl Jahn. Dordrecht, 1968.

Safa, Zabihullah. *Tarikh-i adabiyyat dar Iran*. 4th ed., Tehran, 1362–73/1984–1994.

Sanders, Paula. *Ritual, Politics, and the City in Fatimid Cairo*. Albany, N.Y., 1994.

Schimmel, Annemarie. *Mystical Dimensions of Islam*. Chapel Hill, N.C., 1975

al-Sijistani, Abu Ya'qub. *Kitab al-yanabi'*, trans., Paul E. Walker, in his *The Wellsprings of Wisdom: A Study of Abu Ya'qub al-Sijistani's Kitab al-Yanabi'*. Salt Lake City, Utah, 1994. pp. 37–111.

Smet, Daniel de. *La Quiétude de l'intellect: Néoplatonisme et gnose ismaélienne dans l'oeuvre de Hamid ad-Din al-Kirmani (Xe/XIe s.)*. Louvain, 1995.

Smoor, Pieter. *Kings and Bedouins in the Palace of Aleppo as Reflected in Ma'arri's Works*. Manchester, 1985.

Sourdel, Dominique. 'L'Ésotérisme isma'ilien et ses implications,' *La Civilisation de l'Islam classique*, (1968), pp. 183–8.

Stern, Samuel M. 'Heterodox Isma'ilism at the Time of al-Muizz,' *Bulletin of the School of Oriental and African Studies*, 17 (1955), pp. 10–33, reprinted in his *Studies*, 1983, pp. 257–8.

—— 'The Early Isma'ili Missionaries in North-West Persia and in Khurasan and Transoxania,' *Bulletin of the School of Oriental and African Studies*, 23 (1960), pp. 56–90, reprinted in his *Studies*, pp. 189–233.

—— 'Cairo as the Centre of the Isma'ili Movement,' *Colloque international sur l'histoire du Caire.* Cairo, 1972, pp. 437–50, reprinted in his *Studies,* pp. 234–56.

—— 'Ibn Hasday's Neoplatonist: A Neoplatonic Treatise and its Influence on Isaac Israeli and the Longer Version of the Theology of Aristotle,' *Oriens,* 13–14 (1961), pp. 58–120.

—— *Medieval Arabic and Hebrew Thought.* London, 1983.

—— *Studies in Early Isma'ilism.* Jerusalem and Leiden, 1983.

Storey, Charles A. *Persian Literature: A Bio-bibliographical Survey.* London, 1927– .

Tajdin, Nagib. *A Bibliography of Isma'ilism.* Delmar, N.Y., 1985.

Thackston, Wheeler M. *A Millennium of Classical Persian Poetry.* Bethesda, Maryland, 1994.

Thomas, Thelma K. *Textiles from Medieval Egypt, A.D. 300–1300.* Pittsburgh, P.A., 1990.

Walker, Paul E. *Abu Ya'qub al-Sijistani: Intellectual Missionary.* London, 1996.

—— 'An Isma'ili Answer to the Problem of Worshipping the Unknowable Neoplatonic God,' *American Journal of Arabic Studies,* 2 (1974), pp. 7–21.

—— 'The Ismaili Vocabulary of Creation,' *Studia Islamica,* 40 (1974), pp. 75–85.

—— *Early Philosophical Shiism: The Ismaili Neoplatonism of Abu Ya'qub al-Sijistani.* Cambridge, 1993.

—— *Hamid al-Din al-Kirmani: Ismaili Thought in the Age of al-Hakim.* London, 1999.

Watt, W. Montgomery. *The Formative Period of Islamic Thought.* Edinburgh, 1973.

# Index